FLIPPED LEARNING

FLIPPED LEARNING

A Guide for Higher Education Faculty

Robert Talbert

Foreword by Jon Bergmann

STERLING, VIRGINIA

Sty/us

Published by Stylus Publishing, LLC.
22883 Quicksilver Drive
Sterling, Virginia 20166-2102

Library of Congress Cataloging-in-Publication Data

Names: Talbert, Robert (Associate professor), author.
Title: Flipped learning : a guide for higher education faculty/
Robert Talbert;
foreword by Jon Bergmann.
Description: Sterling, Virginia : Stylus Publishing, LLC, [2017] |
Includes bibliographical references and index.
Identifiers: LCCN 2016055534 (print) |
LCCN 2017013514 (ebook) |
ISBN 9781620364338 (uPDF) |
ISBN 9781620364345 (ePub) |
ISBN 9781620364314 (cloth : alk. paper) |
ISBN 9781620364321 (pbk. : alk. paper)
Subjects: LCSH: Flipped classrooms. |
Education, Higher.
Classification: LCC LB1029.F55 (ebook) |
LCC LB1029.F55 T35 2017 (print) |
DDC 378.1/7--dc23
LC record available at https://lccn.loc.gov/2016055534

13-digit ISBN: 978-1-62036-431-4 (cloth)
13-digit ISBN: 978-1-62036-432-1 (paperback)
13-digit ISBN: 978-1-62036-433-8 (library networkable e-edition)
13-digit ISBN: 978-1-62036-434-5 (consumer e-edition)

Printed in the United States of America

All first editions printed on acid-free paper
that meets the American National Standards Institute
Z39-48 Standard.

Bulk Purchases

Quantity discounts are available for use in workshops and for staff development.
Call 1-800-232-0223

First Edition, 2017

*To my parents, Bob and Jane Talbert—who gave me
the skills and the space to learn things on my own and
the desire to make the world a better place.*

CONTENTS

PART TWO: FLIPPED LEARNING DESIGN

FOREWORD

I first became aware of Robert Talbert's scholarship about flipped learning through his blog, *Casting Out Nines,* and then later through some Twitter chats as he did research for this book. Between these interactions and through the recommendations of the best minds in flipped learning, I invited Robert to be one of the founding members of the Flipped Learning Global Research Fellows. His scholarship, thoughtfulness, thoroughness, willingness to reflect on his practice, and heart for practical strategies have led to an amazing book that all university professors should read regardless of their area of expertise.

As I turned these pages, I was deeply impressed. This book

- is the most accomplished, thorough, and comprehensive treatise on the history of flipped learning written to date;
- explains the variety of frameworks of flipped learning in a clear and cogent fashion;
- practically walks through effective flipped strategies, so that others who flip their university classes will not fall into common mistakes;
- will help professors to learn better how to plan differently in light of flipped learning;
- is a straightforward guide for those who are reticent to start flipping their courses; and
- is scholarly yet still easily digestible.

But what I was most impressed with was Robert's transparency. His story of struggle with his first flipped class did not lead him to give up but rather drove him to figure out how to reach every student in the class. This striving demonstrated to me that Robert cares about not only math and engineering but also the success of each of his of students. He clearly values relationships over content and communicates warmth to every student who walks into his classrooms. Professors everywhere have a lot to learn from Robert.

The book presents flipped learning in simple terms that will lead to greater adoption of flipped learning in universities around the globe. So if you are kicking the tires of flipped learning, stop what you are doing and read this book. After reading it, you will have a clear path to flip your classes.

Jon Bergmann
Flipped Learning Pioneer
Founder of the Flipped Learning Global Initiative

PREFACE

What This Book Is About

This book is about *flipped learning,* an approach to the design and instruction of classes that involves the following simple changes to the way classes are usually conducted:

- Instead of having students gain their first exposure to new concepts and material *in class* (often through a lecture), we set up ways for students to have that first exposure *prior* to class, along with ways to guide them through that first exposure.
- Because all this is taking place *before* class, it frees up large chunks of time *during* class that can now be spent on the activities where students typically need the most help, such as applications of the basic material and engaging in deeper discussions and creative work with it.

This "flipping" of the contexts of student work—first exposure to new concepts before class, then deeper and higher work during class instead of the other way around—is, as we said, a simple idea. But it is also a profound one, and it has the potential to transform education, particularly higher education, in ways we are only beginning to understand.

I began using flipped learning to organize and teach my classes several years ago out of necessity (more on that in a minute) and gradually expanded the scope of my flipped learning designs until, today, every class I teach uses flipped learning: high-level topics courses for majors in my discipline as well as general education courses, large sections and small sections, and face-to-face courses and online courses. The results have been undeniable. Students in these classes not only learn the content of their course as well as or better than in a traditional course setup but also learn to take more responsibility for their work, make greater strides toward becoming self-regulating learners (a concept we will explore in detail in the chapters ahead), work harder and smarter during class time, and are generally *happier* with the course. In fact, in my department (where many of my colleagues are also on board), students now openly complain when a course *doesn't* use flipped learning. As some of our students say, "How are we supposed to learn anything if all the teacher does is *lecture* during class?"

Students *get it*: Higher education today does not have to look like the higher education of yesteryear, or even of a decade ago, when the only reasonable way to guide students through first exposure to new concepts was through having everyone in the same room on a fixed schedule where the information could be disseminated by an expert. In fact, today's students are acutely aware that in a highly competitive job marketplace, their future as professionals depends on their ability to learn on their own, to be able to pick up new skills and ideas on an as-needed basis and then put them to work on difficult, creative applications that matter to them. Someone who *needs* a traditional classroom setup to learn anything will be left behind. They need a higher education that "gets it" as much as they do.

And lest we think of higher education only as job preparation, the notion of *lifelong learning* also is predicated on the idea of having not only the ability but also the *taste* for learning new things on one's own, letting one's curiosity and interests guide one into new ideas and skills, and translating passions and interests into actual knowledge and abilities. Higher education, by its very structure, ought to communicate the vital importance of lifelong learning—but often it fails, again by its very structure, which communicates the opposite of what we want: that learning take place during set times of the day, a set number of times of the week, and only after an expert tells you what you need to know. But those of us who are, or at least like to think that we are, lifelong learners know a different story. Learning is unbounded, deeply personal, deeply rooted in our native human ability to reason for ourselves. The structures higher education places around this process *used to serve* the learning process but are today increasingly *served by* the learning process, so that lifelong learning is not the point any more—attending class and taking tests (that are taken straight from a lecture) and getting high scores is the point. Higher education needs a reboot to come back to the core principle of lifelong learning.

I believe flipped learning is an idea whose time has come. It's a way of doing higher education that shows unique promise for simultaneously getting it back to its intellectual roots while ushering it into the future.

At the same time, flipped learning is, at its heart, a very *simple* idea. How can one possibly write an entire book about it? Well, it turns out that implementing this simple idea is not, itself, all that simple. In fact, this book began with that first attempt at flipped learning that was a pretty massive failure.

Productive Failure

The year was 2009, and I was on the mathematics faculty at a small liberal arts college. As is the case in small colleges, I also did a lot of administrative and service work. One of those administrative jobs was to manage our college's 3+2 engineering program. Like other similar programs at small colleges throughout the United States, students in the 3+2 program attended my college for their first three years to complete the basic science, math, and general education courses needed for an engineering degree; then they transferred to a partner institution, a larger university with an engineering program to take their specialized engineering courses. After five years they received two degrees, one in applied mathematics from my college and one in engineering from our partner.

This was a great program but tricky to manage because of the omnipresent scheduling constraints in small colleges. For example, we could only offer one section of Calculus 2 per year. If there were any schedule conflicts between my college's courses and our partners', it was a serious problem. So to help ameliorate this problem, I proposed a course on computer programming for mathematics majors, using the software MATLAB, that would satisfy a basic course requirement at our partner university.

To ensure sufficient enrollment each time it was offered, the course was made a requirement for *all* math majors, not only the engineering students but also students who don't normally take scientific computing courses, like preservice primary and secondary education majors. The audience therefore included many students who weren't typically very interested in—or comfortable with—the idea of computer programming. To give the full range of students the time and space to learn the subject, I proposed a three-credit course meeting three times a week for 50 minutes each time.

By the time the course was debated and modified by our dean, it had been whittled down to a *one*-credit course—meeting once a week for 75 minutes. This was a serious, if not crippling, problem because I had just one concept in my mind about how a college course should be designed and managed. That setup is the one that I encountered exclusively in college as well as for most of my courses in graduate school, and it goes like this:

- During class meetings, the students in the class get their first contact with the material through a (hopefully well-constructed and logically sequenced) lecture that includes lots of instructor examples, and maybe if there is time, there will be some practice time made available.
- After class is over, the students are tasked with going back to their dorms, homes, and apartments to work on bigger and better

things—things like homework, projects, programming, assignments, and so on.

But immediately I realized that this model simply won't work for a first course on computer programming, aimed at a general audience, done once a week for 75 minutes. First, computer programming is a skill that cannot be learned by listening to a lecture—one has to *do* programming, make mistakes, fix the mistakes, and reflect on those mistakes in order to really learn the subject. I knew this from my own computer programming courses in the past, which had been taught exclusively via lecture. But because I was a skilled learner back in those days and loved technology and had a technical background, it was no problem for me to make the time outside of class for the *real* learning experiences. Second, the students in *my* class were not like I was. They weren't dumb by any means, but they were not expert learners and did not, in many cases, possess even a basic level of comfort with technology, much less skill. Third, even if I were to lecture flat out with no breaks for 75 minutes once a week, and even if the students in the course could absorb all that lecture and put it to good use in their own time, we still wouldn't be able to learn everything we needed to learn in the course.

I needed a different model.

So I did some research, and I eventually came across an article called "The Inverted Classroom in Software Engineering" (Gannod, Burge, and Helmick 2008), by three professors in the computer science department at Miami University of Ohio. These professors at Miami had devised something called the "inverted classroom" (which I later came to realize had been invented by some of their colleagues in the Economics Department, eight years earlier). In the inverted classroom, the direct transmission of information that one normally associates with a classroom lecture still happened, but it happened in a different context: *outside*, actually *before*, the class meeting in the form of prerecorded video and readings. Then, because this activity was relocated outside the class meeting, the meeting was wide open to be spent on active learning activities. Additionally, having the lectures prerecorded allowed students to pause and replay as often as they needed without having to lose themselves in note taking.

After one reading of this article, I knew that this was the model I was looking for. Students would watch videos about certain feature sets of the software prior to the weekly class meeting. MATLAB maintains a collection of professional-quality instructional videos for this purpose (see MathWorks 2016), so I didn't need to *make* any video content, just link to what had already been made and add some viewing notes. I created weekly programming labs in which students would partner and apply the basic feature set of the week—which they learned through watching the videos—to solve an applied problem using MATLAB. Students were assessed on the quality of their solutions as well as on a handful of timed assessments.

This seemed very promising. Students would get to know the software on a basic level before class, thereby liberating tons of time in class to do creative application work. Thus would the flipped learning idea be implemented solidly in my course. This was going to be *awesome!*

Except, as it turned out, it was not so awesome. In fact, it was a resounding failure on a number of fronts:

- I gave students well-crafted video resources, but that's all I did—*gave them* with instructions to "watch this video before class." It turns out this is not enough. Students tried to watch the videos but quickly got lost, did not learn what they needed to learn to be ready for class, and did not retain what they had learned from previous weeks.
- Because students weren't learning from the video preclass assignments, they were showing up to class unready to work on applications of the basic material. Those labs that I so painstakingly constructed for class time? They were nonstarters for the students.
- Students asked me to reteach the material from the videos because they didn't understand them. I refused—maybe I should say "declined"—because I assumed that the reason students were asking was because they had simply refused to watch the videos out of laziness. Perhaps some students *were* lazy, but it's more likely that many of them simply didn't know how to watch a video in the sense of *learning* something from it. Things got tense in the class as a result.
- Students became frustrated that I "wasn't teaching the material." I was mad at the students because, in my mind, they weren't working on their preparatory material hard or well enough. The community atmosphere of the class collapsed in the second week of the semester and never recovered. There was no trust, no sense of mutual help, and honestly very little got learned that semester by anybody.

In short, it was one of the worst experiences in my 20-year teaching career, and it was mostly my fault, and by all rights I should have dropped this model then and there and never looked back.

However, I remained convinced that although going back to the traditional model of instruction might make students (and myself) *happier* it would not result in improved learning, because, again, one cannot learn computer programming by listening to someone talk about computer programming. One has to *try* to program with the time and space to make and repair mistakes while working on an interesting problem that requires basic skills. And those basic skills can, and therefore should, be acquired independently prior to class time, while reserving precious class time for me to *help* students as they do the hard and frustrating work of getting computer code to behave correctly.

In other words, I faced a choice after that initial disaster of a semester: Either try to figure out what was missing from my teaching in the class and then try again or abandon the idea altogether. I chose the former, and it was one of the best decisions of my career.

The Audience for and Structure of This Book

The model that I have described, called the "inverted classroom" by the professors at Miami (and still often called by that name), is the pedagogical model we will call *flipped learning* throughout this book. As mentioned earlier, it is called "flipped" because of the reversal or flipping of the contexts of what students do in their own time versus their time with the entire class. This book, to a great degree, is an extended message to you about what I have figured out in the decade or so since that first attempt, in hopes that you can learn from my mistakes without actually *making* those same mistakes.

I strongly believe that flipped learning is the future of higher education, and therefore all of us in higher education need to be devoting time, attention, and effort in bringing this model into our classes. I also believe that adopting flipped learning cannot happen effectively without a solid set of basic resources and a community to help practice it. In my experiences as a workshop facilitator, speaker, and writer on flipped learning, I've found that although there is a strong interest in flipped learning in higher education, there are few "one-stop shop" resources for how to actually implement it, and only isolated pockets of communities of practice. This situation isn't sustainable. So one of my main hopes for this book is that it would be such a resource for instructors and a starting point for a robust community of practice about flipped learning in higher education.

There are three kinds of instructors who might find this book useful. I think you will find yourself in at least one of these categories:

1. *The curious.* These are college and university instructors who have heard about flipped learning (or perhaps the more popular term, the *flipped classroom*; we'll discuss terminology more in chapter 1) and are interested in learning more. For you, the hope is you'll use the parts of this book of most interest to you and come away with a sound idea of what flipped

learning is and how it might be useful to your students. I also hope that you'll consider graduating to the next category.

2. *The newbies.* These are college and university instructors who are just beginning to practice flipped learning. Maybe you've tried it and it didn't go so well (see my earlier story) and are curious to know what might be missing. Or maybe you are having a great experience with it so far and want to know how to expand your use. Either way, the hope is that you'll find practical tools and research results to help take your use of flipped learning to the next level, and that you will ultimately make it a permanent part of your teaching practice.

3. *The veterans.* These are college and university instructors who have used flipped learning for at least one entire course and are looking to hone their craft. For you, I hope this book provides a bigger picture, some good tips you can use, and some research background that can deepen your understanding of the practice. I also encourage you to parlay your experiences into scholarship that you can share publicly and so build the community of practice. We'll discuss this last item in the final chapter.

I've tried to write this book with each audience in mind, and with a balance of *research* on flipped learning and its theoretical bases, *course design* concepts that will help you set up courses to use flipped learning effectively, *tips and examples* from real-life usage of flipped learning, and *practical considerations* such as obtaining buy-in from students and getting students to do the preclass activities.

The book is *not* addressed toward K–12 (primary or secondary) schoolteachers, unless you are a teacher working with Advanced Placement or International Baccalaureate students or a similar "college-like" audience. This is because the K–12 world already has a great flipped learning ecosystem in place, with several excellent books on the subject (e.g., Bergmann and Sams 2012) and strong communities of practice. It doesn't need this book. The K–12 resources are well worth examining if you are a college or university instructor. However, despite their excellent quality, their applicability to higher education is limited due to the sometimes vast differences between the assumptions and contexts of higher education and K–12 education. For example, in higher education we often assume that students have 24/7 access to a high-speed Internet connection through their institutions; no such assumption can be made for students in a public high school.

Included in our audience is any person involved in education at a higher level—not only professors at four-year institutions, but also community and two-year college instructors, Advanced Placement or International

Baccalaureate instructors in high schools, adjunct instructors who teach classes across multiple institutions or online, even parents with kids who are hungry to learn more. I will often use the terms *colleges* and *universities*; these are always intended as synonyms for any institution of higher education at any level.

This book is divided into three main parts:

- Part One: What Is Flipped Learning? focuses on understanding exactly what flipped learning is, what it isn't, and why instructors have chosen to use it (chapter 1); the research basis and theoretical frameworks that support the concept of flipped learning (chapter 2); and case studies that show different ways that flipped learning is used across academic disciplines (chapter 3).
- Part Two: Flipped Learning Design is all about the practical process of designing (or redesigning) a course around flipped learning. We'll discuss course design paradigms in general and specifically how the model offered by Dee Fink can be adapted to a flipped learning environment (chapter 4), look at a *seven-step model* for flipped learning design that stresses the development of appropriate learning objectives and describe a sustainable model for preclass activities that students actually complete (chapters 5 and 6).
- Part Three: Teaching and Learning in a Flipped Learning Environment transitions from course design to issues of how to make flipped learning a permanent part of your teaching practice. We'll look at variations on the basic flipped design of classes to apply flipped learning to both online and low-tech courses, as well as the idea of "partial flipping" (chapter 7). Then, finally, we look at how to make flipped learning a sustainable and productive everyday part of your career, addressing issues that commonly arise with students as well as ways to parlay flipped learning experiences into your scholarship and service portfolios (chapter 8).

If you don't read the entire book, it's recommended that you read all the way through Part One and then dip into the other chapters as needed.

Flipped learning is an exciting and effective way to teach, and I can't wait for you to learn more about it.

ACKNOWLEDGMENTS

The idea for this book came out of my blog, *Casting Out Nines*, where I have written short articles and passing thoughts about flipped learning and other issues involving mathematics, technology, and education since 2006. On a flight back to Michigan after giving a talk on flipped learning, I wrote a draft for a blog post about flipped learning only to realize that it was almost word-for-word identical to a post I'd written three years before. At that point, I realized it was time to get all my thoughts about flipped learning into one place and into the hands of the general non-blog-reading public. The book you have in front of you is the result, a reasonably cleaned-up and significantly better-researched version of dozens, maybe hundreds, of posts I have made at *Casting Out Nines* through the years.

Because this book is so closely tied to the blog, I want to thank all the readers and commenters (even the trolls!) who have made *Casting Out Nines* such a rewarding avocation, from its days as a self-hosted WordPress blog to its stint in *The Chronicle of Higher Education*'s now-defunct blog network (it's still archived there, at http://chronicle.com/blognetwork/castingoutnines) to its current incarnation on my website (http://rtalbert.org). And thank you to Xarissa Holdaway, Jeff Young, and all of the team at the *Chronicle* who helped shepherd the blog into the national spotlight and keep it there from 2011 through 2015.

As an extension, I want to thank the many people on my social media feeds, mostly Twitter, who resonated with *Casting Out Nines* and helped me sharpen my ideas after the posts were posted. Many of these people simply retweeted links to posts, and I learned how awesomely rewarding it can be to watch an idea take hold and spread. But a few of those people turned out to be kindred spirits and fellow travelers, who began to follow my writing (and vice versa) and eventually became colleagues and friends. These include Spencer Bagley, Lorena Barba, Bret Benesh, Brian Bennett, Derek Bruff, Justin Dunmyre, Dana Ernst, Joshua Eyler, T. J. Hitchman, Patrick Honner, Sarah Kavassalis, Mitch Keller, Vince Knight, Peter Newberry, Frank Noschese, Kate Owens, Chuck Pearson, Kris Shaffer, Calvin Smith, Bonni Stachowiak, and many, many others. It's a pleasure to interact with these people and an honor to be in their circles. Anybody who thinks Twitter is a waste of time for academics is doing it wrong.

I want to give a special thanks to all the faculty with whom I consulted in the making of this book. You will see some of their names in the chapters but all of them contributed and I appreciate their time and efforts: Bret Benesh (College of St. Benedict), Kevin Karplus (University of California–Santa Cruz), Kieran Mathieson (Oakland University), Nathalie Neve (Portland State University), Malissa Peery (University of Tennessee), Drew Walker (University of California–San Diego), and Ed Webb (Dickinson College). I want to thank particularly some of the "big names" who took time to respond to out-of-nowhere e-mails and Twitter direct messages about their experiences in the early days of flipped learning, particularly J. Wesley Baker, Jon Bergmann, Eric Mazur, and Glenn Platt.

I'm particularly grateful that those unsolicited Twitter direct messages I sent to Jon Bergmann in May 2016 led to a longer conversation about flipped learning, which in turn culminated in a working relationship with the Flipped Learning Global Initiative, a program Jon began in 2016 to create awareness and help the implementation of flipped learning around the world. I am truly honored to be one of the inaugural cohort of Flipped Learning Research Fellows for this organization. It just goes to show that sometimes bugging people can pay off. Go to http://flglobal.org to find out more about the Flipped Learning Global Initiative.

As the idea of this book began to take shape, I wasn't exactly sure how to proceed, or even if proceeding was a good idea—I had never written a book before. So I consulted the person whose knowledge and experience I respect possibly more than any other: Linda Nilson is the best in the business when it comes to promoting effective and innovative teaching, whether it's through one of her many great books or the seemingly endless series of workshops and keynote addresses she gives. She also happens to be my former boss; she hired me into a Master Teaching Fellowship when I was in graduate school at Vanderbilt University and she was the director of Vanderbilt's Center for Teaching. In the one all-too-brief year I spent at the Center for Teaching working under Linda's supervision, I think I learned most of what I know about effective teaching and the scholarship of teaching and learning. Her mentorship and friendship throughout the intervening years have been a constant blessing both professionally and personally, and her imprint will be seen in this book by anybody who knows her or her work.

It was on Linda's advice that I contact John von Knorring at Stylus Publishing with the idea for this book. John has been incredibly supportive and helpful through the process of bringing this book to completion, and I couldn't have asked for a better group to work through than the team at Stylus.

Finally, I have three groups of people to thank, without whom this book definitely would not be a reality.

First are my students from Bethel College (Indiana), Franklin College, and Grand Valley State University (GVSU). My use of flipped learning got its start at Franklin, and I've honed it at GVSU since moving there in 2011, but my Bethel students first made me aware of the deeply human element of teaching that motivates me to be excellent in the classroom. Without the students at these institutions—their feedback, their hard work, their patience, and their inherent goodness as people—all the innovative teaching in the world would just be chasing after the wind.

Second are my colleagues from the mathematics department at GVSU. More than once, outsiders have remarked to me that the GVSU math department is like a superhero team, so studded with amazing talent that it must be intimidating to work there. Let me be clear: It is. I haven't been the smartest person in the room since arriving in Allendale, Michigan, in 2011. But the mixture of crackling intellectual energy, heartfelt care for students, and incredible kindness among my colleagues makes GVSU a place to work like none other, and I have thanked God every morning when I drive onto campus that I am privileged to work in a university like Grand Valley. I particularly want to thank Ed Aboufadel, David Austin, Matt Boelkins, David Clark, David Coffey, Marcia Frobish, John Golden, Jon Hasenbank, Jon Hodge, Karen Novotny, Darren Parker, Shelly Smith, Ted Sundstrom, and Clark Wells—these particular colleagues have given me direct feedback, honest questions, deep conversation, and blunt criticism about flipped learning and other teaching and learning issues that have made the ideas in this book better than they would have been otherwise, and me a better teacher.

Third and finally, I want to thank my family for their support and love during the process of writing this book. The summer of 2016, when most of the words in the book went to the page, was spent juggling writing and teaching on the one hand, with shuttling kids back and forth from camp, making breakfast and lunch and snacks for kids, mediating conflicts with the TV, remodeling the kitchen, and making sure we had at least some time to enjoy another beautiful summer along the west coast of Michigan on the other. By pulling together as a family, I think we made it. So Cathy, Lucy, Penelope, and Harrison—I love you all very much, and thanks.

PART ONE

WHAT IS FLIPPED LEARNING?

WHAT IS FLIPPED LEARNING, AND WHY USE IT?

When my father was a young man working on an electrical engineering degree at Texas Tech University in the 1950s, there was no issue about the *way* that his academic courses were set up and executed. Students went to class at fixed times during the week and in fixed locations. In class, an expert instructor would lecture about a topic in electrical engineering, physics, or mathematics. Students took notes and, possibly, asked questions. Then the class was over, and students went back to their dorms to work on the problems and design projects. Then the cycle repeated. There might have been some variations among courses at the university, but the similarities to how those courses were designed and taught along the lines of this model far outweighed the differences.

This education served him well through college and into the first couple of decades of his career as an engineer. He worked for General Motors and was at one point contracted to NASA to help design the electrical and guidance systems for the Gemini and Apollo spacecraft. His education served him well because, despite having to move around from one job site to another and jumping from General Motors to NASA and back, he still basically just did one *thing* in his work: design electrical systems for vehicles. After his stint at NASA and General Motors, he and my mom (and at that point, my sisters, too) moved to Tennessee, where he took a job at the public electric utility for the city of Nashville. I came along shortly after that move. And for the great majority of my childhood I remember Dad still doing just one *thing* day in and day out: Design electrical systems for the city of Nashville. It was like NASA, except with cities instead of spaceships.

But then one day Dad was promoted to supervisor, and he was working on a wide assortment of tasks, only a fraction of which had to do with engineering. The biggest of those projects occurred when the Houston Oilers of the National Football League moved to Tennessee. He was in charge of designing the electrical grid for the new stadium that was to be built. This sounds like engineering, but many nonengineering tasks lurked below the surface. For example, in order to build that stadium, several blocks of the near east side of Nashville needed to be cleared, and he was involved in the civil engineering—and the politics—of this process. He had to manage people and learn whom to talk to to learn what he needed to learn to get the day's work done. He had to pick up new skills rapidly, in the moment, and with a minimum of help from third parties. He certainly did not have the luxury of taking a course from the local college in whatever it was he needed to know. In short, he was now responsible for a complex arrangement of tasks and projects that had very little to do with the book knowledge that he gained, indeed mastered, as an undergraduate.

My dad's story illustrates a larger truth: that the nature of life and work has changed significantly just in the last few decades. Consequently, the way we conceive of education should change to match. Models of higher education that are based on a scarcity model of information and on training undergraduates in a single, narrow discipline are fast becoming (if they are not already) obsolete. Higher education needs a new way to present itself, a way that continues the best of its long intellectual traditions without being tone deaf to the needs of the world around it.

The Traditional Model

To understand how we might address these issues, we will start with long-held basic assumptions about how college and university courses are structured and how learners are expected to use their time.

For centuries in higher education, the most efficient (or perhaps the *only*) way to teach students was to gather them into a fixed place on a fixed schedule, disseminate pertinent information, and then have students work with that information in activities involving cognitive processes more complex than just writing down disseminated information. This is still the predominant mode of instruction in universities today, and it should be familiar to nearly everyone. Students arrive at a class meeting with their classmates, engage in first contact with new material through a lecture (which could include elements of activity such as group work or question/answer exchanges), and then go home to work with that new material through homework, labs, essays, projects, and the like. This cycle of meetings, followed by higher-order work, followed by meetings continues, punctuated by occasional summative assessments.

Throughout this book, we will refer to this model of course design as the *traditional model.* It has the following main features:

- The class meeting is used primarily for introducing students to new material for the first time and disseminating further, related material (often through the form of a lecture).
- Higher-level work on that material—work that focuses on application, synthesis, evaluation, and creativity—is done following the class meeting, by students individually. Students *might* be allowed to work in groups or might work in groups even if not allowed, or might work alone even if groups are allowed. There is not much regulation or supervision by an expert (i.e., the professor or teaching assistant) in this individual phase, and if the student wants help, she will have to rely on her peers (assuming collaboration is allowed) or interaction with the instructor that is possibly time delayed.

Note that this is a model of *design,* not necessarily a model of a particular *instructional method.* The class meeting might consist of lecture, or it might be something different. *What makes the traditional model is not the specific pedagogy used in the class time, but the way the class time itself is purposed.* Students encounter new material and related material during class time, and then work with it on a higher level afterward.

As we mentioned, the traditional model is *traditional*—it is the way that most people will describe how college works if you ask them. The traditional model can, in the right hands, lead to a learning environment in which deep learning is facilitated. And many of us who went to college can recall memories of profound insight, or just plain fun, from the many hours spent taking courses modeled in the traditional way. We should also emphasize that this model does not describe all instances of higher education from the past. Instructional design and pedagogical models such as the Oxford tutorial, case study methods, practica, and laboratory experiences do not fit this mold. Still, the typical and traditional way of conceiving of college classes is as described.

However, there are crucial issues with the traditional model that are becoming more and more apparent as the world around us—the world that gave birth to the traditional model—changes:

- *The traditional model creates an inverse relationship between cognitive difficulty of student work and student access to support.* This means that in the traditional model, students are doing the simplest work when their channels of support are most readily accessible and the hardest work when the support is least available. When the resident expert (the instructor) is physically available in the same space as the students, representing the maximum point of accessibility to help, the students' job is often simply to take notes. Conversely, students are doing the most complex work when the channels of work are least accessible—their work on higher-level cognitive tasks like application and synthesis tasks takes place after the instructor has left the building. We often hear this inverse relationship play out in statements that students make, such as *This material made sense in class, but when I try it, I'm lost.* This happens because taking notes, although not a trivial cognitive task, is still at its heart an information-processing task. It is more cognitively complex to take the information represented by student notes and apply that information to a real problem, or to compare and contrast the concepts contained in the notes. (And this is assuming that students take notes as experts would take notes, which is hardly the case—for most students, "taking notes" means raw transcription and nothing more.) Students are more likely to need help on the latter tasks than on the former. However, the problem is that the instructor is *present* in the former and *not present* in the latter. Students then find themselves in situations where they need the support of their instructors when they are in precisely the context where that help is least available: when they are alone.

- *The traditional model takes time away from social, guided exploration of deeper learning.* In a traditional classroom setting where lecture is predominant, the time devoted to nonlecturing activities—where students will put their newly received knowledge to the test and explore the big ideas of a lesson—is a fraction of the entire class meeting. In some cases there may be *no* time in the class meetings devoted to these sorts of activities; rather, students are left to their own devices to explore deep ideas, a task to which many students today are singularly unsuited due to a lack of experience with deep learning or critical thinking, or a lack of skill with regulating themselves as they learn. If there is time set aside in class to do active learning tasks, often time runs out far ahead of any meaningful process. And so this deeper learning is left up to the students to do on their own time—again, in a context where help is least accessible.

- *The traditional model does not promote self-regulated learning behaviors.* Self-regulated learning is a complex psychological concept with its own entire research literature, and entire books can and have been written on the subject. But briefly, *self-regulated learning* refers to learning that "encompasses full attention and concentration, self-awareness and introspection, honest self-assessment, openness to change, genuine self-discipline, and acceptance of responsibility for one's learning" (Nilson 2013, p. 4). The much-used notion of *lifelong learning*, part of so many mission statements for institutions of higher education, is expressed well in self-regulated learning. All instructors who care about teaching hope that their students will eventually come to practice all of these behaviors and that their one course can help them along the path. A course taught in the traditional model *can* do this, but the behaviors themselves are not explicitly *part of* the model. A successful student in a traditional model (or any model) will exhibit a combination of these behaviors, but practice and assessment of these behaviors are only rarely an actual part of the class specifically taught and practiced alongside the discipline-specific content of the course. Indeed, by promoting a model in which the instructor is the source and gatekeeper of knowledge, many of these self-regulating behaviors are downplayed.

- *The traditional model creates undesirable intellectual dependencies of students on instructors.* All of these issues tend to create an environment in which the student–professor relationship can tend toward unhealthy dependency. When the professor is the gatekeeper for information, as in the traditional model, students can come to believe that the professor is *necessary* for learning and then exhibit traits that are consistent with this belief. In mathematics, for instance, we see this when students claim they are unable to start a solution to a mathematics problem without the professor's guidance. In disciplines involving writing, we can see this when students believe they cannot self-check work reliably. (*Can you tell me if this is on the right track, professor?*) Other times, because the professor is the gatekeeper not only to knowledge but also to grades, the student can see the professor as an *obstacle*—the person who takes away the points—and develop an adversarial relationship. All of us who work in higher education want the best for our students, and that includes a healthy, productive working relationship that leads students to become effective, independent thinkers. This *can* happen in the traditional model—but it doesn't seem to be the default.

These issues have a single common denominator: *They happen because of the way space, time, and activity are used in the course design.* Because the traditional model uses class meetings for initial contact with new material and dissemination of related material, with higher-order tasks relegated to the students' individual spaces, the issues with support for higher-order tasks, time in class for exploration of deep ideas, self-regulation, and healthy professional relationships take root. This suggests that if we treated time, space, and activity differently, these issues might be ameliorated. In fact, if we *completely reversed* how space, time, and activity are used, we might end up with a radically better model.

A Definition of *Flipped Learning* (First Attempt)

Reversing the ways in which space, time, and activity are allocated in a class would have several ramifications:

- Students' first contact with new material in the course, and their first steps at basic cognition using that material, would take place *outside* of class meetings because students might benefit from having unstructured time to interact with that material at their own pace, and also because the basic cognitive tasks do not require the kind of intensive expert guidance that higher-level tasks do.
- Having relocated the first contact experiences outside of class, the entire class meeting is now open for targeted questions and for higher-level tasks—the kinds of hard, demanding work that students need to do in order to assimilate the information they've seen and that will benefit them the most from social interactions with their peers and close guidance from an expert.

This model of pedagogy is what we mean by *flipped learning.*

We call it flipped because of the reversal (flipping) of the activities that take place in the various contexts of a course. The term *flipped learning* is intended to apply to an entire philosophy of teaching and learning that encompasses the design of a course (which we will sometimes call *flipped learning design*) and the expectations not only for *what* students learn in a course but also for *how* they go about learning it.

By using a flipped learning model, all of the issues in the traditional model mentioned previously can be addressed:

1. In flipped learning, the relation between cognitive difficulty and access to help is now *direct* rather than *inverse*. Students are using their class meetings to work on cognitively advanced tasks, where they have peers and an instructor at their side to get help as they work.
2. In flipped learning, the entire class meeting is opened up for the instructor to plan whatever active, creative, rigorous activities best serve the needs of the students. There are no more internal negotiations for class

time in order to fit in the lecture and no instances where the lecture runs over time and leaves no room for activities. Further, because in flipped learning the first contact with new material often takes place *prior* to the class meeting, there is time for students to "soak in" the new material and ask questions before being asked to apply that information to a more advanced task.

3. Flipped learning promotes self-regulation because self-regulated learning behaviors are forced to get to the point on a daily basis. Students may be provided lectures prior to class, but they are in control of how they learn from those lectures. For example, students are in control of deciding for themselves when their understanding of a recorded lecture is not adequate and then taking action in the form of stopping the video and replaying it, and trying something different to understand it. Students have to practice self-regulated learning behaviors on a regular basis as part of the basic infrastructure of the course, rather than having this left up to chance.

4. Because students are now in charge of working with basic material, the instructor is free to abdicate the role of knowledge gatekeeper and instead shift to a role of coach, helper, and consultant as students work on higher-order tasks. A more productive, professional, and "grown-up" relationship between student and professor is therefore engendered.

This should give the general idea behind flipped learning. However, it will be important for us to move toward a more precise definition of *flipped learning*, for several reasons, which we will take up later in this chapter. To do so, we need to discuss in greater detail the concepts of *time, space,* and *activity* that make the flipped learning model what it is.

Time and Space

We mentioned that the traditional and flipped learning models are reversed from each other in terms of what students do in various contexts of experience in the course. Those contexts fall into two categories: the context of *individual space* and the context of *group space*. Note that by *space,* we do not necessarily mean only physical space but rather the physical, emotional, intellectual, and psychological contexts that students encounter when they are doing work.

Individual space refers to the context in which students operate when they are working mainly by themselves, or perhaps in a small informal group that meets apart from a formal class meeting. A student encounters individual space when working alone in a dorm room, library, or coffee shop.

The student also encounters individual space when working in a tutoring center receiving help on demand, or meeting after dinner with a study group, or working with a friend on Skype. Work done in the individual space is focused on the *individual student's efforts*, even though there may be more than just the individual present.

By contrast, *group space* refers to the context in which students operate when they are working with a formal group as part of the class itself. Group space is what students encounter, in other words, when they are learning *with the entire class* or some intentional, regulated subset of that class such as small groups formed during class by the instructor or a designated breakout group in an online course. A student is encountering group space when she attends a scheduled class meeting. She is also encountering group space on a field trip with her class, or during a meeting in a scheduled tutorial session run by the instructor, or in an online class interacting on a discussion board or video chat as part of a scheduled group activity.

Note that group *space* does not always involve group *work*. Indeed the prototypical group space—the stereotypical large lecture section—is a group space in which possibly hundreds of students are gathered in a single room, but little to no group interaction is taking place. Although we consider this a group space, the work that is done is largely performed by the individual. Likewise, individual space does not necessarily mean working alone. Indeed, for many of us, some of our liveliest college experiences were small group interactions that took place in the individual context—late night study sessions in the lounge, heated philosophical discussions over pizza, and so on.

You may find these definitions of *group* and *individual space* abstract or overly complicated. Why not just say "class time" instead of "group space" and "outside-of-class time" instead of "individual space"? In a traditional in-seat, face-to-face course—that is, a course in which students gather physically in a fixed space at fixed times—group space really *does* just mean the class meeting, and individual space is everything else. However, we want our notion of flipped learning to extend beyond face-to-face courses and be applicable to the emerging world of *online* and *hybrid* courses.

Although definitions of *online* and *hybrid courses* vary from institution to institution, generally speaking an *online course* is a course delivered without significant face-to-face elements—perhaps without *any* face-to-face elements. An online course may be *synchronous*, meaning that the course meets on a fixed schedule but entirely on the Internet. For example, such a course may require students to log into a video chat room three times a week at the same time of the day, similar to a face-to-face class. Online courses may also be *asynchronous*, meaning that no fixed meetings exist at all, either in time or in physical space. A *hybrid course,* on the other hand, has a significant component of regular, fixed meeting times in a fixed location like a traditional class, along with significant online instruction. Survey research led the Babson Survey Research Group to define a *hybrid course* as one delivering less than 80% of the course online and an *online course* as one delivering 80% or more of the course online; many institutions define *online course* to be one in which 100% of the course is delivered online (Allen and Seaman 2010). Moreover, there are further finer distinctions between these two categories, including blended classroom courses, blended online courses, and web-enhanced courses (Sener 2015). These differences, and the applicability of flipped learning to each one of them, will be taken up in chapter 7.

Neither online nor hybrid courses maintain the traditional notions of before-class, in-class, or after-class times and spaces that traditional in-seat courses have. Asynchronous online courses, for example, have no class time or preclass time—there is only *time*, and how it is used depends on individual student choice in the moment, and those choices create the contexts of individual or group space. If a student, for example, chooses to spend an hour in the morning working with a full-class discussion thread on a discussion board, this would be considered *group space* even though it is not a group meeting. During the same interval of time, possibly even in the same physical space, another student in the same class might be working on a task individually or in a small informal study group, which would be considered *individual space* for our purposes.

Definitions of *flipped learning* that assume fixed meeting times and spaces are therefore inadequate to the task of applying flipped learning to a modern higher educational environment. We therefore will use the notions of individual space and group space instead.

Direct Instruction and Active Learning

The distinction between traditional and flipped learning models hinges not just on the existence of group and individual space but on what students are *doing* in the group and individual spaces. Therefore, we need a clear idea about not only *space* and *time* but also *activity*. In particular we need to understand the balance between *direct instruction* and *active learning*—a balance that must always be dealt with in any pedagogical model but that takes on a particular importance in the flipped learning model.

Direct instruction has many definitions and interpretations. For our purposes, we will define *direct instruction* as any teaching technique in which information being taught is presented in an organized, sequenced way by a teacher, explicitly directed toward the student. This definition is an amalgamation of definitions found in the literature and it is not to be confused with Direct Instruction, a specific pedagogical program founded by Siegfried Engelmann and Wesley Becker (Engelmann 1980) that is a subset of this larger definition.

Direct instruction can look like many different things:

- The stereotypical lecture, given in a one-way oral transmission from a professor to students who sit listening and taking notes in a lecture hall, *can* be a form of direct instruction. It is not *necessarily* direct instruction, because direct instruction presupposes organization and logical sequencing, and we have all experienced lectures that fail on these fronts. In order to be direct instruction, the pedagogy must at least attempt to *instruct*.
- Students who watch a (well-organized, sequenced) lecture that has been recorded to video are receiving direct instruction.
- An instructor whose students are working in small groups in a class meeting who notices that one group is falling behind and briefly gives a fully worked-out example to that group to get them back on track is engaging in direct instruction.
- A student in an online mathematics course who reads a discussion board post that contains a worked solution to a problem written up by the instructor and who is actively processing the steps of that solution is receiving direct instruction.

Direct instruction, then, is not just one form of teaching. Rather, it describes a range of pedagogies that—like all pedagogical methods—has contexts in which it can support learning and contexts in which other methods would be better for supporting learning. It can and should be part of every instructor's toolbox, to use well when the context is right. The key idea is identifying the context in which direct instruction leads to the best results in student learning.

The counterpart of direct instruction is *active learning*. The range of definitions and interpretations of this term is staggering and far too great to include in its entirety here. For our purposes, we will include as active learning *any instructional method that engages students in the learning process, in an active way, as part of the group space activities*. This definition follows established descriptions of active learning (e.g., Prince 2004) and is broad enough to include a wide range of pedagogical activities but also precise enough to screen out "activities" that we don't normally associate with the term *active learning*, such as doing homework. Certainly doing homework is an active process, and we hope students learn something in the process, but when we talk about active learning, we are generally thinking about something students do to learn *while in the classroom*, which for us means in group space and not individual space.

Active learning, and its effect on students, has been studied countless times, and many studies show a strong relationship between the use of active learning and student achievement. It is not our intent to give a full review of those results; however, two of the most authoritative and widely discussed studies are worth mentioning:

1. In 1998, Richard Hake, a physicist at Indiana University, conducted an analysis of 62 introductory physics courses in a variety of institutions across the United States, studying a total of over 6,500 students in those courses. The students were given the Force Concept Inventory (FCI; Hestenes, Wells, and Swackhamer 1992), an instrument that assesses students' understanding of the basic physics notion of "force," at the beginning of their course and again at the end. Hake found that students who were enrolled in courses focused on active learning (what he termed *interactive engagement*) showed gains on the FCI of over two standard deviations beyond those of similar students enrolled in courses focused on lecture. Other factors such as the size and type of the institution, student background, and so on did not factor into these gains; they were explained solely through the use of active learning (Hake 1998).

2. A report by Freeman and colleagues (2014) through the *Proceedings of the National Academy of Sciences* described a meta-analysis of 225 studies of STEM (science, technology, engineering, and mathematics) courses that focused on active learning and its effects on student outcomes. The study found that

   on average, student performance on examinations and concept inventories increased by 0.47 SDs [standard deviations] under active learning ($n = 158$ studies), and that the odds ratio for failing was 1.95 under traditional lecturing ($n = 67$ studies). These results indicate that average examination scores improved by about 6% in active learning sections and that students in classes with traditional lecturing were 1.5 times more likely to fail than were students in classes with active learning. (p. 1)

   The study went on to suggest that if active learning were thought of as a treatment for a disease, and the treatment were undergoing a clinical trial, then the clinical trial would be "stopped for benefit." That is, the trial would be ended because the treatment is so obviously beneficial.

These studies of active learning, along with many others, strongly suggest that active learning, when carefully planned and skillfully executed, can help students improve in learning. These benefits can occur in any discipline. A cursory look through the research literature on active learning reveals it is not just a single method of teaching but rather encompasses a vast array of specific activities, all with the common denominator that students are actively engaged in the learning process while in group space.

Does this mean that active learning is "good" and direct instruction is "bad"? Like most things, it's not that simple. Direct instruction and active learning are often seen as opposite ends of a spectrum, and in some sense they are. However, this dichotomy has unfortunately led to a long-running and often rancorous feud between two camps of educators and education pundits. On one side are those who support active learning over and against direct instruction and sometimes even advocate for the elimination of direct instruction. On the other side are those who believe the opposite. The "Math Wars" of the early 2000s and many of the current arguments over the Common Core State Standards are instances of this feud, which sometimes resembles the Hatfields versus the McCoys in its intensity and longevity.

For the benefit of our students, these feuds need to be put aside. Educators need to think of direct instruction and active learning as *complementary* rather than opposed or even mutually exclusive. A skilled educator will know when direct instruction is best for students and will use it skillfully and in the proper context and measure. The same is true for active learning. Direct instruction and active learning are *tools*, not religions. There is a correct context for each of them, and they can support each other to provide a rich learning environment for every student. In this book, we will not choose sides but rather seek ways to set up learning environments for our students where the strengths of both kinds of instruction are maximized and in which our students benefit the most.

The flipped learning idea claims that some contexts are better than others for both direct instruction and active learning and that those contexts are the opposites of what the traditional model uses. That notion is at the heart of our second attempt at defining *flipped learning*—which this time attempts to operationalize the idea.

A Definition of *Flipped Learning* (Second Attempt)

Now that we've examined the ideas of group versus individual space, direct instruction versus active learning, and the general idea of flipped learning versus the traditional model, we are ready to refine the definition of *flipped learning* we saw previously. In creating definitions, we do not wish merely to play semantic games. Instead, we wish to isolate the essence of flipped learning and accurately describe what makes this idea what it truly is, so that we can study it further.

This second attempt at a definition is from the Flipped Learning Network (2014):

> Flipped Learning is a pedagogical approach in which direct instruction moves from the group learning space to the individual learning space, and the resulting group space is transformed into a dynamic, interactive learning environment where the educator guides students as they apply concepts and engage creatively in the subject matter.

This definition describes *flipped learning* in terms of the use of time, space, and activity as we discussed before. However, the Flipped Learning Network definition goes significantly further than just defining a concept. It also lays out four pillars of flipped learning, conveniently arranged as the acronym *FLIP*:

1. *Flexible environment.* Flipped learning is based on allowing learners to learn in different ways and at different speeds, and to give learners choice in how they demonstrate evidence that they have mastered course content. Flexibility also refers to the instructors in a flipped learning environment, who are expected to be flexible in their plans, making on-the-fly adjustments for individual learners or for entire classes if formative assessment data suggest that changes need to be made.

2. *Learning culture.* A flipped learning environment is a community that values the learning process in all its forms, including all the warts, with learners at the center rather than the instructor. Students in a flipped learning environment are using their precious group space on high-impact, meaningful activities that place their work at the center of attention. Meanwhile, the instructor provides scaffolding and feedback with a view not simply toward gathering numbers for a gradebook but to help students learn.

3. *Intentional content.* Materials used in flipped learning are honed to a sharp edge, with explicit connections to learning targets that are clearly stated; text, video, and online content that is tightly constructed with high educational quality and very little "fluff"; and materials are differentiated so that students at different places in their learning can work on something meaningful.

4. *Professional educator.* An instructor in a flipped learning environment carries out a number of difficult jobs. The instructor has to prepare the content and set up the learning environment. She has to observe the students as they work and know when to intervene and when to let students struggle. She has to collect formative assessment data to know where the "hot spots" are as students learn and make appropriate in-the-moment adjustments. And after the fact, she should be a reflective teacher, taking time to evaluate her own performance and share her results as well as being well connected with an active community of practice, whether at her university or online or both.

Along with each of the pillars is a rubric of indicators of effective flipped learning implementations, so instructors can be aware of the characteristics of effective flipped learning instruction. For example the *L* pillar ("learning culture") has checkboxes for "I give students opportunities to engage in meaningful activities without the teacher being central" and "I scaffold these activities and make them accessible to all students through differentiation and feedback."

This definition and the FLIP rubric that accompanies it allow us to confront some common misconceptions about flipped learning:

- *Flipped learning is putting video lectures outside class and doing homework in class.* One finds this description often in the popular media, where simplicity and succinctness are key elements. Unfortunately, that description loses some of the nuance of the concept of flipped learning.
- *Flipped learning requires video.* Included in the previous misconception is an assumption that you *must* have lectures recorded to video in order to have a "true" flipped learning environment (e.g., see Cheshire and Leckhart 2012). Although having recorded lectures available on prerecorded video is common among flipped courses, and there are real advantages for doing so, it is neither necessary nor is it always the case. In fact, as we will discuss further in the next chapter, one of the original implementations of what we now identify as flipped learning—by Harvard's Eric Mazur in the form of *peer instruction*—used no videos at all. Under the Flipped Learning Network definition, *flipped learning* can be done without any electronic tools at all. What determines flipped learning is not the technology being used but what activities take place in the individual versus group spaces that students encounter.

- *Flipped learning is a new, untested concept—a buzzword or a fad.* It's true that the *terms* used—whether *flipped learning* or its cousin, *the flipped classroom*—are relatively new. As we will see in the next chapter when we discuss the history of flipped learning, the adjective *flipped* was introduced around 2007 to describe what instructors were doing. But in fact, the first published study of flipped learning was made in 2000—almost two decades ago—and the concept of using active learning to replace portions of a traditional class meeting goes back much further. And in fact, as we've noted, some older "legacy" models of pedagogy have strong similarities with flipped learning. Among these are the Oxford University tutorial model, in which students' group space consists entirely of discursive assessment focused on the students' abilities to present, defend, and critique their own ideas as well as those of others, and of the tutor. (A valuable and detailed description of the Oxford tutorial is Palfreyman, 2008) The time-honored methods of the case study, practicum experiences, and laboratory pedagogy also prefigure flipped learning. More modern pedagogies such as service learning and teaching with simulations provide further examples of learning experiences in which students gain contact with information in the individual space, and then put their learning to work in the group space. Far from being a fad, flipped learning encompasses some of the best intellectual traditions in the long history of higher education, and a move toward flipped learning is in some sense a return to our roots.

- *Flipped learning is* not *a new concept.* That said, it would not be entirely correct to say that flipped learning is not new and has been around since the Middle Ages. This view is sometimes used in a dismissive way, to suggest that the excitement around flipped learning is just some people rediscovering the wheel and that professors who have been requiring readings or problems outside of class and then discussing them in class are already doing flipped learning (and so no further professional progress is needed). It's certainly the case that legacy pedagogies like the Oxford tutorial have characteristics of flipped learning and fit parts of the definition we have given. However, other aspects of flipped learning extend those ideas. For example, the Oxford tutorial model as it is situated historically does not allow the kinds of flexible learning environments (the *F* in FLIP) that our definition suggests they should have. Also, an unstated intention of flipped learning is that *all students* should be placed in the flipped environment and supported in their learning, regardless of the type of institution or the background of the student; the Oxford model, for all its benefits, has a very different set of assumptions. So although older models of instruction may prefigure flipped learning, our notion of flipped learning intends to enhance and extend the aims of instruction. It's very possible that, after reading this book, you may create a kind of "Oxford Tutorial 2.0" that takes the best of the historical Oxford model and adds new ideas that produce the full benefits of a flipped learning environment to all students.

Attaching a description of *professional practice* sharpens the definition of *flipped learning* by not only defining what we mean but also describing how it works and what it looks like in "real life" when employed in the classroom. Flipped learning is more than just a teaching technique—it is an entire philosophy that encompasses course design, specific teaching practices, and professional engagement.

And yet there is still one more thing to tweak with this definition of *flipped learning*.

A Definition of *Flipped Learning* (Third Attempt)

So far, we have defined *flipped learning* as a pedagogical approach that, among other things, moves direct instruction from the group space to the individual space. By putting direct instruction into the individual space, that instruction is to be used as a way of preparing students to participate actively and productively in the group space, where there are challenging and creative activities planned that will involve the whole class in a wide range of cognitive tasks.

What our second attempt at the definition of *flipped learning* doesn't address is that *direct instruction may not be the only way to prepare students for the group space activities.* There could be other activities that students could do besides simply watching video lectures or doing guided readings. In fact, in some cases, students' preparation for group space activities might be best accomplished by leaving direct instruction completely out of the picture.

Lorena Barba, associate professor of mechanical and aerospace engineering at George Washington University, teaches Practical Numerical Methods with Python as an introduction to scientific computing (Barba n.d.). It is taught locally on several campuses and also as a massive open online course (MOOC) through the OpenEdX platform. In the course, students learn about numerical methods and scientific computing through solving basic problems in physics and engineering, learning all the theory they need in the context of working on the problems. Students engage with the course primarily by working through a sequence of computational notebooks, using the Jupyter platform (http://jupyter.org) running the programming language Python. In the MOOC, and in the face-to-face versions of the course, students experience what we could easily call a flipped learning environment. In their individual spaces, students explore new material by working through the notebooks. In the group space—a class meeting for the face-to-face version of the course, a discussion board for the MOOC version—students are applying their basic explorations to more complex problems and working with the instructor and their classmates. And yet no direct instruction takes place in the individual space or in the group space, for that matter, apart from a tutorial on how to navigate Jupyter notebooks and some basic Python programming lessons. In fact, despite the stereotype that a MOOC is composed of video lectures, there is only one video in the entire course (Barba 2015).

The unusual structure of this online course illustrates what one group of researchers at Stanford University discovered about the structure of a flipped learning environment: that in some cases, student learning is improved when the direct instruction (if any) is *preceded by* guided "discovery learning" activities, rather than having higher-level activities necessarily follow direct instruction (Schneider, Bumbacher, and Blikstein 2015). The researchers in this study provided learners with a "tangible user interface" for exploring the human auditory system with a physical model fitting on a tabletop, which learners manipulated through physical, literally hands-on activity. Students in the study were enrolled in a psychology course and had no prior experience with studying the human hearing system. One group was given a professionally made video that gave step-by-step instructions describing the human hearing system; a second group was given the tangible interface and asked to build the human hearing system without guidance. Following this initial phase, both groups completed a quiz on the human hearing system, and then they read a professionally written text on hearing and completed two more activities and a posttest. Students in the "discovery" group, who began with free exploration of the auditory system via the tangible interface, performed significantly better on both the mid- and posttests than the "listen" group that began with a high-quality video.

What the Stanford study suggests and the numerical methods MOOC instantiates is the idea that first contact with new material in a lesson need not happen via direct instruction. In some cases, it may be better for student learning in the long term for students to engage in structured hands-on activities first and then provide direct instruction later (along with more active learning). In fact, guided exploration and discovery of ideas before being given a normative explanation is one of the key tenets of the "constructivist" approach to learning (Bransford and Schwartz 1999).

What this means for our previous attempt at defining *flipped learning* is that we need to be clear about what is supposed to happen with the students in their individual spaces. What we intend is that *first contact with new material* takes place in this space and not in the group space as the traditional model would have it. However, we also see now that "first contact" need not happen via direct instruction. It *might* be best implemented by direct instruction in some cases; but in other cases, a guided discovery activity with little to no direct instruction might be best.

We also should point out that in the Stanford study and in Barba's MOOC, the discovery activities that precede the group space activity are not free-for-alls but rather are *structured* and *guided*. In the numerical methods course, discovery takes place by working through a sequence of highly structured computer notebooks that contain a mixture of text, graphics, and executable Python code that learners manipulate. In the Stanford study, subjects' interaction with the tangible interface was preceded by a description of the parts of the interface and a problem to solve by manipulating the components of the interface. Students were not, in either case, simply placed in a learning environment with no directions. Although there was not a traditional provision of direct instruction, there was plenty of *structure* to make the "free" discovery activities fruitful and unlikely to go off into the weeds.

So for our third and (possibly?) final attempt at a definition of *flipped learning*, we are merely going to modify the Flipped Learning Network definition to recognize the real purpose of the individual space and the multiplicity of ways this can happen:

> *Flipped Learning is a pedagogical approach in which first contact with new concepts moves from the group learning space to the individual learning space in the form of structured activity, and the resulting group space is transformed into a dynamic, interactive learning environment where the educator guides students as they apply concepts and engage creatively in the subject matter.*

In chapters 2 and 3 we will explore some specific case studies of flipped learning environments, all of which instantiate this definition despite a wide diversity of academic subjects, levels of difficulty, institutional profiles, and instructor teaching styles.

Why Instructors Choose to Use Flipped Learning

The remainder of this book will lay out the history and theory behind flipped learning, which in turn support the course design and implementation of classes that use flipped learning. As you'll see, and as you might guess, this is hard work. It's helpful, before we dive into this process, to hear from real professors who practice flipped learning about *why* they chose to shoulder the work and use flipped learning in their classes.

I posted an open invitation on Twitter to respond to a survey that simply asked for respondents' names, disciplines, and institutions as well as a brief response to the question, *Why do you use flipped learning?* Although the respondents represented a wide variety of disciplines including science, technology, engineering, and math (STEM) as well as humanities and social sciences, and no doubt their actual implementations of flipped learning look quite different from each other, their responses tell a coherent story.

All of the respondents mentioned that they chose flipped learning because they wanted more time in class to focus on higher-level activities in their subject, particularly those activities that involved the application of basic ideas, critical thinking, and problem-solving. Lori Ramey, who teaches writing and English at Erskine College, says it this way:

> For a student to really dig into a text, we need to prepare them to do that work on their own, so they can bring their insights into the classroom. Flipping allows teachers to focus attention of the group on details that truly matter, and gives the students the opportunity to work like experts in the discipline. Gathering data, reading novels, writing initial responses: these are the kinds of activities that professionals do to prepare for the collaborative work that drives knowledge forward. When we allow students to work like professionals, trusting them to prepare beforehand, we maximize their time in the classroom with a discipline expert.

Ramey's last sentence highlights another reason instructors chose flipped learning: Flipped learning exercises those skills that students will need after college, such as the ability to self-teach, self-assess, and self-regulate. In other words, flipped learning gives them practice in working like professionals.

One aspect of this metacognitive focus of flipped learning is simply the ability to process information. In a comment that demonstrates further that flipped learning does not require the use of video or other high technology, Justin Dunmyre, who teaches mathematics at Frostburg State University, describes his use of flipped learning:

> My particular flavor of flipped learning is to eschew video lectures in favor of having the students read a textbook. Reading a textbook, especially a mathematically oriented one, is a skill that is best improved through practice. This gives students a skill that will help them in all of their classes going forward, and it will also help them develop into autonomous, lifelong learners.

Noel-Ann Bradshaw, who teaches mathematics at the University of Greenwich, takes the professional development aspect of flipped learning a step further by pointing out that students who experience flipped learning environments have concrete evidence that they and their professors can pass on to employers about their ability to work in a professional environment:

> I have found that it has developed my students' ability to learn for themselves, which has increased their confidence. When they apply for jobs they can tell employers that they have the ability to learn new skills for themselves as they have done this for themselves during this year.

Bryan McCabe, who teaches civil engineering at the National University of Ireland, echoes this point about professional development and practice:

> Engineering degrees are professional qualifications and upon graduation, it isn't enough for engineers to "know" things; they must be able to "do" things. I had been trying to increase the amount of student activity in my classes over the years, and flipped learning allowed to me to commit to it fully. Students really appreciate the active workshop environment in scheduled class time and the opportunity to study short, concise videos beforehand in preparation.

Theron Hitchman, who teaches mathematics at the University of Northern Iowa, expands the idea of professional development to include teaching students not only the content of a subject but also the discipline itself:

> I can more effectively guide my students through their difficulties, and introduce them to the culture of mathematical work, if I structure our class time together around *their work* and *their ideas*. That means that students have to do other work outside of class, so we can spend our class time on deeper conversations focused on their understanding and thinking.

This comment brings us back to one of the chief benefits of flipped learning—namely, the creation of expanded time to do active learning in the group space and increase student engagement in the material. Matthew Winslow, who teaches psychology at Eastern Kentucky University, highlights the importance of engagement:

> "The person doing the work does the learning." I wanted to get off the stage and get my students engaged because I think they learn more that way. So the ultimate answer [to why I use flipped learning] is because I think it enhances their learning.

Behind all of these comments about creating time and space for active learning, teaching metacognitive skills, and preparing students for their future work is a profound sense that the *classroom experience in higher education ought to be student-centered.* For example, Tiernan Henry, who teaches earth and ocean sciences at the National University of Ireland, says that he uses flipped learning

> to encourage student engagement with classes and to facilitate this by meeting them halfway. Courses [are] now taught in six-week blocks so there's less time to ease into the topic for the students. Flipping the class initially was about giving them control of practical preparation, and it's gradually moved on to me uploading short videos . . . that demonstrate field techniques and methods; however, the students can access these at any time for revision and for prep for class.

Giving students control over the sources from which they learn, and over how they use those sources, is a key element of flipped learning—the *F* in the FLIP acronym—and promotes a strongly student-centered environment.

The respondents also noted that flipped learning promotes *relationships* between the students and the instructor that are positive and personal, another key aspect of a student-centered learning environment. Anne Gardner, who teaches civil engineering at the University of Technology in Sydney (Australia), says:

> I use flipped learning because it means that the scarce face-to-face time I have with my students can be spent on the confusions, misconceptions, and what they don't know yet (the interesting bits of the syllabus), rather than on material that most people can understand. This means the time I have with them can be time that I really value-add to their understanding.

Finally, Carolina Buitrago, who teaches English language instruction at the Institución Universitaria Colombo Americana, notes that the student-centered environment fostered by flipped learning includes enhanced opportunities for active learning, intentional metacognitive and professional development, student-centered environments, and more positive relationships in the course—and it's liberating for instructors:

> I use flipped learning because it allows me to easily create student-centered environments and learning-rich classrooms. I also use it because I can differentiate learning for my students by creating/curating materials. I use it because I have seen it make my learners more autonomous people and because it engages them. I use flipped learning because it allows me to be

myself in the classroom. I can be a teacher who cares, I can facilitate, I can experiment and learn while I teach.

In the words of these college and university professors—who, again, come from a wide variety of geographical settings, academic disciplines, and institutional types—an image of flipped learning begins to emerge that is a compelling model for higher education. In flipped learning, we address all the great pedagogical goals of higher education throughout history: not only mastering content skills but also developing higher-level thinking skills, self-regulatory behaviors, understanding of the cultures of academic disciplines, readiness for professional work, personal relationships with professors, and willingness to become lifelong learners.

This chapter has been focused on describing flipped learning, laying out its component parts and its essential ideas. We've also seen why university and college professors have chosen flipped learning over traditional models. At this point, it's appropriate to dig deeper and look at the body of research literature that supports the concepts of flipped learning we have presented. We will do that in the next chapter.

2

THE HISTORY AND THEORY
OF FLIPPED LEARNING

In the previous chapter, we gave a detailed description of flipped learning. We saw the contrasts between flipped learning and the traditional model of course design; the essential components of time, space, and activity that make flipped learning what it is; the problems that flipped learning attempts to address; and why instructors from across different disciplines have chosen to use flipped learning in a variety of contexts. At this point, you should have a good idea of what flipped learning *is* and what it *is not*, and begin to see why it could be a compelling model for instruction in higher education.

But as professionals in higher education, we often want more than just good explanations and compelling stories when thinking about a new idea. We also want *evidence*, preferably from sound scholarship and reputable research. After all, we are talking about a pedagogical model that seems experimental and novel. Insofar as a professor might be *switching* to flipped learning from a traditional approach to teaching, she would like to have some reasonable expectation of why this way of running a class should work as well as or better than the methods higher education has adopted for a very long time. On the other hand, a professor who has used flipped learning before can benefit from knowing *why* certain things about it are potentially transformative for student learning.

In this chapter we will focus on providing that evidence, in the form of a historical survey of flipped learning, some seminal results, and a look at the current state of what we know about flipped learning. This chapter is not intended to be a comprehensive literature review. Indeed, the literature on flipped learning is expanding at an increasing rate; an ERIC database search on peer-reviewed articles with "flipped classroom" or "flipped learning" in the title or the abstract returns over 100 results for 2015 and 2016 alone, compared to just 43 articles in 2013 and 2014 combined. The common criticism that flipped learning lacks justification from research is losing traction month by month. This is good news, but the downside is that it is actually hard to keep up with the sheer quantity of scholarship that flipped learning is producing. So in this chapter, we will focus on the *frameworks* that support flipped learning, and later in the book we will discuss how to navigate, and add to, the scholarship on flipped learning.

A Short History of Flipped Learning

Finding the Origins of Flipped Learning

Where did flipped learning originate? And what problems were its originators trying to solve?

To answer these questions, we will first need to recall our definition from chapter 1:

> Flipped Learning is a pedagogical approach in which direct instruction moves from the group learning space to the individual learning space, and the resulting group space is transformed into a dynamic, interactive learning environment where the educator guides students as they apply concepts and engage creatively in the subject matter. (Flipped Learning Network 2014)

Under this definition, individual instances of flipped learning might go back hundreds of years, in the form of single professors who organized their courses in this way. Many of those names will be lost to history. In tracking down the time and place in which flipped learning as an organized, intentional concept first originated, we are looking for instances where the intention was something greater than just an individual professor's practice, times and places in which flipped learning was done *with* purpose and *on* purpose, with the intent of making it a program of pedagogy transcending the boundaries of an individual course.

This is an important distinction, due to the misconception that flipped learning is just a modern name for the very old practice of *giving students work to do before class and then having active participation in class.* Early pedagogical models such as the Oxford tutorial method, case study methods, and laboratory experiences are predicated on this model. They often share characteristics of flipped learning, such as the emphasis in the group space on debate and discussion of readings assigned for individual space. We want to emphasize that these models have significant historical value and measurable benefits for students today if the context is right. However, despite the positive aspects of those models, they do not fit our definition exactly, for at least two reasons.

First, models in which students are simply assigned readings before class and then encouraged or required to discuss those readings in class are not really stressing *direct instruction* in the individual space. Simply giving a student a text to read is not the same as direct instruction. In direct instruction, the instructor *guides* students in their encounter with new material in a sequenced and organized way—she does not merely hand off a book to read. Nor is setting aside time for discussion the same as the "dynamic, interactive learning environment" guided by the instructor that flipped learning requires. To be clear, these models *can* fit the description of flipped learning. But they do not do so merely by definition. Many instances of these models can be as traditional as classes designed solely around lecture. The difference is in the *guidance*.

In flipped learning, the instructor provides guidance in both the individual *and* group space. In the individual space, that guidance often is in the form of direct instruction. This can take several forms. For example, the instructor might structure outside readings with activities that students complete to show evidence of fruitful engagement with the readings. For example, the instructor might assign not only a reading but also an activity (writing an outline, summary, or mind map of the reading), or the instructor could assign metacognitive questions asking students to describe how they approached the reading to help them become better readers. Flipped learning does not assume that students simply know, natively, how to take disciplinary content and extract meaningful information or ask good questions. It assumes, rather, that guidance in students' first contact with new material is a necessity; it plans for this, and these plans are intentionally part of the instructional model. To the extent that this intentional planning is not present in an instructional model, that model is not flipped learning, no matter how much reading or discussion is done.

Second, models in which students are simply gathered together to discuss preclass readings do not necessarily support active learning. Discussions of readings *can* be active, dynamic learning experiences—but only if the students participate. How will the instructor ensure that each student participates? If this is left simply to chance, then only a few vocal students will participate, and not all learners will be included in the learning process. At this point, the promise—and the definition—of *flipped learning* is left unfulfilled. Instead, in flipped learning we must see an *intentional* approach to getting *all* students involved in dynamic, creative activities that support deep learning. A discussion class, for instance, can be kicked off with a think-pair-share exercise or a think-pair-share-square exercise (Kothiyal, Majumdar, Murthy, and Iyer 2013) that gets pairs of students involved, gradually leading up to a whole-class discussion. Or discussions can be kick-started using technology in the form of classroom response systems (commonly called "clickers"), in which students individually, and anonymously, respond to provocative questions first and then share their responses with others (Bruff 2009). We will see more examples of creating an active, social, dynamic learning environment in the group space throughout the book. The point, for now, is that a class meeting that simply assembles students in one place and *expects* discussion without intentional guidance does not fit our definition of *flipped learning*.

Therefore, to look for the first organized instances of flipped learning in the published literature, we are looking for *coherent and intentional* approaches to learning that put guided exploration of new material into the individual space and use the group space for active learning, not implemented merely by individual faculty in a one-time-only scenario but rather with the intent of making flipped learning a coherent, long-term program of pedagogical work.

We are also going to restrict our search to those instances where flipped learning was implemented *by faculty in their courses* as opposed to others who might have suggested or reported the idea. For example, Barbara Walvoord and Virginia Johnson Anderson (1998) contrasted a "traditional model" and "alternate model" of classroom teaching in which "first exposure" learning was done during class in the "traditional" model and before class in the "alternate model." They go on to describe the use of this model in history, physics, and statistics. This model was promoted not so much as an organized paradigm for course design but as a method for maintaining control over one's grading workload. But it is also clearly a description of what we now identify as flipped learning. Perhaps Walvoord and Johnson Anderson's book motivated the faculty members we will meet next.

Again, isolated instances of this approach to course design and teaching can be found throughout the history of higher education. But in the published research record, we can trace the origins of flipped learning back to three major sources.

Harvard University: Eric Mazur and Peer Instruction

Eric Mazur is a physicist at Harvard University who began teaching the introductory physics course for engineering and science majors in 1984. For years, his instruction, focusing on lecturing in class supplemented by demonstrations, was decidedly traditional but was well received by students in terms of course evaluations and success on exams. In 1990, however, when Mazur encountered a series of articles by physics education researchers Ibrahim Halloun and David Hestenes (1985, 1987), he began to wonder how effective his teaching actually was. Halloun and Hestenes's articles suggested that although students may perform well in traditional introductory physics courses, their personal beliefs about physics are essentially unchanged by physics instruction. As a result, a student may enter a physics class—even a Harvard student entering a Harvard physics class—with a concept of the notion of force firmly situated in pre-Newtonian ideas, do well in the course, and leave with the same outdated ideas about the fundamental concept of force.

Halloun and Hestenes developed a simple instrument for gauging students' conceptual understanding of force called the Force Concept Inventory (FCI; Hestenes, Wells, and Swackhamer 1992). The questions on the FCI require no mathematical computation and no technical knowledge of physics; they are commonsense questions about everyday occurrences that involve forces. Mazur gave this instrument to his introductory physics students with the expectation that *his* students—the cream of the crop of university students, highly skilled with excellent intellectual backgrounds—would show fewer misconceptions than the students from Halloun and Hestenes's work. However, as Mazur puts it:

> The first warning [that something was wrong] came when I gave the Halloun and Hestenes test to my class and a student asked, "Professor Mazur, how should I answer these questions? According to what you taught us, or by the way I *think* about these things?" (Mazur 1997, p. 4)

Mazur discovered that although his Harvard students were adept at physics problems that involved memorization and computation, even quite complex computation, their conceptual understanding remained in many cases stuck in the Aristotelean era despite an entire semester of skilled direct instruction in class that was highly rated on course evaluations.

Mazur was rightfully shocked and disturbed. In response, he did what a professional scholar-educator should do: Examine his teaching based on the evidence, and make changes to help students learn his subject better. The result of his labor was a system of course design and instruction that has become known as *peer instruction* (Mazur 1997).

In peer instruction, the focus of class time is on exposing and correcting student misconceptions on the major ideas of an individual lesson. To prepare for the class, the instructor identifies three to five essential concepts in the upcoming lesson. The instructor then prepares, for each essential concept, a short (five to eight minutes long) "minilecture" or demonstration that presents this concept in some way. This is done to set up a thorny conceptual question about that concept—a question that doesn't require mathematical computation—presented as a multiple-choice question (which Mazur calls a "ConcepTest") to students on a large screen. Students are instructed to think quietly for a short period of time, around one to two minutes, to arrive at their answer to the question.

When they are ready, students vote for their answer using a classroom response device or clicker. Software attached to the instructor's computer registers all the student votes. At the end of the voting period, the instructor observes the voting data. If a significant percentage (Mazur uses 75% as a cutoff) of students select the correct answer to the question, then the answer is revealed and the instructor provides a follow-up explanation and time for further questions. If, on the other hand, there is not a significant consensus on the right answer, then students are instructed to pair off with another student to take turns arguing in favor of their answer for two to five minutes; then at the end of the debate, students are instructed to revote on the same question, and the instructor can see from the data whether students are moving to the right answer. Quite often, students converge on the right answer on the second round of voting after discussing their misconceptions, or else the vote becomes split between the right answer and one other wrong answer, spurring class-wide discussions on the answers. In this way, peer instruction allots roughly 10 to 15 minutes of class time ("group space") to demonstrations followed by question/discussion time to each essential concept of the lesson.

The effectiveness of peer instruction has been well documented across academic settings (see Crouch and Mazur 2001 for an overview of the first 10 years of peer instruction research). In Mazur's original studies, he found that students in peer instruction classes showed gains in their FCI scores from the beginning to end of a semester that were two to three *standard deviations* greater than those of students in traditional lecture courses.

Mazur did not use any particular terminology other than *peer instruction* to describe this technique. However, today peer instruction is viewed as an instance of flipped learning. It certainly meets the definition of *flipped learning* we have given in this book. The focus of the group space is on dynamic application of basic content, specifically a lively interaction among peers to isolate and correct common misconceptions about fundamental concepts. In order to have time to do this in class, students in peer instruction classes are required to learn the basic content independently prior to class. In Mazur's classes, this was simply done by reading a textbook; the technique predates the emergence of online video by several years. But as alluded to previously, simply asking students to *read a physics book* is not sufficient guidance to ensure they get something out of the reading. At Harvard, Mazur developed software to allow students to read the textbook online using an early version of social annotation software, so that students could comment and ask questions on the text in a way that other students and the instructors could read and reply to. In this way, students could help each other in the individual space to learn from the book while reading.

From Mazur's example, we can see that flipped learning emerged as a solution to a concrete pedagogical problem associated with students' conceptual understanding of a complex subject. But Mazur wasn't the only person at the time coming up with the idea of flipped learning, and Harvard wasn't the only place where it was happening.

Cedarville University: J. Wesley Baker and the Classroom Flip

Meanwhile, in 1995 at Cedarville University, a small liberal arts university in Ohio, communications professor J. Wesley Baker had a revelation (Baker 2015). He had been teaching a course on multimedia program screen design, a subject we might today call "user interface design." There was no textbook written for this subject, so he used a book for traditional print graphics design along with lectures that applied the concepts to the design of computer screens. In 1995, there were no projection systems at Cedarville, no computers installed in the classrooms, and no campus computer network until the fall of that year. Baker had to come to class with a computer and two monitors on a cart each time he taught.

Once the new campus network was installed in fall 1995, he was able to put his lecture slides on the network and use the new classroom systems for presentations. He realized something soon after the new system was in place:

> I remember vividly the day in that class when I was clicking through the slides, with the students dutifully copying down the information in their notes. In the middle of the lecture, I stopped and said, "This is really stupid! The information on the slides is going from the screen to your notes without passing through either of our brains. The presentation is on the network. Just access them online before class and let's not waste time in class just copying down slides." My office was located on the other side of campus from the classroom and I can remember getting about half-way back to my office when it suddenly dawned on me, "I just gave away all of the content for the class. What am I going to do in class the rest of the term?" (Baker 2015, p. 1)

Upon returning to his office, he wrote out the memo shown in Figure 2.1. Baker announced his intentions to students at the very next class meeting, and then redesigned his classes from that point forward by putting his lectures on the campus network and, rather than lecturing in class about graphic design, bringing in a poorly designed user interface and letting students work in groups to improve it.

Figure 2.1. J. Wesley Baker memo.

```
Here is my vision for what I would like to see accomplished during class
time:
-CLARIFY by discussing any questions you have from reading and class slides
-EXPAND on the material by adding to the "mix" material from your own
reading or things covered in other classes, which inform the current topic
(e.g., some of the students have read some research articles for Electronic
Media Research, which deal with experiments on screen design; we should
have the benefit of those findings for our discussion)
-APPLY the material by looking at and analyzing sample screens based on the
principles discussed in the text and slides
-PRACTICE the application by spending time in design groups working on the
project steps (this will come more once we get past the mid-term exam)
```

This restructuring of class is the epitome of flipped learning. Direct instruction, via lecture, is moved from the group space to the individual space. It is truly direct instruction because the lectures are more than just resources to read; they are organized and sequenced attempts at instruction directed from the instructor to the student. Class time is therefore freed up to spend entirely on answering questions, adding student perspectives, and doing the eminently sensible thing to do in a design course—namely, to design things.

Baker continued structuring his classes this way and, in his role as faculty liaison to the Computer Services Department at Cedarville, was able to disseminate his ideas to colleagues in training sessions, during one of which a faculty member remarked: "So, what you're doing is flipping the classroom and homework around" (Baker 2015, p. 4). Although an early conference presentation on the model given by Baker to the faculty at Northwest Nazarene University in November 1997 did not use the term *classroom flip*, the name eventually stuck. Baker began to refer to his method as the "classroom flip," the earliest documented use of the term *flipped classroom* to describe this instructional method. Baker went on to engage in an active schedule of professional development workshops focusing on the "classroom flip," mostly for faculty at small independent colleges in the Midwest, until the mid-1990s, when he gave up this schedule to return to a greater focus on teaching in his discipline.

Later, in March 2000, Baker gave a conference presentation (Baker 2000) that laid out his fully realized vision for flipped learning, using the term *classroom flip* to describe it.

Miami University: Lage, Platt, and Treglia's Inverted Classroom

At nearly the same time that Baker was redesigning his graphics design courses using the classroom flip at Cedarville, three professors in the economics department at Miami University—also in Ohio—were uncovering issues with student learning in economics that were different but no less serious than the issues Mazur was finding with his Harvard physics students.

Maureen Lage, Glenn Platt, and Michael Treglia (2000) were finding that students in their introductory economics courses at Miami were struggling at times because their *learning styles* were not fully suited to traditional lecture-based instruction; conversely, instructors were constrained in their ability to vary instructional methods by class time. In order to serve all students in the best way, sufficient time needed to be created to allow instructors to provide not only traditional direct instruction but also significant time for activities that reached a broader range of students.

By "learning styles," Lage, Platt, and Treglia were referring to a wide range of ideas in the educational psychology literature. One notion of learning styles identifies a student as a *dependent, collaborative,* or *independent* learner depending on whether the learner learns best through, respectively, direct instruction, working with others, or working on his or her own (Reichman and Grasha 1974). Another uses the Myers-Briggs Type Indicator (MBTI; Briggs and Myers 1977) to identify four axes of personality types (Introvert-Extrovert, Sensing-Intuitive, Thinking-Feeling, Judging-Perceiving) whose combination can determine or at least affect how one learns. Finally, students can be identified in terms of how they process information, *assimilation* versus *convergence,* on the one hand (describing learners who take in information through abstract conceptualization), and *divergence* and *accommodation,* on the other (describing learners who take in information through concrete experience) (Kolb 1981).

What Lage, Platt, and Treglia learned not only from practical experience but also from existing research literature on teaching and learning in economics (e.g., Charkins, O'Toole, and Wetzel 1985) offered a basic truth about effective teaching: Student learning can be improved by using a variety of teaching methods that reach learners of different learning styles. And yet, behind this sensible idea is a nagging question: Where are instructors going to find the time to cover all the material if they are busy varying the methods of instruction?

The idea that Lage, Platt, and Treglia invented to address this problem was first realized in their introductory economics courses in 1996 and published in the *Journal of Economic Education* in 2000 (Lage, Platt, and Treglia 2000). It is one of the clearest pictures we have of flipped learning in its infancy, and it was the first peer-reviewed journal article intended for a broad audience giving a formal framework for flipped learning.

With a course setup covering one main topic per week (in which the class met for two 75-minute periods), students engaged in a two-phase process:

1. Before the first day of discussion, students were to complete a reading from the course textbook. Students were also encouraged (though not

required) to watch prerecorded videos on VHS that could be checked out from the library or viewed as PowerPoint slides with sound recordings in the department's computer labs and on the Internet. Students were instructed to arrive at class with questions about the reading and viewing.

2. In class, there would be time (10 minutes) for students' questions over the preclass reading and viewing. An absence of questions was interpreted as a clear understanding of the assigned content. Then the remainder of class time for the week was spent on a variety of lively activities including economic experiments and lab assignments designed to engage students in essential economic questions and concepts, along with time for practice worksheets and review questions.

This format of class was dubbed the *inverted classroom* by Lage, Platt, and Treglia. It is instantly recognizable as *flipped learning* under our definition. Their journal article gives a full discussion of their findings from the 1996 introduction of the inverted classroom. As with Mazur's peer instruction and Baker's classroom flip, the class time ("group space") is focused on active learning to approach deep conceptual ideas, with the entire class and the instructor present, and to make time for this, students are given guided engagement with new material outside of class as a preparatory activity.

Interlude: Connections Among the Origins

So, where did flipped learning as a coherent, organized instructional model begin? It's impossible to pinpoint an exact moment, but Mazur at Harvard; Baker at Cedarville; and Lage, Platt, and Treglia at Miami came to similar conclusions about the traditional model of instruction in their respective disciplines and invented what we now recognize as flipped learning to solve specific pedagogical problems, all around the same time—namely, the latter half of the 1990s. We credit all three equally, because their instructional methods fit the definition of *flipped learning* and because their approach was not just the insular instructional style of one professor but rather promoted as a coherent instructional paradigm.

Interestingly, it appears that none of them were aware of the work at the other schools, despite coming up with and implementing their ideas at almost the same time. Glenn Platt indicated (personal e-mail correspondence, May 20, 2016) that he, Lage, and Treglia were not aware of Eric Mazur's experiments with peer instruction. And though Baker was working with flipped learning simultaneously only 53 miles away and published his work on flipped learning at almost the same time as Platt and his colleagues, neither were aware of each other; the Miami group only became aware of Baker because a fourth Miami faculty member happened to be in the audience of Baker's classroom flip conference talk in March 2000 and happened to discuss the talk with other Miami faculty upon returning, at which point Platt e-mailed Baker to let him know about the work being done with Lage and Treglia (Baker 2015). Such a near miss among these professionals, all working on the same ideas at the same time but unaware of each other, should motivate today's flipped learning practitioners to connect with each other and promote strong communities of practice—a concept to which we will return in chapter 8.

All three approaches to flipped learning share common elements that drove their development:

- All three approaches were motivated by concrete pedagogical problems that arose in the everyday practice of the traditional model. In Mazur's case, he had evidence both from his own students and from those in the Halloun and Hestenes studies that indicated serious issues with conceptual knowledge in basic physics that were unchanged by traditional lecturing. In Lage, Platt, and Treglia's case, students in their introductory economics courses were encountering mismatches between their learning styles and the one-size-fits-all nature of traditional lecturing. In Baker's case, it was simply that students weren't getting the best possible practice in class on designing web pages if all they did was listen to someone talk about the design of web pages.
- All three approaches to flipped learning were motivated by the same practical problem: finding sufficient time in class to address their respective issues. For Mazur, the concept of peer instruction presupposes that class time should be liberated in order to engage in the peer instruction process. In Baker's case, it was a question of finding time in the class to have students work on actual design problems and share their experiences. For Lage, Platt, and Treglia, it was finding time in class to include a wide enough variety of activities that students of varying learning styles would be fully included.
- All three approaches were motivated by technological innovations. For Mazur, the classroom response system or "clicker" opened up the possibility of efficient, anonymous classroom voting on his ConcepTests. For Baker, the installation of a campus computer network suddenly made it viable to distribute his lecture notes online for students to access easily outside of class. For Lage, Platt, and Treglia, the advent of the World Wide Web (invented in 1989,

opened to the public in 1991) made it possible to place multimedia sources on a large network. It is conceivable that flipped learning could have developed outside the range of these innovations; our earlier discussion of "legacy" pedagogies indicates that something *like* flipped learning has been in place for a very long time. But historically, flipped learning came into its own with the assistance of new technologies and possibly *because of* those technologies.

Finally, it is worthwhile to note that in Lage, Platt, and Treglia's case, the inverted classroom was invented to solve what was essentially a problem about *diversity and inclusion*, and not merely a logistical problem. The diversity issue that the inverted classroom addressed was specifically *intellectual* diversity—namely, diversity of learning styles. However, the link between learning styles and other forms of diversity including gender, racial, and socioeconomic diversity is more pronounced than we often think.

Conspicuously absent from the discussion so far is the popular term *flipped classroom*. This didn't come along until several years later, in the work of two high school chemistry teachers in the American West.

Secondary Education: Bergmann and Sams and the Flipped Classroom

In 2007, Jon Bergmann and Aaron Sams were teaching high school chemistry in Woodland Park, Colorado. Among the everyday problems that they faced as teachers were students who missed class and needed to be retaught the material. Sams came across a magazine article about software that would record PowerPoint lectures with a voice-over track added, and then save it to an electronic video file. Instantly they knew that they had a partial solution to their teaching problem. As Bergmann (2011b) puts it:

> Thus, we began to record our live lessons using screen capture software. We posted our lectures online so our students could access them. When we did this, YouTube was just getting started and the world of online video was just in its infancy. . . . In all honesty, we recorded our lessons out of selfishness. We were spending inordinate amounts of time re-teaching lessons to students who missed class, and the recorded lectures became our first line of defense.

What began as a simple and effective way to simplify classroom instruction became something of a revolution. Bergmann and Sams's students—both the ones who missed class and needed to catch up and the ones who were in class but needed a review—readily took to the video lectures. Because the videos were posted online, other students and teachers from outside Woodland Park found them, and soon the videos were being used to replace in-class lecturing, initially for days when substitute teachers needed to come into a class. As interest in the videos grew, eventually Bergmann and Sams were invited to present their work in professional development workshops. Other teachers began to see the usefulness in recorded video and started to make their own. Eventually, Bergmann and Sams's work found its way into the news (Bergmann 2011a), and before long, their idea had caught on like wildfire.

At first, their method of using prerecorded online video to shift direct instruction away from class time had no particular name. They referred to the videos themselves as *vodcasts* (a portmanteau of *video* and *podcast*) and at first the method was called *pre-vodcasting*. Bergmann and Sams saw this term as being too technical for a general audience of teachers, so they suggested the term *reverse instruction,* which was used in accounts of this method at the time (e.g., Walsh 2012) and continues in some cases up to the present day.

However, in 2010, Dan Pink of the London newspaper *The Daily Telegraph* wrote an online article (Pink 2010) describing reverse instruction, specifically highlighting the work of another Colorado teacher, Karl Fisch, who used the reverse instruction method in his mathematics classes. In the article, Pink offhandedly referred to Fisch's technique as "the Fisch flip." It was here that this instructional method and the term *flipped* were first joined, and the term *flipped classroom* was born (although that term does not appear in Fink's article). Fisch, for his part, learned the reverse/flipped instructional method from a Bergmann and Sams workshop, and so the term *flipped classroom* has become inextricably linked with this instructional method and with Bergmann and Sams's original work. Indeed, two years later, Bergmann and Sams (2012) published their widely read book *Flip Your Classroom: Reach Every Student in Every Class Every Day*, which has resulted in the production of several follow-up volumes and stands as one of the most, if not the most, widely used source on flipped instruction for K–12 teachers worldwide.

Before Pink's article, while the reverse instruction concept was gaining in popularity rapidly, Bergmann and Sams did extensive research to see if a similar idea was being used elsewhere and, finding nothing, at one point even consulted a lawyer to investigate copyrighting the term *reverse instruction* (Bergmann 2011b). Interestingly, Bergmann and Sams's research did not turn up the seminal article from Lage, Platt, and Treglia discussed previously, even though the article appeared almost a decade earlier and was cited at least 46 times in other articles between the years 2000 and 2008 (in a search of Google Scholar for "inverted classroom"; see http://bit.ly/1Xg3dvg). Bergmann (personal e-mail correspondence, May 16, 2016) stated that he and

Sams became aware of the Lage, Platt, and Treglia article only just as their *Flip Your Classroom* book was on its way to press.

We can only speculate why the connection between Bergmann and Sams's work and the work of others did not appear sooner, but two explanations seem plausible. First, there was, and still is, a disconnect in terminology. What we are calling *flipped learning* in this book has been known by the terms *inverted classroom, pre-vodcasting, reverse instruction, flipped instruction*, and *flipped classroom* among several others, and in some instances (e.g., Mazur) by either no terminology at all or else by specific, localized terms that refer to specific pedagogical techniques (e.g., *peer instruction*) rather than overall frameworks. Second, there was, and again still is, a disconnect between the work of instructors in higher education and that of instructors in primary and secondary education. It is worth noting that whereas the earliest instances of flipped learning were in universities, Bergmann and Sams's work has been primarily addressed to K–12 teachers. The research literature and professional publications (where reports of flipped learning would typically appear) for higher education and those for K–12 education often have little to no overlap, so that a person doing research for K–12 teaching and learning findings is unlikely to find a result from higher education and vice versa, unless the researcher has deliberately crossed over and searched both audiences.

There remains today a distinction between flipped learning work done for higher education and similar work done for primary and secondary schools. Although flipped learning first emerged in higher education and has a longer history there, it has been decidedly more enthusiastically adopted among primary and secondary instructors, and the communities of practice for those using flipped learning are more fully developed in K–12 education than in higher education.

Flipped Learning in Higher Education Since 2000

We have now seen that flipped learning developed on parallel tracks, originating in higher education in the period from around 1996 to 2000 and then being rediscovered independently in K–12 education between 2006 and 2008. The popularity of flipped learning really began to take off with the work of Bergmann and Sams, as K–12 educators (and the school systems for which they worked) embraced the idea. This popularity has had an effect on its use in higher education as well, and practitioners in higher education— being arguably more oriented toward research methodologies than teachers in primary and secondary schools—have produced a steadily deepening body of scholarly literature on flipped learning.

Prior to 2011, however, not much was happening in research on flipped learning. One of the sole exceptions was the PhD dissertation of Jeremy Strayer at the Ohio State University (Strayer 2007). (The connection between flipped learning and the state of Ohio was thereby continued.) Strayer's dissertation was one of the first (if not *the* first) truly scientific study of flipped learning in the sense of using a systematic experimental design to study the effects of flipped learning environments on students. In Strayer's study, two versions of an introductory statistics course were offered: one using the traditional model and lecture and the other using a flipped model with an intelligent tutoring system to deliver content and some form of direct instruction outside the classroom. Strayer's study focused not on student mastery of statistics knowledge but rather student satisfaction and affective responses to being in a flipped learning environment. His findings were useful but not entirely positive; students in the flipped learning environment were found to be less satisfied and more unsettled in their learning process than those in the traditional environment. However, the study draws conclusions about how better to set up and manage a flipped learning environment as a result.

Five years later, Strayer (2012) would publish another study again finding that students in flipped learning environments are more unsettled and possibly less satisfied than counterparts in a traditional classroom, although students in a flipped learning environment gradually become more open to cooperative learning and innovations in teaching methods than their counterparts.

Since 2011, and particularly following the rapid popularization of "the flipped classroom" by Bergmann and Sams in 2010 through 2012, there has been a steep increase in the research done on flipped learning. A search on the ERIC database reveals the trend of increasing contributions to the scholarly literature on flipped learning. Table 2.1 shows the number of peer-reviewed articles listed at ERIC that have the terms *inverted classroom, flipped classroom,* or *flipped learning* in either the title or abstract, by year from 2011 to 2015.

These data show a roughly 250% increase *per year* in the number of peer-reviewed articles being published about flipped learning. These numbers do not include other forms of scholarly writing such as master's and doctoral theses, nor do they include a vast number of non-peer-reviewed items such

TABLE 2.1

Number of Peer-Reviewed Published Articles Containing References to Flipped Learning by Year: 2011–2015

Year	2011	2012	2013	2014	2015
Number of articles	0	5	14	35	89

as magazine articles and op-ed pieces that shed further light on flipped learning. This suggests that flipped learning is not just a fad or a buzzword but a pedagogical model being seriously explored and examined by a rapidly growing segment of the academic population.

What Does the Research Tell Us About Flipped Learning?

With this significant of an increase in the number of scholarly publications about flipped learning, is there a coherent message emerging that describes what generally happens when students are involved in flipped learning environments, or that outlines best practices to elicit the greatest gains in student learning? At the time of this writing, the answer is a definitive "Not yet." Although flipped learning as a concept and classroom practice is nearly two decades old and although it has been the subject of great public attention and informal writing, the body of scholarly literature on flipped learning is still finding its footing, despite the quantity of literature produced in recent years. Articles on flipped learning published in 2016 were first written and submitted in 2013 in some cases, when the number of existing peer-reviewed publications on the subject could still be counted on one's fingers and toes.

We can, however, draw some solid conclusions about less broad questions:

- There is much that is known about specific implementations of flipped learning. For example, Eric Mazur's peer instruction idea has been the subject of extensive scholarship. An article published in 2001 to mark the 10-year anniversary of the introduction of peer instruction at Harvard (Crouch and Mazur 2001) outlined many of the research findings about peer instruction. For example, students in introductory physics classes based on peer instruction significantly outperformed their counterparts in a traditionally structured class on a variety of validated assessment instruments and showed significant improvements in both conceptual mastery and computationally based problem-solving. Another study on peer instruction (Lorenzo, Crouch, and Mazur 2006) showed that peer instruction reduced the "gender gap" in performance in introductory physics between male and female students. There is a similar body of research for specific teaching methods such as peer-led team learning (PLTL) and process-oriented guided inquiry learning (POGIL), teaching methods often associated with the natural sciences.
- We now know that active learning, generally speaking, can lead to dramatic improvements in student performance, at least in the STEM

disciplines. For example, a landmark metastudy (Freeman et al. 2014) in the *Proceedings of the National Academy of Sciences* aggregating the results of 225 other studies on active learning in the STEM disciplines found that students tended to be 1.5 times more likely to fail their course under traditional lecture-based teaching than in an active learning–focused course, and it found significant improvements in academic performance using a variety of assessments. This study followed an earlier one (Hake 1998) that studied 6,000 students in 62 different introductory physics courses and found that students in "interactive engagement" courses showed gains on the FCI that were two *entire standard deviations higher* than students in traditionally structured courses. Insofar as flipped learning is intended to create time and space for active learning, a result about active learning is really a result about flipped learning.

- The phenomenon that active learning in general, and forms of instruction that promote active learning in particular, improves student learning is not unique to the STEM disciplines. Indeed, there is a broad and deep body of literature on active learning in the humanities, fine arts, social sciences, and languages, as well as in vocational training and even outside academia in the areas of workforce training and religious education.

These more limited bodies of knowledge indicate that the scholarly literature on flipped learning rests upon broader principles that are well established (e.g., what we know about active learning) and specific instances that are well studied.

Theoretical Frameworks That Support Flipped Learning Practice and Research

What will be useful in thinking about flipped learning moving forward, both as a classroom practice and as an object of study, is to examine some theoretical frameworks from deeper in the study of educational and cognitive psychology that support the concept of flipped learning and provide a sound structure for both its use and its study.

The originators of flipped learning did not invent flipped learning as the result of a chain of reasoning about theoretical constructs. Rather, they were interested in solving practical pedagogical problems: finding ways to improve students' conceptual understanding about "force," finding time to vary instruction to match students' learning styles and address the concomitant diversity issues in their classes, finding ways to leverage a newly installed computer network to provide more time with hands-on work, or devising a means of delivering content to students who couldn't attend class. Still, these approaches were motivated by existing scholarly work (e.g., Mazur's knowledge of Halloun and Hestenes's studies), which is in turn rooted in pedagogical theory. Today, our understanding and practice of flipped learning can be similarly bolstered by understanding the theory behind the practice.

In a recent survey of flipped learning, Lakmal Abeysekera and Phillip Dawson (2015) propose the critical examination of flipped learning through the lenses of two major psychological theories: self-determination theory (SDT) and cognitive load theory (CLT).

Self-Determination Theory

The first theoretical framework is SDT, a theory of human motivation first proposed by psychologists Edward Deci and Richard Ryan (1985). In SDT, rather than focusing on the *amount* of motivation a person may have for learning, the focus is on the *type* of motivation the person has. Because the success of a flipped learning environment depends heavily on student motivation—motivation to complete the preparatory activities, to participate actively in class, and so on—SDT has much to say about flipped learning.

SDT makes two different distinctions between motivation types: between *intrinsic* and *extrinsic* motivation, on the one hand, and between *autonomous* and *controlled* motivation, on the other.

Intrinsic motivation is described by Ryan and Deci (2000) as "the inherent tendency to seek out novelty and challenges, to extend and exercise one's capacities, to explore, and to learn" (p. 70). It refers to the motivation to seek out challenges and learning opportunities from an internal desire and from an enjoyment or interest in the thing being sought, independently of any other rewards. By contrast, *extrinsic motivation* "refers to the performance of an activity in order to attain some separable outcome" (Ryan and Deci 2000, p. 71). The contrast between intrinsic and extrinsic motivation should be immediately clear and personally relevant to anyone involved in teaching and learning. When we learn something new, in any context, we can be motivated by external rewards that can be separated from the task. For example, we might be motivated to work on completing a research paper because our job performance is partially based on research output; this is separate from rewards that are inherent in the task itself, such as when we complete the paper because we like to write, or because the research question is interesting.

Autonomous motivation, "comprises both intrinsic motivation and the types of extrinsic motivation in which people have identified with an activity's value and ideally will have integrated it into their sense of self" (Deci and Ryan 1985, p. 182). In other words, autonomous motivation refers to motivation that is endorsed by the individual, regardless of whether that motivation is intrinsic or extrinsic. By contrast, *controlled motivation*

> consists of both external regulation, in which one's behavior is a function of external contingencies of reward or punishment, and introjected regulation, in which the regulation of action has been partially internalized and is energized by factors such as an approval motive, avoidance of shame, contingent self-esteem, and ego-involvements. When people are controlled, they experience pressure to think, feel, or behave in particular ways. (Deci and Ryan 1985, p. 182)

In this way, a person can feel extrinsic motivation that is autonomous, such as when we complete work on a research paper because we need to finish that paper in order to get a positive performance evaluation (the "extrinsic" part) and when we personally place a high value on professional advancement and doing well in our jobs (the "autonomous" part). If, however, we are completing that paper not because we value professional advancement but because we have been made to feel inferior to our colleagues if we don't publish, this is extrinsic motivation that is controlled in nature.

Deci and Ryan point out that although human beings are naturally inquisitive and curious and are strongly intrinsically motivated from birth, intrinsic motivation can be affected by external conditions and the satisfaction of certain needs. Specifically, to maintain intrinsic motivation, humans need to satisfy three basic cognitive needs: *competence*, *autonomy*, and *relatedness*. In an educational setting, the need for competence simply refers to the need to believe that one has mastered the "knowledge, skills, and behaviors necessary to be successful in a social context" (Abeysekera and Dawson 2015, p. 4). The need for autonomy refers to the need for a sense of control over one's knowledge and a sense of independence. The need for relatedness, by contrast, refers to the need to feel that one belongs to a social group in a given context. According to SDT, under conditions that satisfy these three basic needs, intrinsic motivation will flourish throughout one's life span; conversely, if these needs are not met, intrinsic motivation will atrophy (Ryan and Deci 2000).

SDT provides a useful way to think about course design and teaching in general, and flipped learning in particular. As mentioned previously (and reiterated in Parts Two and Three of this book), the success of flipped learning depends in large part on student motivation. Ideally, we would like students to be intrinsically motivated by the subjects we teach them. If nothing else, we would like them to experience *autonomous* motivation, so that if they are not intrinsically motivated to learn, they are at least in control of what motivates them. We want students to be "engaged" in their work, in other words. Conversely, what we hope to avoid are situations in which students are "learning" merely because of an external reward on which they place no significant personal value or, worse, because of feelings of pressure or shaming. Because of this, we should consider what kinds of course designs provide a learning environment that facilitates the satisfaction of the basic needs for competence, autonomy, and relatedness.

The traditional model of education *can* provide such an environment in the right hands and under the right conditions, but it is not the default. As Abeysekera and Dawson (2015) point out:

> The traditional lecture is caricatured as a passive, transmissive experience, effectively eliminating any sense of autonomy or competence in students. In fact, feelings of autonomy and competence are most likely to be experienced by the teacher within a learning environment created through this approach. (p. 5)

Note the word *caricatured*. Again, lecture environments *can* be quite productive for students, but the research cited by Abeysekera and Dawson indicates that this is not the natural outcome.

By contrast, *flipped learning* as we have defined it is structured precisely so that the group space is focused on supporting students as they progress through difficult, creative tasks by working with other students and with the instructor. In this way, flipped learning naturally caters to the needs for competence and connectedness. And by placing moderate responsibilities for students to acquire basic knowledge in their individual spaces, it also promotes the satisfaction of the need for autonomy. Abeysekera and Dawson propose that flipped learning environments, for these reasons, promote both intrinsic motivation and autonomous extrinsic motivation, more so than environments based on the traditional model. (We note that Abeysekera and Dawson *propose* this statement, framing it in the form of three research questions that merit further study. Their paper was published in 2015 but written in 2013 before the boom of published work in flipped learning began in earnest; a close meta-analysis of the research published from 2013 to the present may reveal evidence for or against this proposal. But in the meanwhile, the proposal is reasonable to state given the framework of SDT.)

Cognitive Load Theory

The second theoretical framework proposed by Abeysekera and Dawson (2015) for the study of flipped learning is CLT. This framework builds on the observations of cognitive psychologists such as George Miller, who observed that human working memory has strict limitations. Miller, for example, observed that human working memory can hold only between five and nine "chunks" of information at any given time (G. Miller 1956).

If human memory capacity is so limited, can some approaches to learning become counterproductive by overwhelming that memory capacity and making it impossible to learn deeply? Psychological research, especially the work of John Sweller, investigated this idea in the 1980s and continued through the 1990s. Sweller's work related to the acquisition of *schema*, or an organized pattern of thought that connects disparate but related bits of information into a systematized whole. Sweller's work, which drew on studies of schema acquisition among expert chess players (Groot 1965), has discovered that certain forms of problem-solving actually interfere with schema acquisition. Specifically, his work found that "means-end analysis"— an approach to problem-solving where a subject with an initial problem state and a goal state chooses an action by searching through a space of possible responses and selecting the one that reduces the distance between the initial and goal states—imposes a heavy burden on working memory. This burden has become known as "cognitive load," and Sweller's work formed the basis for what is now known as CLT.

In CLT, learning tasks can have three forms of cognitive load. A task's *intrinsic load* refers to the effort required to perform the task that is inherent in the task itself and cannot be reduced. Tasks also have *extrinsic load*, which is cognitive load that is not inherent in the task but that merely adds to the difficulty of performing it, for example, in the way that the task is presented. Finally, a task can contain *germane load*, which is cognitive load that is added to the task but that aids the formation of schema.

For example, if a person is learning how to bake a cake from scratch using a recipe, certain aspects of this process provide a cognitive load that the person simply can't eliminate. The person has to know what the ingredients are, make a trip to the store to purchase them, and know how to measure them out and then follow a recipe. This is part of the intrinsic load of cake baking. However, the process of cake baking can be made harder than this without a corresponding benefit. For example, if the recipe is poorly written, or given only in pictures with no measurements, additional load is put on the baker to finish the task that doesn't help him learn how to bake. (The process would arguably be made simpler by *adding* information—for example, including both text and pictures.) A recipe could additionally provide germane load by including, for example, not only instructions on how to bake the cake but also notes about the kind of flour used, the science behind why cakes bake in the first place, and so on. This is additional load, but it helps the baker acquire a coherent and organized schema about cake baking apart from just the recipe.

The implications of CLT for course design and teaching are immediate. As instructors, we want students not merely to gain a facility with facts and tricks; we want them to develop schema in our subjects and show a nuanced, connected understanding of what they have learned. Our course design and instructional choices should work together to point students in this direction. As Sweller puts it,

> The implications of working memory limitations on instructional design can hardly be overestimated. All conscious cognitive activity learners engage in occurs in a structure whose limitations seem to preclude all but the most basic processes. Anything beyond the simplest cognitive activities appear to overwhelm working memory. Prima facie, any instructional design that flouts or merely ignores working memory limitations inevitably is deficient. It is this factor that provides a central claim of cognitive load theory. (Sweller, van Merrienboer, and Paas1998)

Abeysekera and Dawson provide a few propositions about flipped learning and cognitive load, similar to those they provide for flipped learning and SDT. First, they propose that flipped learning environments that provide prerecorded video might reduce cognitive load because of students' abilities to pause and replay the video in their individual space. Particularly among lower-achieving students who may struggle more with managing cognitive load than higher-achieving students, prerecorded video has been shown to help with learning gains (Owston, Lupshenyuk, and Wideman 2011), and so flipped learning environments may provide significant help to struggling students. Second, Abeysekera and Dawson propose that flipped learning environments, with their focus on using group space for active learning, might provide more opportunities for instructors to offer individualized instruction to students, thereby helping students manage their cognitive load more effectively. This is as opposed to the traditional classroom model, which takes a "transmissive" approach, crafting a single activity centered around direct instruction that is intended for the entire class; as Lage, Platt, and Treglia (2000) point out in their work, a typical undergraduate class could contain a multitude of learning styles and therefore this one-size-fits-all approach might overwhelm some of the most intellectually vulnerable students.

A Third Framework: Self-Regulated Learning

Finally, we discuss a third theoretical framework supporting flipped learning that was not mentioned explicitly by Abeysekera and Dawson (2015)—namely, the concept of *self-regulated learning*. Self-regulated learning is a well-studied psychological theory developed by Barry Zimmerman (2002) and Paul Pintrich (2004), among many others. According to Zimmerman,

> Self-regulation is not a mental ability or an academic performance skill; rather it is the self-directive process by which learners transform their mental abilities into academic skills. Learning is viewed as an activity that students do for themselves in a proactive way rather than as a covert event that happens to them in reaction to teaching. Self-regulation refers to self-generated thoughts, feelings, and behaviors that are oriented to attaining goals. (2002 p. 65)

Self-regulated learning refers to learning behavior that exhibits the following characteristics (Nilson 2013):

- *Strategic knowledge.* A self-regulating learner knows about strategies and heuristics for certain kinds of tasks, the procedures and workflows for various kinds of problem-solving situations, and effective strategies for monitoring and executing the act of studying—for example, task and time management strategies, methods for memorizing and rehearsing, and different methods of organizing and connecting information.
- *Knowledge about cognitive tasks.* A self-regulating learner has the ability to comprehend the directions of a task, assess its difficulty and time requirements, and choose the right time and context for different learning behaviors.
- *Self-knowledge.* A self-regulating learner is aware of his own strengths and weaknesses as a learner and has the ability to monitor and adjust his affective response to successes and failures in studying; he knows what works personally in a given situation and can modify his behavior to make study more effective.

Self-regulated learning involves more than just knowledge. It involves having a mind-set of *taking initiative* over various aspects of learning and a degree of *control* over those aspects. For example, a self-regulating learner studying for a mathematics test needs to have knowledge not only of the content being covered; she also has to have reasonable goals set for herself, a means for knowing whether her knowledge is sufficient to attain the goals (e.g., through practice problems and their solutions), the ability to practice when feasible, and the initiative to do so, along with the ability to monitor and control her affective responses so as not to lose motivation when the practice goes poorly (or become overconfident when it goes well).

Pintrich (2004) presents a rubric (see Table 2.2) for self-regulation in the form of four *areas* of self-regulation—cognition, motivation/affect, behavior, and context—as well as four *phases* of self-regulation—forethought/ planning/activity ("Phase 1"), monitoring ("Phase 2"), control ("Phase 3"), and reaction/reflection ("Phase 4"). Performance on a learning task can be characterized by the 16 combinations of area and phase this rubric creates.

For example, activities in Phase 1 (forethought, planning, and activation) could include the following:

- *Cognition.* Reviewing prerequisite knowledge; remembering what worked well for study on previous material; setting goals for what one should know.
- *Motivation/affect.* Thinking about why the cognitive goals are important to the learner, personally; self-examining what difficulties one might encounter and weak spots that are relevant to the task; perceiving how difficult the task is inherently (i.e., judging the task's inherent cognitive load).
- *Behavior.* Planning out a schedule for studying; making plans for how one will examine one's own behavior.
- *Context.* Reviewing the efficacy of the physical space used for study.

A fully self-regulating learner will proceed through each of the phases in each of the areas of the task at hand—first planning and thinking ahead; then monitoring aspects of cognition, behavior, affect, and context as the task proceeds; exerting control over the tasks by making informed changes to cognition, behavior, affect, and context based on feedback from the monitoring phase; and ultimately reflecting back on the task to determine what worked well and what worked less well in all areas.

Flipped learning and self-regulated learning go hand in hand because of the privileged position of independent learning activities in flipped learning. Every time a student engages in a flipped learning environment, the "muscles" of self-regulation get practice. During the individual space activities students do to prepare for later activities, they have an opportunity on a small, safe scale to exercise all four phases in all four areas of Pintrich's model of self-regulation. The student is the one responsible for learning in this space, not the instructor, as is often the case in traditional class structures where first contact with the material comes in a transmissive mode. The student,

TABLE 2.2

Areas and Phases of Self-Regulated Learning

Phases and Relevant Scales	Areas for Regulation			
	Cognition	Motivation/Affect	Behavior	Context
Phase 1				
Forethought, planning, and activation	Target goal setting	Goal orientation adoption	Time and effort planning	Perceptions of task
	Prior content knowledge activation	Efficacy judgments	Planning for self-observations of behavior	Perceptions of context
	Metacognitive knowledge activation	Perceptions of task difficulty		
		Task value activation		
		Interest activation		
Phase 2				
Monitoring	Metacognitive awareness and monitoring of cognition	Monitoring of motivation and affect	Awareness and monitoring of effort, time use, need for help Self-observation of behavior	Monitoring changing task and context conditions

(Continues)

Table **2.2** (*Continued*)

Phases and Relevant Scales	Areas for Regulation			
	Cognition	Motivation/Affect	Behavior	Context
Phase 3				
Control	Selection and adaptation of cognitive strategies for learning, thinking	Selection and adaptation of strategies for managing, motivation, and affect	Increase/decrease effort Persist, give up help-seeking behavior	Change or renegotiate task Change or leave context
Phase 4				
Reaction and reflection	Cognitive judgments Attributions	Affective reactions Attributions	Choice behavior	Evaluation of task Evaluation of context
Relevant MSLQ Scales	Rehearsal Elaboration organization Critical thinking Metacognition	Intrinsic goals Extrinsic goals Task value Control beliefs Self-efficacy Test anxiety	Effort regulation Help seeking Time/study environment	Peer learning Time/study environment

to be effective in the individual space, must think ahead and plan out cognition, motivation, behavior, and context; pay attention to these four areas as the guided activity is completed; make changes based on feedback from self-monitoring and other sources (e.g., questions asked to the instructor); and ultimately think about how well the task went, to be sure to do well or better next time. During the group space, the same progress can take place on harder tasks with increased feedback present from classmates and the instructor.

Flipped learning environments encourage and support the development of self-regulated learning skills and behaviors perhaps more thoroughly than any other kind of instructional model. We will see in Part Two of this book that in order to maximize growth in self-regulation, it takes intentional focus on self-regulated learning when designing learning experiences; we cannot expect self-regulation to happen spontaneously in a flipped learning environment, although there is some evidence that it might. However, flipped learning environments set the stage for thinking about self-regulation in ways that other instructional methods do not.

Looking Ahead

We've seen that far from being a fad, buzzword, or flavor-of-the-month educational craze, flipped learning has a lengthy history, is well grounded in sound psychological theory, and is enjoying a prodigious growth in serious scholarship that points to its effectiveness. Next, we will see how the idea of flipped learning is being put into practice through the work of actual professors in a variety of disciplines.

3

MODELS OF FLIPPED LEARNING

I n the previous chapters, we have taken a good look at what defines *flipped learning*, how and why flipped learning was invented, and the theoretical frameworks we can use to understand flipped learning. Although this body of knowledge by itself forms a compelling case to consider flipped learning environments, it is even more convincing to see examples of its use, especially from ordinary college and university instructors in a variety of disciplines and institutional settings, who operate under the same sets of conditions that most of us do.

In this chapter we will look at several case studies of flipped learning implementations and ask the following questions in each one:

- What is the context of this course?
- Why was flipped learning used in this course?
- What do students do when they participate in this course? What does the instructor do when participating in the course?
- Why does this particular implementation fit our definition of *flipped learning?*
- What are the benefits for students in this environment?

We will begin with two of my own courses in mathematics and then proceed to look at other implementations in other subject areas.

Case Study: Calculus

What Is the Context of the Course?

Grand Valley State University (GVSU) is a public university of 26,000 students located in western Michigan in the United States. At GVSU, the standard first-semester course in calculus is taken by a wide range of students. The course is populated mostly by students majoring in engineering, with students in the life sciences forming another large constituency. The course satisfies a core general education requirement at GVSU and is a gateway course to many higher-level mathematics and science courses. As such, Calculus 1 is a course that constitutes a major hub of activity for the mathematics department, with offerings of 8 to 12 sections each semester and 2 sections (including a fully online section) in the summertime.

Importantly, Calculus 1 also serves as the entry point into both the academic major and minor programs in mathematics at GVSU. The mathematics degree program is the home not only for those aspiring to be mathematicians but also for all those wanting to become mathematics teachers in primary and secondary schools. A significant percentage of these students do not begin their college careers in calculus; many need to take preparatory courses in algebra and trigonometry before they have satisfied the prerequisite requirements for calculus. Still, Calculus 1 is the place where most mathematics majors, again including preservice mathematics teachers for primary and secondary schools, get their first impression of university-level mathematics—an impression that inevitably colors and informs all subsequent encounters with the discipline.

Why Was Flipped Learning Used in This Course?

Before teaching calculus at GVSU, I had taught calculus dozens of times at other colleges and universities, always using a decidedly traditional approach. Class time was focused on communicating normative explanations of ideas and on modeling problem-solving steps, through lecture. Although I had always included significant group work in the class, that group work was contingent on my lecturing—I would lecture, and then get students into groups to work on problems based on what they had seen in the lecture. Outside of class, students were responsible for working on homework problems and coming to office hours if they needed to discuss their work. In the language of our earlier discussion of the traditional model, the students' group space (my class meetings) was focused mainly on communicating information and modeling some very basic applications, whereas the individual space (post- and preclass) was focused on students taking the basic material from class time and doing more advanced things with it.

I taught calculus in this way for over 15 years, with hundreds of students and in a range of institutional types, before I ever considered using a flipped learning model. Each time I taught the course in the traditional format, I encountered the same issues:

- Students would attend the lectures, but participation in group work was shaky because in group work I was asking them to work with concepts they had seen only moments before. What was intended as a step up the Bloom's taxonomy pyramid, with students applying basic concepts to new problems, often became merely reteaching the material I had just taught in lecture—or worse, just groups of students looking at each other without working.
- If a student did *not* attend the lecture, the student was behind and had only the textbook to use as a resource for catching up. Occasionally a student would come to office hours to ask me to reteach the material to her; this isn't a bad instinct, but when *several* students do this on a regular basis, it becomes problematic. Or if there is a student who missed several days of class in a row and wants all of that material retaught one-on-one, it becomes hard to be helpful.
- Even students who attended class regularly and participated actively developed a sort of addiction with my teaching, and not in a good way: They came to believe that they were not capable of starting a solution to a problem on their own without me there to give them a push. Even after giving direct instruction on problem-solving techniques proven capable for starting a solution (Polya 2014), students seemed unwilling or incapable of taking initiative to apply those techniques, to set out on their own and try to solve new problems related, but not identical, to the ones they had seen in lecture. In the language of our theoretical frameworks from the last chapter, students were showing no signs of self-regulation and few signs of being able to transfer their learning from lecture examples to new problems.

After teaching calculus for so long and seeing the same issues over and over again every year, whether in a large top-20 research university or a small liberal arts college, I began to realize that my learning environment in those courses was not serving students well. Students may have been getting As in the course, but they were not proficient with the later courses in science, mathematics, and elsewhere that require the ability to apply calculus to new and difficult problems in context. Worse, they were building dependencies on me as an instructor that took away from their own personal agency to show initiative, take risks, and evaluate their own results when solving problems.

Of greatest concern was the effect that my learning environment was having on future teachers. If students think that calculus is about effective parroting of the teacher's lecture and if calculus is the course that informs all those students' future experiences with mathematics, then what necessarily will happen is that those students will become the teachers who communicate this flawed understanding of mathematics on to the next generation.

Based on these concerns and realizations, I decided to redesign the calculus course using a flipped learning design. The intention was that students would get direct instruction via prerecorded video to be viewed prior to class time, and then class time would be spent *entirely* on answering questions and working through more difficult problem-solving tasks. My hope was that students would begin to learn what professional mathematicians already know about our discipline: that it is not confined to basic hand calculations, that it involves taking risks and initiative to explore problems before developing solutions, and that it is inherently social and intended to be done in the company of others.

What Do Students Do in the Course? What Does the Instructor Do?

Calculus 1 at GVSU is a four-credit class, meaning that it meets 200 minutes each week over a 14-week semester. Typically, this occurs four days a week in 50-minute blocks, although other configurations equivalent to this are possible. Of those four blocks, one is designated as a "lab" period dedicated to having students work in pairs on applied problems in calculus involving the use of computing technology.

In the Individual Space

Prior to a class meeting (including lab days), students completed an assignment called *Guided Practice* in which they encountered new material for the first time in a structured way. Guided Practice assignments consisted of the following parts:

- An *overview* that gives a general description of what students will be learning in the upcoming lesson along with brief descriptions of how the new material will connect to previous material and real-life problems
- A list of *learning objectives*, or specific learning tasks, for the lesson that are split into two sublists: a list of *basic* learning objectives that describe what students should be able to do when they arrive at the class meeting and a list of *advanced* learning objectives describing

tasks students should be able to do in the long term after the class is over and with further work

- A section of *resources* for learning, typically involving a portion of the textbook (Boelkins, Austin, and Schlicker 2014) to read and a selection of videos to watch (a collection of 93 videos made specifically for this course was accessible in a YouTube playlist, at http://bit.ly/ GVSUCalculus) along with additional optional video resources when further direct instruction or examples were considered useful (e.g., when a new topic built on a topic from a prior course and review might be needed)

- A collection of *exercises* that provided students with ways to practice the tasks outlined in the basic learning objectives list

- A set of *instructions* on how to submit their work, typically by entering basic information (name, section number) and the responses to the exercises into a Google Form

The Guided Practice model will be discussed extensively in chapter 6. A typical Guided Practice assignment is shown in Figure 3.1.

Guided Practice assignments were posted at least 10 days in advance of the class meeting to which they were attached. Students were expected to work on these at least 24 hours in advance, and the submissions were due (via the Google Form) at least 1 hour before class time. Before class time, I (the professor) would open up the Google Spreadsheet created by the form submissions and look for patterns—common incorrect answers, different approaches to solutions, common misconceptions, and so on—that would inform what I would do in class. By working the Guided Practice assignment, students would have structured first contact with the new material by having clearly stated learning objectives, a reliable set of resources for learning about those objectives, and simple exercises to gauge their understanding before setting foot in class.

As the professor, my role was to provide support for students as they learned. Students were encouraged to consult me during office hours or by e-mail for any questions they had about the reading, viewing, or exercises; in some sections, a discussion board was set up for the purpose of asking those questions asynchronously.

In the Group Space
Upon arrival at the class meetings, the first five minutes of class was set aside for students to form into groups of three or four and discuss their answers to the Guided Practice assignment for the day; then another five minutes

was set aside for debriefing of that assignment, focusing on patterns of misconceptions that might have appeared in the response spreadsheet.

After this debriefing session, typically 30 to 40 minutes of class time remained to engage in any form of active learning that might fit the material at hand. These would often include peer or group activities, such as the following:

- Peer instruction activities using clickers and ConcepTests (Mazur 1997) for conceptual material
- Group work on applications of basic material to more advanced computations and to real-life applications
- Groups working through the derivation or proof of an important idea

Figure 3.1. Guided Practice assignment for Calculus 1.

Guided Practice for 1.8: The tangent line approximation

Overview

This section is a little different because we will be doing most of the work in your lab session with a computer. But this is appropriate since it's a very computationally oriented section. We will be looking at a common application of the derivative to making accurate predictions about a function when we don't have complete information about the function. This is the basic idea behind such applications as weather forecasts, financial forecasting, laboratory estimates, and more. We know by now that the derivative $f'(a)$ at a point $x = a$ gives the slope of the tangent line to the graph of f at $x = a$. This tangent line is also called the **local linearization** of f at $x = a$, and we will learn how to compute local linearizations and use them to estimate values of a function.

Learning Objectives

BASIC learning objectives

Each student will be responsible for learning and demonstrating proficiency in the following objectives PRIOR to the class meeting. **The entrance quiz for the class meeting will cover these objectives.**

- (*Algebra review*) Given the slope of a line and a point (not necessarily the *y*-intercept) on that line, state an equation for that line in *point-slope form* and in *slope-intercept form*.
- Given the value of the derivative of f at *a* point $x = a$ (i.e., given $f[a]$), write the *equation of the tangent line* to the graph of f at $x = a$.
- Explain what is meant by the *local linearization* of a function f at the point $x = a$.
- Use a local linearization of a function at $x = a$ to approximate values of f near $x = a$.

(Continues)

Figure 3.1 (*Continued*)

ADVANCED learning objectives

The following objectives should be mastered by each student DURING and FOLLOWING the class session through active work and practice:

- Given a function f, find its local linearization at $x = a$.
- If $L(x)$ is the local linearization of a function $f(x)$ at $x = a$, and if b is some point near a, determine whether $L(b)$ is greater than, less than, or equal to $f(b)$ and explain.

Resources

Reading: **Read Section 1.8, pages 71–77 in Active Calculus.** We will work some of the activities in class, but you may also work on them outside of class for further understanding.

Viewing: Watch the following videos at the MTH 201 YouTube Playlist. These have a total running time of 18 minutes, 34 seconds:

- Quick Review: The tangent line approximation (2:18)
- Calculating a tangent line (5:42)
- Using a tangent line (3:27)
- Using the local linearization (7:07)

Exercises

These exercises can be done during or after your reading and video watching. They are intended to help you make examples of the concepts you are reading and viewing. Work these out on scratch paper, and then you will be asked to submit the results on a web form at the end.

1. A line has a slope equal to –3 and goes through the point (4, 6). State the equation of this line in point-slope form and then in slope-intercept form.
2. The function f has the following features: We know that $f(2) = -3$. State the equation of the tangent line to the graph of f at $x = 2$ in point-slope form and then in slope-intercept form.
3. The tangent line to the graph of f at $x = 2$ that you calculated in question 2 is called the local linearization of f at $x = 2$. Use the local linearization to predict the value of $f(2.1)$ and explain briefly what you did.
4. What specific mathematical questions do you have about the reading and viewing that you would like to discuss in class?

Turn-in instructions

Go to the web form located at the following link and type in your answers: http://bit.ly/14FjsHH

Responses are due **one hour before your section's class time.** If you do not have access to the Internet where you live, please let me know in advance and we will make alternative arrangements.

Included and implicit in all of these activities was the potential of needing to provide targeted direct instruction with specific individuals or groups on specific points. If a group was stuck on a problem involving an application of the derivative, for instance, because they were not fluent with the basic notion of a derivative, I was able to take a few moments to give them a brief tutorial and get them on their way again. Really, anything that benefited the students could be done during class time without the pressure of having to complete a lecture first.

Why Is This Flipped Learning?

This was an example of a flipped learning environment because students' first contact with new concepts in calculus occurred primarily in their individual spaces, by working through the Guided Practice assignment. That contact was a combination of direct instruction (via the videos) and a structured inquiry activity (via the Guided Practice exercises). Students were not simply given the book and a section to read; they were given a *structured activity* that provided *guidance* as they met the new material for the first time.

It is also an example of flipped learning because the group space was refocused on active learning through challenging, interactive work on higher-level tasks that would have ordinarily been relegated to time out of class when students are separated from the instructor and many of their classmates. In the group space, I was able to listen in on student conversations; intervene when necessary with questions of my own; offer suggestions, observations, and the occasional brief tutorial; and guide students as they engaged in dynamic, rigorous, creative work with the basic concepts.

What Are the Benefits to the Students?

After the first time I taught this course with a flipped learning environment, I felt that it was the first time in 15 years of teaching calculus that students had adequate time and space to explore the concepts of calculus with sufficient levels of support. Instead of being constantly on the clock to rush through a group activity in 10 or 15 minutes, we had three times as much time to work together, ask questions, air out misconceptions, and get our issues resolved.

Teaching the class in a flipped format also allowed me to get to know students' individual learning tendencies and preferences in a way that I could never approach before. Each day, I had the ability to talk face-to-face with each student, or at least a small group of students. I was able to tailor my interactions to their precise needs, communicate in person without having to wait for them to come for office hours, and help them work together to boost group productivity.

I also began to notice subtle shifts in students' perceptions of their roles as learners. At the beginning of the semester, students would ask, "Could you show me how to get started on this problem?" just like in the older classes where students felt powerless to take a step to try a solution of their own. As the semester moved ahead, the questions changed to "I've tried the following to get started but I think I'm stuck. Can you help?" And better yet, students would ask, "Could you point me in the direction of a good set of resources that would give me more practice?" Gradually, students moved from being dependent on me for success toward becoming self-regulated learners.

The greatest benefit from a flipped learning environment for students was the support that they received as they worked on more difficult material, and not being forced to work on this at home by themselves. This was reflected in the students' own words on course evaluations. One student said, "If I ever needed help during the in-class work, there was plenty of time for Professor Talbert to make it around to all the students." Another student made a similar point: "It just makes more sense to do practice problems in the presence of an expert on the material, rather than at home, alone."

Case Study: Communicating in Mathematics

Another course that occupies a central place in the mathematics program at Grand Valley State University (GVSU) is Communicating in Mathematics, a second-year course in methods of mathematical proof.

What Is the Context of the Course?

Whereas Calculus 1 is the entry point for students studying mathematics at the basic level at GVSU, Communicating in Mathematics is the gateway course for all higher-level mathematics courses. The focus of the course is on *methods of mathematical proof* and on *mathematical writing* (hence the name). The course requires Calculus 1 as a prerequisite and is targeted at second- and sometimes third-year students who intend to take higher-level courses such as abstract algebra and real analysis, subjects that are founded on abstraction and proof-based problem-solving.

Due to its heavy emphasis on writing, the course satisfies a university "supplemental writing skills" (SWS) course requirement. In order to be designated as an SWS course, the course must base at least one-third of the semester grade on student writing (assessed by quality), require at least 3,000 words of writing, contain explicit instruction on writing, and allow students to engage in a revision process for their writing. The Mathematics

Department developed its own textbook for the course (Sundstrom 2013) that includes guidelines for mathematical writing.

The course is a four-credit course, meaning (as with Calculus 1) that it meets 200 minutes per week over a 14-week semester. The 200 minutes are split up in different ways for different sections. However, the credit amount for the course at the time I taught it was three credits, meaning 150 minutes of meeting time, usually arranged in two 75-minute meetings per week.

This course had, at the time, the record of the greatest percentage of nonpassing course grades of any mathematics course in the GVSU catalog, including remedial mathematics courses, by a wide margin. In fact, historically almost 40% of students taking this course either withdraw or receive grades of D or F. An in-house student survey revealed patterns suggesting why this might be the case. Many students voiced that the methodology of the course—working with abstract ideas, experimenting with mathematical phenomena and looking for patterns, phrasing those patterns in the form of well-formed mathematical conjectures, and then supplying a cogent and well-written argument for them—was not their idea of what "mathematics" was supposed to be. Rather, the prevailing student conception of mathematics as a discipline remained firmly on a far more basic level—specifically, that mathematics is concerned with computations that have one solution method and one right answer, and making computations by hand as quickly and with as few mistakes as possible. Further, the way of determining if an answer is correct is by the teacher telling them or by checking an answer key. Professional mathematicians strongly disagree with this, instead affirming that mathematics is a process of obtaining knowledge about abstractions (and communicating that knowledge to others), and this is the philosophical thrust of the Communicating in Mathematics course. This conflict of "sociomathematical norms" (Yackel and Cobb 1996) is one key source of tension and stress for students as many struggle not only with the significant workload of the course but also the need to shift a paradigm about the very discipline in which they are majoring.

From a cognitive load theory perspective, the course also requires significant resources and commitments from students that many are not used to making. Many students when asked why they are choosing to study mathematics would say that "it comes easy for me," mostly because the process of "mathematics" for them involves not much more than computations of easy- to medium-level difficulty involving symbolic or numerical manipulation. The *intrinsic load* of studying for this course, however, is quite heavy; students must learn about symbolic logic, number theory, and other abstract concepts as well as professional standards for writing and communication involving both specific mathematical rules for writing and general rules for good writing in any context. Additionally, the *germane load* of the course (additional load that helps students form coherent schema about the subject) is also significant: Students must engage in metacognition almost constantly to determine whether their proofs are sufficiently clear and correct, discover how to make corrections to drafts of proofs based on instructor feedback, and so on. Nor does this account for any of the *extrinsic load* that may be a part of the instruction.

Many students—quite possibly a significant piece of the 40% who eventually withdraw or fail—simply are unprepared to handle this level of cognitive load, and either drop out or try to approach the course using the paradigms of their previous experiences with mathematics courses. Specifically, many students do not attempt to build schema for the subject in a way that views all the moving parts as a cohesive whole, and so they view the course as a thousand different pieces when it is, rather, one construct with a thousand parts. Because there is no coherent schema in place, students have to invest far more time and energy in keeping up with the course (because 1,000 pieces take much more effort to maintain than one construct), and the results are predictable: failure or withdrawal from nearly half the students and exhaustion and widespread confusion even among the other half that passes.

Why Was Flipped Learning Used in This Course?

I was first assigned this course in 2011, when I was new to GVSU as a faculty member. I had taught a similar version of the course elsewhere, using a traditional format along with structured group work in class. I continued with this format when I taught the class for the first time at GVSU. The class met on Tuesdays and Thursdays for 75 minutes each time.

Prior to class, students were given reading assignments from the textbook and asked to work through some of the "Preview Activities" that introduced sections of the book. Reading Questions designed to focus students' reading were assigned. Both the Preview Activities and Reading Questions were taken up and graded. Along with those grades, students completed homework assignments outside of class, had four timed exams and a final exam, and completed a proof portfolio that consisted of extended proof-based problems with a system of revision in place to allow them to submit multiple drafts. There was also a light participation grade. The class would begin with announcements and then a lecture on the day's material, with time for questions during the lecture, and then this was followed by structured activities intended to apply what had been taught in the lecture.

Then, postclass, students worked on homework and their proof portfolios and studied for tests.

The results that I obtained were exactly as described previously. The course demands a paradigm shift for students, many of whom are caught flat footed by the rigors and demands of the subject. For many, it was as if I were participating in a bait-and-switch operation, advertising the course as "mathematics" but not giving students the "mathematics" that they were used to. Despite the excellent quality of the textbook and the engaging nature of the Preview Activities, many students completed the Preview Activities only out of obligation and did not really understand what they were doing. Many didn't do the Preview Activities at all. Despite what I considered to be clear, organized lecture material (including giving out the slides for the lecture in advance) and engaging students in evidence-based active work (using a variant of peer instruction for the lecture portion of the 75 minutes), when students began work on group activities to apply what they knew, they just didn't know *enough* to make a reasonable attempt at the activities. I was asking them, for example, to apply what they had just heard about mathematical induction to set up a proof by mathematical induction; meanwhile, they were still struggling with the basics of mathematical induction. In the end, my drop/failure/withdraw rate closely approximated the historical 40% figure.

This was not an acceptable result for me, and I chose to redesign the class using a flipped learning model with the following goals:

- *Have actionable data about student knowledge of basic concepts before coming to class.* Students were turning in Preview Activities and Reading Questions *on paper, at the beginning of class* in my traditional setup, and I would look over that work usually after the class was over. But this was doing neither me nor the students much good, because by the time I saw their preliminary work it was too late to address their misconceptions. By using a flipped learning framework, first contact with new material would not only be more structured but also have a way of getting formative assessment data on their initial contact *prior* to class so any misconceptions could be brought up explicitly *in* class.

- *Free up as much time as possible for students to work on proof and writing exercises while in class.* The most important activity in the course is forming and then proving mathematical conjectures. After the first iteration of the course, I found that taking time away from these activities was seriously detrimental to all facets of student learning in the course. My lecturing was the main culprit of that time being taken away. The learning environment in class needed to be focused on working together on the activities that mattered most: making and proving mathematical conjectures. Lecture was getting in the way; it needed to be moved.

- *Help build students' self-regulation behaviors in a concrete way.* At the time, I had not heard of "self-regulated learning," but the behaviors and skills it describes are a precondition for student success in this course (and probably many others). Many students expected the teacher (me) to do most of the work: Tell them if they are on the right track, work examples for them, even in some cases tell them what to say in their proofs. This is not setting students up for success in the courses that use Communicating in Mathematics as a prerequisite. Rather, in addition to learning the technical content of the subject, I needed students to build their muscles in taking initiative, checking their own work, evaluating the quality not only of their work but also of their approach to the work in terms of cognitive tasks and affect and context—and all the other phases and areas of self-regulation that we have discussed in this book. By consistently centering the course on in-class lecture, this was depriving students of the opportunities to work on these crucially important skills.

What Do Students Do in the Course? What Does the Instructor Do?

To set up the flipped environment for the course, I created a YouTube playlist of videos (www.youtube.com/playlist?list=PL2419488168AE7001) that closely mirrored what I would cover in an in-class lecture. These short lectures did, in fact, replace formal in-class lecturing. These plus the textbook we normally use for the course formed the main body of learning resources for students.

In the Individual Space

Prior to class, students were given Guided Practice exercises to do, similar in structure to those used in Calculus 1. They contained an overview of the new material, specific learning objectives for the lesson, a list of resources (textbook and video), exercises, and submission instructions. These Guided Practices were essentially the Preview Activities and Reading Questions that I had previously used in the course, wrapped inside structured "rules for engagement" that gave students explicit learning outcomes for which they should aim, a varied list of resources to use, and exercises that were specifically targeted at items in the learning objectives lists. To address one of the issues mentioned earlier (not seeing the students' preclass activities until later), students submitted their work using a Google Form. Just as with Calculus 1, the Google Form puts student responses into a spreadsheet, and before class I would scan the spreadsheet for patterns and trouble spots.

In the Group Space

Upon arrival to class, students took a five-minute quiz using clickers on questions taken directly from the Guided Practice exercises. This provided a level of quality-control checking and accountability to make sure students had fully engaged with the Guided Practice exercises. Then we would reveal the solutions to the quiz and take questions. This would normally occupy about 10 to 15 minutes of a 75-minute period. The entire remaining time—more than an hour in most cases—was spent on active learning tasks related to forming and proving mathematical conjectures, the activity at the heart of the course (and the discipline). My role during this time was to ensure each group was being active and progressing forward, to answer questions, to give additional exercises to those who finished early, and to furnish some very short and targeted tutorials to groups who were stuck on basic concepts. We would end the time with questions and answers, and then students were tasked with completing their group work individually and turning it in. If students had completed their group work in class, they could turn it in on the spot.

Why Is This Flipped Learning?

Why *wasn't* the *original* iteration of the course flipped learning? After all, students were given reading questions and activities outside of class, and then did group work in class. Isn't that flipped learning?

My answer is "Almost." In fact, one could say that the first iteration was "somewhat flipped" because, indeed, students were doing preparatory work before class and then active work in class. What keeps this structure from fully fitting our definition of *flipped learning* is the focus of the *in-class* period. The in-class activities were focused on two things: lecture and then group work. But, really, lecture was the main focal point. Not once did I preempt a lecture in order to give more time to group work; much more frequently it was the other way around, cutting group work short so that I could keep lecturing. Although my structure does fit, in a way, a *part* of what makes flipped learning what it is—namely, that first contact with new concepts had moved from the group learning space to the individual learning space in the form of structured activity—the other part was not clearly in place; namely, my group space was not fully transformed into a time for dynamic, interactive work, done by students and guided by me, on difficult concepts. It was mainly a time to lecture, and hopefully there was enough time for group activities left over.

The revised iteration fixed this deficiency. The preclass work students did was not really changed that much; there was merely additional structure added onto what was already there, and video was introduced as part of the "diet" that students consumed for preparation. However, the class period became much more intentional about students working together on the heart of the course—making and proving mathematical conjectures. The philosophy was that anything that significantly took time away from actually working on such activities should be relocated to before class or after class, or else eliminated. So the group space of the second version of the course was focused, as it should be, on students working together on hard problems with my guidance.

What Are the Benefits to the Students?

Initiating a flipped learning environment didn't completely solve the problem of conflicting sociomathematical norms or managing a high cognitive load, nor did it completely reverse the high rate of drop/withdraw/fail grades. However, the grade distribution was somewhat better than the historical average, with 32.5% of students (13 out of 40) either dropping or earning D or F grades. This is not a point of pride, but it does suggest some progress.

Student comments from the course evaluations tell a story of growing self-regulatory abilities. As one student pointed out,

> This course has taught me more how to problem solve on my own because we did so much work outside of the classroom on our own; we didn't have the professor lecturing us, then doing homework at home. We worked through the lecture on our own, and it gave us the opportunity to work through our problems first, without instantly being rescued. It was frustrating at times but I guess overall I have benefited from it.

Another student noted an improved sense of self-efficacy, a critical component of Pintrich's model of self-regulation:

> I'm much more comfortable with not having a cookie-cutter version to solving a problem. This kind of thinking was hard to do at first but now I feel more capable.

A third student made a similar point, along with what appears to be a coming to terms with the sociomathematical norms of the subject:

I realize now how much more complex math is. This course is a different type of math. It's not working with basic algebra. It's not learning formulas and plugging things in. It's different. In the beginning, I thought this course was going to be really really difficult but everything was dealt in strides and everything was built off of other things we were learning, which is what many math courses are.

Finally, this student noted not only improved confidence but also enjoyment of the process:

At the beginning of the semester I was very stressed out and worried about this class. But as time has gone by, I am much more confident in this course and I actually enjoy this new type of thinking that the course has challenged me to do.

Case Study: Mathematical Biology

Our next case study comes from the subject of mathematical biology, which focuses on constructing mathematical models of biological processes. A course on this subject was taught at the University of Wisconsin at LaCrosse (UW-LaCrosse) by professors Eric Eager, James Peirce, and Patrick Barlow (Eager, Peirce, and Barlow 2014).

What Is the Context of the Course?

Mathematical Biology 201 is offered as a second-level course at UW-LaCrosse, indicating a level suitable for advanced first-year students or beginning second-year students. The course typically enrolls 25 students with academic majors in the life sciences (biochemistry, microbiology, physical therapy, etc.) along with some mathematics majors. These students must complete first-semester Calculus 1 before enrolling, and the course serves as a substitute for second-semester Calculus 2. The course is taught in the mathematics department and it has a strong mathematical focus, but its audience is scientists, and the science plays at least as large a role as the mathematics does.

Why Was Flipped Learning Used in This Course?

The design of this course around a flipped learning model was driven by the needs of its client disciplines in the life sciences, as well as the perceived learning goals for the course by the faculty in the mathematics department who teach it, reflected in the questions the instructors asked when designing the course:

> What do faculty members in the life sciences want their students to bring to their courses from the mathematical courses they require as a part of their major? Or, possibly more importantly, what mathematical/quantitative skills and experiences do students need once they graduate and embark on careers in the life sciences?

An answer from the perspective of the life sciences was found in a 2004 report by the Mathematical Association of America (MAA; Ganter and Barker 2004), in which several client disciplines of mathematics courses were surveyed on this very question. The MAA report found that faculty in the life sciences highly value conceptual understanding as well as the ability to construct mathematical models, solve problems effectively, and interpret the meaning of data. Experience with working outside disciplinary boundaries and synthesizing and analyzing information that connects concepts from different subjects are also considered important.

In a similar vein, the instructors of the course had a clear idea of what they would like students to learn in their course as well. Students should be able to identify when a particular biological problem could benefit from a quantitative model. Students should then be able to construct a rough conceptual model for the problem, identify potential mathematical structures embedded within the conceptual model, and then analyze a quantitative model to make predictions about the biological system that is being modeled. Students should also be able to reason about the uncertainty inherent in quantitative models of biological processes and analyze the results of a mathematical model with a critical eye, proposing improvements to the model when appropriate.

This is a long list of quite complex cognitive activities in which students should engage. The instructors chose a flipped learning model for the course because, quite simply, they felt students cannot learn these skills from listening to a lecture, and the amount of time needed to practice and finally attain these skills precludes the possibility of spending time in class on lecturing.

What Do Students Do in the Course? What Does the Instructor Do?

In the Individual Space

The instructors created a collection of 75 video lectures, ranging in length from 5 to 25 minutes, for students to use in preparation for class. These videos covered all the basic mathematical knowledge needed for upcoming class activities in the context of biological models. Although there was no formal means of holding students accountable for comprehending the videos (e.g., through beginning-of-class quizzes), the instructors made participation in the in-class activities difficult or impossible without first thoroughly viewing the video lectures. The lectures were made using simple technological tools such as free screencasting software that runs on an iPad.

In the Group Space
The class meeting was the highlight of the course. During the class meetings throughout the semester, students worked in groups of two or three on a series of 35 biological case studies of varying lengths. Some were very short and could be done in 15 to 20 minutes; others were so complex that multiple class meetings were devoted to them. In the case studies, students were presented with biological problems and required to build and analyze quantitative models for those problems. The modeling process combined elements of communication (both interpersonal communication within a group and technical communication of the results), mathematics, and computer programming. During this time, the instructor played several roles. The instructor would simply gauge students' progress in the model-building process and be on alert for issues with student work. If needed, the instructor could intervene to answer questions, provide a nudge to a group that was stuck, or even pull the entire class together for a short "breakout" session to address a common problem through a brief, targeted lecture. (Note that this implementation shows that the group space in a flipped learning environment need not be *devoid* of lecture or direct instruction; it is merely no longer *focused* on that kind of instruction.)

Students could finish up their case study in class or complete it outside of class if needed. To place a check on students freeloading within the case study groups, each week a randomly selected case study was chosen as a "group quiz" and taken up for a grade. Also outside of class, students engaged in homework from the textbook and writing projects.

Some class meetings were spent on assessment tasks. There were two kinds of assessments given. Individual quizzes were scheduled on regular dates; the quizzes consisted of three questions involving small modeling problems, and students selected two of these and worked through them using their notes, programs, homework, and the video lectures. Another form of assessment was a "modeling competition" intended to replace timed exams, in which students were given open-ended modeling problems and 24 hours in which to complete them in groups. Students with the best modeling solution were given perfect homework scores until the next modeling competition.

Why Is This Flipped Learning?

The UW-La Crosse mathematical biology course is a great example of our definition of *flipped learning*. Students gain first contact with the new material—mathematical and quantitative methods for modeling biological processes—in the form of direct instruction provided by online video made by the instructors. Then the group space is transformed into a place of lively, creative work on difficult problems in biological modeling. Students are working on the hardest part of the course—the actual construction of quantitative models of biological systems—in a place and a context in which they have the greatest access to help from the professor and from each other.

It is worth noting that like the original instances of flipped learning we discussed in chapter 2, flipped learning in the UW-La Crosse mathematical biology course was instituted to solve a specific pedagogical problem, not simply because flipped learning was a "fad" to try or because an administrator said it should be done. Namely, the instructors had a vision for what they wanted students to be doing in their course, and they realized that intentionally following this vision meant freeing up time in class. By simply relocating the "structured first contact" experience to the individual space, relatively vast amounts of time were liberated and put to use. It is likely that the client disciplines for the course appreciated this as well.

What Are the Benefits to the Students?

Aside from the clear benefits to students in the form of providing them dedicated time and space to work on the most important and difficult parts of the course, the UW-La Crosse faculty found several other positive effects of using flipped learning.

The instructors administered the Class-Level Survey of Student Engagement (CLASSE) to their students (Ouimet and Smallwood 2005), an instrument that gauges engagement and metacognition, and found that in the most recent offering of the course (in 2014)

- 77% of students reported "[putting] together ideas or concepts from different courses when completing assignments or during class discussions" more than five times (Eager et al. 2014, p. 148). Note that this is one of the desired outcomes of mathematics courses from the client discipline of the course.
- 62% of students reported "applying theories or concepts to practical problems or in new situations" was emphasized in the course work "very much" (Eager et al. 2014, p. 148).

- 77% of students reported participating in a study group for a quiz or test at least twice, with 54% reporting this happened more than twice (Eager et al. 2014, p. 148).

Although we cannot conclude that the flipped learning environment *caused* these results, certainly the flipped learning environment crafted by the instructor enabled and supported the behaviors that underlaid them.

Student comments on the course in semester evaluations were generally very positive (see Eager et al. 2014). Students commented that the flipped learning environment made them have better feelings about mathematics and that they learned more than in any other mathematics course they had. In fact, one of the instructors reports (personal e-mail communication from Eric Eager, June 22, 2016) that 5 of the 65 students who have taken the course decided, following the course, to become mathematics majors or minors despite having to go back and take Calculus 2 and extend their schooling by a year. Many commented that they not only looked forward to taking more courses using a flipped learning environment but also wished *every* course they had could be taught this way.

Case Study: Flipped Learning in Business-Related Courses

The College of Westchester, located in White Plains, New York, is a college serving around 1,000 students, focusing on business and information technology (IT) in a career-focused context. The college offers two-year associate in applied science (AAS) degrees as well as four-year bachelor of business administration (BBA) degrees in a variety of business- and IT-related areas.

After seeing the mounting evidence for the effectiveness of flipped learning environments that began to accumulate in 2012 and 2013, Chief Information Officer Kelly Walsh approached Provost Warren Rosenberg to discuss the introduction of flipped learning at the college through a structured pilot program, bolstered through a competitive grant program. The Flipped Classroom Competitive Grant offered two grants of $1,000 each for instructors who proposed flipped learning redesigns of existing courses. Of the submissions received, professors Christopher Nwosisi and Alexa Ferreira were selected, and their courses were then redesigned using flipped learning principles (Nwosisi, Ferreira, Rosenberg, and Walsh 2016).

What Is the Context of the Course?

The two courses involved were Cisco Networking Basics, taught by Nwosisi, and Adult Development in the Workplace, taught by Ferreira.

Cisco Networking Basics is the first of a four-course sequence in the Cisco Networking Academy program, a program that prepares students to take the Cisco Certified Network Associate (CCNA) exam, which provides an entry-level certification for the Cisco certified professional program for those wishing to become computer network administrators. The course is also designed to help students prepare for the Cisco Certified Entry Network Technician (CCENT) entry-level certification exam. It is a prerequisite for several other network administration courses at the College of Westchester and is required for the computer networking administration degree. The other course, Adult Development in the Workplace, is quite different in its focus. It is a general education course that is part of the BBA programs in accounting and business administration, focusing on the psychology and sociology of adult physical, cognitive, and personality development.

Although these courses are different in their approach and clientele, we will treat them together because they were developed simultaneously as part of a competitive grant at the College of Westchester and were redesigned under similar principles. In particular, a feature of these courses that distinguishes them from the others in this chapter is that only a portion of each course was converted into a flipped learning environment. In both courses, only those meetings in *alternate weeks* were conducted using a flipped model. These are the first two "partially flipped" courses we have encountered so far; the question of whether a course can be "partially flipped" will be taken up in a later chapter, but these two courses serve as a useful introduction to the idea.

Why Was Flipped Learning Used in This Course?

We already mentioned the main reason flipped learning was even considered at the College of Westchester—namely, the rapidly accumulating evidence for its effectiveness. For these two courses in particular, the reasons for wanting to introduce flipped learning closely mirror the nature and demographics of the course.

Christopher Nwosisi, professor of the Cisco networking course, stated that he observed weakness in some students' problem-solving skills, with difficulties in understanding networking concepts and hence problems in following in-class lectures as well as they could; he wanted to create a flipped learning environment in order to provide more coaching on problem-solving tasks involving actual computer networking. Nwosisi's reasons are reminiscent of those of Wes Baker, one of the originators of flipped learning, who wanted to give his students more time and experience with actual user interface design instead of listening to lectures about design.

Alexa Ferreira, professor of the adult development course, wanted to see her students more engaged and participatory during class. Like general education courses at any number of colleges, students sometimes struggle to see the relevance and importance of this subject matter. Through creating a flipped learning environment, Ferreira could use multiple teaching modalities and active, engaging classroom activities freely and without as many concerns about running short of class time.

What Do Students Do in the Course? What Does the Instructor Do?

In the Individual Space
In both courses, the flipped learning model was used in alternate weeks. During those weeks, Nwosisi's networking class accessed video and audio lecture resources, participated in an online discussion forum, and took online quizzes to gauge their understanding (and provide accountability for completing the work). In Ferreira's adult development course, the new topic was briefly introduced *in class*, and then students learned more through direct instruction outside of class and participation in learning activities that included games and interactive demos. The instructors in both cases gave support on demand to students as they learned.

In the Group Space
Student activities in the group space were quite varied. Nwosisi's networking students worked on lab activities involving computer networks designed to drive home conceptual understanding. They worked either independently or in groups, with the instructor available as a resource and a guide. Ferreira's adult development students participated in realistic case study–like activities, such as designing educational intervention programs for older adults.

Why Is This Flipped Learning?

Even though this was only a *partial flip*, the structure during the *flipped weeks* was clearly identifiable as flipped learning. First contact with new concepts was moved from the group space to the individual space in the form of a structured activity. Note that in Ferreira's case, giving an introduction to the new material in the group space rather than individual space did not negate the flipped learning criteria; indeed, giving students a "teaser" prior to their individual space activities helped them navigate those activities and could be considered part of the "structure" for the activity done outside of class. Likewise, the group space was changed from a time for information transfer and "telling" to a time for activity and "doing," in which students engaged in valuable activities where they applied concepts and engaged creatively in the content, under the guidance of the professor.

What Are the Benefits to the Students?

There were slight overall grade improvements in the two courses—a 2.6% improvement in one and a 3.5% improvement in the other—but neither change was statistically significant. This is typical of many studies of flipped learning that measure improvements in grades: Often, there is no significant *improvement* nor sign of a significant *drop* in numerical measures.

However, when looking at grades in the aggregate, namely the percentage of students earning a D, F, or W (withdraw) grade versus the percentage of those who do not, we begin to see impressive results. When looking at all sections of both courses during the 2012–2013 academic year, 24.1% of students earned a D, F, or W grade. During the flipped learning pilot, across all sections this number dropped to 20.6%. Additionally, the DFW percentage was all but eliminated in the adult development course in the flipped learning version (Nwosisi et al. 2016).

Additionally, students responded positively in their feelings about flipped learning. A survey was given to the students in these courses, with 94% of students agreeing with "I like this approach to learning" and 72% agreeing with "This approach helped me learn the material better." Only about half (55%) thought that the flipped approach required more work than the traditional approach, and about half (55%) indicated that they would like more of the material in the course taught this way.

Case Study: Flipped Learning in Online and Hybrid Education Courses

Online and hybrid courses are increasingly common across the higher education spectrum and pose interesting questions for flipped learning. Can a flipped learning environment be applied to an asynchronous online course in which there are no real-time meetings? Can you create a "flipped classroom" when there is no classroom? Conversely, in a hybrid course—one that has occasional in-seat, face-to-face meetings along with a significant online component—is the learning *automatically* flipped because of the online portion of the course, or does additional planning and forethought need to take place?

This case study addresses these questions. (We will also discuss them further in chapter 7.)

What Is the Context of the Course?

Mark Hale is an associate professor of higher education at Dallas Baptist University, an institution near Dallas, Texas, with around 5,500 students, including almost 2,000 graduate students. Hale is also the assistant provost and director of hybrid programs, and he teaches hybrid courses in higher education to graduate students. These courses have typically involved face-to-face meetings on alternate weeks for two and a half hours, with online activities during the remaining weeks. The face-to-face meetings were conducted in a traditional fashion, with lectures followed by discussion and presentation. During the "online" weeks, students would read course readings or watch lectures and then engage in an online discussion board with each other and the professor.

Why Was Flipped Learning Used in This Course?

After hearing about the peer instruction technique developed by Eric Mazur, which we discussed in chapter 2, Hale became interested in converting his hybrid courses into a flipped learning environment. Hale began to feel as though students were lacking the preparation to engage in deep discussions during the face-to-face meetings, because they were engaging in discussion and presentation very shortly after seeing the material for the first time. Students did engage in some independent learning during the "online" weeks and had opportunities to show their learning during the face-to-face meetings but sometimes lacked the ability to analyze concepts deeply or apply their knowledge to new contexts. In Hale's words (from an e-mail communication in 2016),

> The real reason I wanted to try the method was to encourage, if not force my students to enter the class more prepared for an active and engaging learning environment. So many times I felt as if my students were arriving for our traditional class meeting unprepared. They expected me to deliver the content and then engage in discussion based on their limited knowledge of the topic. I wanted to go deeper. I wanted my students arriving in class with significant and important questions about the topic we were planning to address that day. I also wanted to move away from a lecture heavy group space of course content delivery to a more collaborative learning experience. (Personal e-mail communication from Professor Hale, June 25, 2016)

The courses targeted by Hale for redesign were Legal Issues and Finance in Higher Education and History and Philosophy of Higher Education. As a first step toward creating a true flipped learning environment in these courses, the setup of the meetings was changed so that instead of having face-to-face meetings alternate with online activities every other week, *each* week contained *both* face-to-face and online components. Students would now meet face-to-face for 75 minutes each week, with this face-to-face meeting preceded by online activities each week.

What Do Students Do in the Course? What Does the Instructor Do?

Hale divided the weekly course schedule into "quadrants." The first two quadrants took place online whereas the second two took place during the face-to-face meetings.

- Quadrant 1 consisted of students accessing and processing course content online. The content type depended on the topic. There was a textbook for both courses that was used along with supplemental readings as primary sources. From there, Hale would bring in video to support other topics when applicable. Some of that video would be created by Hale whereas others would be curated from online sources. For example, students watched a documentary about the Kent State University shootings as a supplemental video. Note that video was not *required* for all of these lessons, and when it was required, it was not necessarily created by the professor.
- Quadrant 2 had students engaging in an initial assessment, again still online. This was a short, formative assessment to be completed the day before the weekly face-to-face meeting. Because the assessment was done prior to the meeting, Hale could review the students' responses and identify areas where additional time could be spent to fortify students' understanding and areas where the plans for the face-to-face meeting might need to be altered.
- Quadrant 3 moved into the face-to-face meeting. Hale spent almost no time addressing the class in a lecture format. This quadrant was focused on discussion rather than lecture—perhaps engaging in targeted question/answer sessions with students over issues from the first two quadrants, but otherwise with a view toward active engagement.
- Quadrant 4 consisted of collaborative learning activities. These included point/counterpoint debates, case studies, and process development exercises. Most activities would involve a brief introduction by Hale, followed by time for students to work through the activity and report, discuss, and debate their findings. During this time, Hale visited each group to guide their work, made sure the whole class was

making sufficient progress, and recorded the results of the group's reports.

Why Is This Flipped Learning?

Before considering why this is an example of an effective flipped learning environment, it's important to note that *simply having an online component prior to a face-to-face meeting does not constitute a true flipped learning environment.* Flipped learning involves much more than simply putting resources online, telling students to read or view them before class, and then expecting discussion in class. Even if students comply with those directives (which is far from a safe assumption), if the first contact with new concepts is not guided and structured in some way, students may frequently lack the depth of understanding needed to go further with their learning in class. And in fact, many students may not engage with the new concepts at all in the reading or viewing if they know that the professor is just going to lecture over it when they come to class.

Rather, a true flipped learning environment requires that first contact with new material be moved into the students' individual space, *packaged in a structured activity* to "teach" that material—or rather, to give students support as they teach themselves the basics. The structured activity serves as a model for self-regulated learning as students learn how to set learning goals, identify effective learning resources, and self-evaluate how well they are learning and make informed choices about whether they should seek help or make changes in their learning processes.

This structured activity can be something as simple as an online assessment, as Hale provided for his students, that serves as a guide through the reading and occasional viewing as well as a "stick" for making sure students complete it. The assessment also provided Hale with actionable data on student learning prior to the face-to-face meetings. Importantly, the structured reading and viewing was not optional; it was a required first contact with new concepts that would not be "retaught" in a lecture later. Hale stressed to students that if they did not complete the preparatory work, they would be unable to participate actively in the face-to-face activities.

Likewise, even though the group space in Hale's classes already included time for discussion, this by itself did not create a flipped learning environment. Instead, the structured first-contact experiences done by the students allowed the group space to be transformed from lecture-plus-discussion into a truly active and dynamic learning environment. Hale describes the group meetings as "fast paced and exciting" with so much activity that a tight schedule was required to ensure that all activities were brought to a satisfactory conclusion.

What Are the Benefits to the Students?

Hale reports that according to course evaluations, students had an "overwhelmingly positive" response to the change in course design from traditional (though hybrid) to a truly flipped learning environment. Many students requested additional opportunities to experience a flipped learning environment. (This is a theme for our case studies so far—that once students are given the chance to learn in a flipped learning environment, they tend not to want to go back to the traditional model.) Students expressed appreciation for using the very limited face-to-face meeting time not to rehash basic concepts that could and should be learned independently in the online setting but rather to go deeper on topics that require additional thought and areas in which the preclass structured activities indicated a need for further exploration.

Case Study: Flipped Learning in Engineering Courses in Sweden

All of our case studies so far have focused on courses at colleges and universities in the United States. However, as this case study indicates, flipped learning is not an exclusively American phenomenon. In fact, there is a growing involvement in flipped learning in universities across the globe.

Lennart Svensson is an associate professor in the Department of Signals and Systems at Chalmers University of Technology in Gothenburg, Sweden. Among the courses that Svensson teaches are specialized advanced courses in signals and systems, including a course called Sensor Fusion and Nonlinear Filtering. This course, like many others in the STEM disciplines, involves acquiring skill not only with computation but also with conceptual understanding. Svensson found that his students were becoming skillful with computation but lacked the conceptual understanding of the subject to apply it meaningfully to research or applied industrial problems. In this, his situation was similar to that of Eric Mazur teaching physics at Harvard in the 1990s. And like Mazur—and drawing upon Mazur's previous work—Svensson looked to flipped learning to make a change.

What Is the Context of the Course?

Sensor Fusion and Nonlinear Filtering is an advanced undergraduate course, taught in a master's degree program and typically enrolling PhD students as well as participants from industry. The course enrollment is capped at 70 due to the design of the learning space used, but the enrollment often goes over this amount because of the PhD and industry-based students in the course.

The course was traditionally conducted by lectures in class, followed up with homework assignments and projects outside of class and no written exams.

Why Was Flipped Learning Used in This Course?

Svensson liked the idea of flipped learning initially because it allowed him to create a set of curated online videos for his students to use whenever and however they liked, with the ability to pause and replay, freeing up time in class for other activities. The real strength of the flipped learning model, though, to him was not merely the existence of materials outside class but what those materials implied for how he could use class time. His overall goal was to refocus class time on building conceptual understanding of the subject rather than transmission of information. In the traditional model, he states, "Most of my students ended up knowing how to solve problems but often seemed to only have a vague idea about what they were doing" (personal e-mail communication from Professor Svensson, June 26, 2016).

In keeping with this plan, Svensson created a set of videos for students in the course (an example can be found at http://goo.gl/nQHme4) along with in-class activities intended to stress conceptual understanding.

What Do Students Do in the Course? What Does the Instructor Do?

In the Individual Space

Before class meetings, students would watch a collection of videos that were posted to YouTube. Svensson used a platform called Scalable Learning (www.scalable-learning.com) that allows users to upload video and embed quizzes into the video, so that viewers have to stop at intervals and check their learning. The Scalable Learning platform also collects data from the quizzes, and the data were used both as information for adjusting plans for in-class activities and to check that students had done the viewing.

In the Group Space

The preclass videos were present primarily to set students up for productive in-class experiences. Those experiences took three different forms:

1. Students would sit in groups of three to five and work through "warm-up" activities, such as working together through quizzes that showed evidence of misconceptions or a lack of understanding. Other warm-up

activities involved what Svensson calls "retrieval" activities in which students first sit quietly for a few minutes and summarize the preclass viewing to themselves on paper, and then take turns explaining the material to others in their group and choosing one thing they found interesting or confusing, and then cycling through the groups to see what they selected. About 10 minutes was dedicated in each class for this activity. The concept of retrieval is well known as an effective study method (Bjork 1975; Karpicke and Blunt 2011) and serves the purpose not only of allowing students to process their preclass viewing but also preparing students to engage in other in-class activities.

2. Students would also often engage in peer instruction activities, as we described in chapter 2. Peer instruction was invented specifically to improve students' conceptual understanding of a topic and was specifically introduced for large lecture courses in physics, so it finds a natural home in Svensson's classes.

3. In addition to (or sometimes instead of) peer instruction, students would work in groups of three to five to solve a sequence of small problems, and illustrate and reflect on the results they obtained.

Afterward, in the individual spaces once the group space activities were done, students still worked on homework assignments and projects—just as they did in the traditional setup of the course.

Why Is This Flipped Learning?

This design of the course fits our definition of *flipped learning* because the students' first contact with new material comes in the form of a structured experience in their individual spaces, as a preparatory activity, in the form of videos with embedded quizzes. This structure is the electronic equivalent of the lecture with strategic pauses built in. The advantage here is that students could access the lecture materials on their own devices and on their own schedules, with the ability to pause and replay at will. And we note again that this was not simply telling students to watch videos; there was a *structure* placed around the viewing in the form of the embedded quizzes, which provided actionable data about student learning in real time as well as a layer of accountability to check to see who was watching the videos, and when.

But the main reason this is flipped learning is because of what happened in the group space. That group space, previously reserved for lecturing, became a laboratory for students to find and repair their misconceptions on the material through guided collaborative activities that were known to be valuable for learning. In our language, the group space was transformed into a dynamic, interactive learning space where students worked on the most advanced cognitive ideas—namely, the acquisition of correct conceptual understanding and applications of highly technical material—guided by the instructor. The work in the individual space was mainly aimed at preparing students to participate productively in this learning environment.

What Are the Benefits to the Students?

In a study of the effects of this design of Svensson's course (Svensson and Adawi 2015), students in the course were surveyed about their perceptions of the flipped learning environment. Although these kinds of surveys are only an indirect measure of actual learning gains—unlike, for example, the methods in Hake's (1998) classic study of physics students—they do give an indication of student engagement and whether students are emotionally and psychologically ready to learn in such an environment.

The results of the survey were quite strong. Over 95% of the students surveyed (all but one student) responded "agree" or "strongly agree" with the statement "I would rather watch a video with quizzes than a live lecture." Over 86% responded "agree" or "strongly agree" to the statement "Having in-class sessions where we focused on conceptual understanding was useful." Finally, over 91% responded "agree" or "strongly agree" to the statement "The flipped classroom teaching led to improved learning and better understanding of concepts."

When given open-ended free-response questions about their perceptions of the flipped learning environment, students expressed strongly positive opinions about it, with a particular appreciation of being able to view lectures at their own pace and with the option of pausing and replaying (and being able to review while working on homework and projects). Students also found the redesigned group space activities valuable, citing greater interaction with the professor and classmates as one of the chief benefits.

We end by noting that Svensson converted another course (Svensson and Hammarstrand 2015), a PhD-level course called Probabilistic Graphical Models, into a flipped learning environment with a similar structure, and with similar results, but instead of making his own videos, he used video lectures already made for a massive open online course (MOOC) developed by Stanford University (Koller n.d.). This indicates that, if a flipped learning environment is to be built on the foundation of online video, the instructor does not necessarily have to *create* the videos but instead can *curate* them.

We have now seen a wide variety of examples of flipped learning environments used throughout the spectrum of higher education: introductory courses and advanced courses, highly specialized courses and general education courses,

courses in large universities and small colleges, courses in traditional four-year universities and private career-focused colleges, courses at universities in the United States and outside the United States, face-to-face courses and online/hybrid courses, courses in the STEM disciplines and outside the STEM disciplines. Indeed, no two of these flipped learning environments are exactly alike. And this only covers a very small sample size; all indications suggest that flipped learning is being used in one way or another in many more places and contexts.

And yet all of these flipped learning environments are instances of the same basic idea: that first contact with new concepts has been moved from the group space to the individual space in the form of structured activities, and the group space has been transformed into a dynamic, interactive learning environment with students working actively on the most cognitively demanding tasks while the instructor is fully present to guide them.

Just as we do with our students, we now want to move from basic ideas, concepts, and examples to applying what we've learned to a new situation—namely, our own courses. In the next part, we'll take an extended look at how to design or redesign your own courses around the flipped learning model, to make your courses the next great case study of flipped learning.

PART TWO

FLIPPED LEARNING DESIGN

4

DESIGNING A COURSE
AROUND FLIPPED LEARNING

W e've now seen a definition of *flipped learning*, explored the history and theory behind flipped learning, and seen several examples of ordinary professors in a wide variety of contexts building and running courses using flipped learning with great results. At this point, I hope your curiosity is piqued, and you are wondering how you might design or redesign one or more of your own courses to use flipped learning too. If so, then the natural question is, *How do I do it?*

In this chapter we will present some basic ideas about *course design—* structured workflows for putting together a course starting with the basic facts about the course all the way to the first day of class and beyond. We will focus particularly on a course design model proposed by Dee Fink that stresses "significant learning" at its core and see how that model can be adapted for designing a flipped learning environment. We will end with a preview of the next two chapters, which describe a seven-step model for flipped learning design at the individual lesson level.

Course Design in General and Why It Matters

One of the great traditions of working in higher education is getting one's courses ready for an upcoming semester. Those of us who work in higher education do this at least twice a year. We think about the readings we want to assign, the number of tests we want to give, how to allocate grades, and the calendar for the semester. But sometimes, even the most experienced college educator doesn't think about the *design* of her courses during this preparation period, by which we mean the *infrastructure of choices we make about the nature and structure of the course*: what we want students to learn, how we will craft environments in which that learning is possible or likely, what students will do to build their understanding and show evidence of their learning, and how we will evaluate the degree to which that evidence shows that learning has taken place. Without a clear understanding of the design of a course, the choices we make about assignments, grading, and scheduling will be confused at best and self-destructive at worst.

A well-structured design of a course generally involves several steps:

- Determining the *facts* about a course, including facts about students (how many are enrolled, what are their fields of study, why might they be taking the course, what needs will they have, what skills will they bring, etc.), facts about the course itself (is it a prerequisite for something else, does it have a prerequisite, where does it fit in the curriculum, does it fit any special designations such as writing across the curriculum, etc.), and facts about the physical context (what technology is available, how is the classroom laid out, are the seats fixed or movable, is the course face-to-face or online, etc.).

- Determining the *learning goals* for the course—that is, what students should be able to do once the course is over. These goals include a mixture of high-level course objectives and low-level topic objectives.

- Determining the *activities* in which students will engage in the course to generate evidence for whether the learning goals are being met. These include day-to-day group space activities and, for our purposes, activities that take place in the individual space, as well as the assessments that will be given to generate information about the extent to which learning has taken place.

- Determining the *structure of the class*, including when topics will be introduced, how the topics link together, and how the individual and group space activities will be conducted.

- Determining the *grading system* for the course, meaning how the evidence that students present of their learning, through their work, will be translated into short-term assignment grades and long-term course letter grades.

- Determining any *contingency plans* that one might need for the course. These can include finding loopholes in assessment plans; making plans for late work, inclement weather, and the like; making a plan for academic honesty and dishonesty considerations; and so on. Especially included here are taking *accessibility* issues into consideration—for example, making sure that students with visual impairments have as equal access to course content as those without visual impairments.

It's only after thoroughly *designing* a course in this way that we are ready to write a syllabus and prepare individual classes. This takes significant time and effort. However, there is also significant payoff. By having a sound course design, you will save yourself time later (e.g., you can create shorter and more effective tests if you have a clear idea of your course's learning goals), and students will find your course to be a richer and more enjoyable learning environment.

However, because proper course design does take time and effort, it would be helpful to have some established patterns for course design that we can use to guide us. Let's look at two well-established course design frameworks that are especially amenable to flipped learning.

Wiggins/McTighe and Backward Design

In their book *Understanding by Design*, Grant Wiggins and Jay McTighe (2005) propose the process of *backward design*. To understand backward design, consider the stereotypical method of course design that many of us who teach in higher education may have used in the past (or may currently use):

- First, we determine what we are going to cover in the course. For example, we might decide which sections of the book we are going to teach, or what readings we want students to work through. We also determine how we are going to cover it, although this often doesn't involve much forethought because our default mode of teaching is lecture.
- Second, we decide how many assessments (quizzes, tests, papers, etc.) we will give in the course and when they will take place.
- Third, we put the syllabus together, which is mainly a record of the first two steps along with a calendar (if it's a good syllabus) and a grading system, and perhaps some additional policies about late work and other items.

In other words, quite often instructors start with *coverage* first, then *assessment*, and only at the end of the process is there some form of determination of what students have actually learned—unless there is no determination at all but rather just a totaling of points, which is assumed to be a reliable proxy for learning outcomes.

Backward design, on the other hand, is so called because it reverses this process:

- First, the instructor *identifies the desired results* of the course. What should students know, understand, and be able to do both during and after the course?
- Second, the instructor *determines acceptable evidence*. How will I know whether and to what extent students have attained the results that I said I desire? What will I accept as sufficient evidence that learning or mastery has taken place, or is taking place?
- Third, the instructor *plans learning experiences and instruction*. Given the list of desired results for a topic and given what I will accept as sufficient evidence of learning, what activities can and should I plan for students to generate this evidence? What activities create a learning environment in which it is possible, even likely, that real evidence of progress toward the desired results will happen?

In backward design, *student understanding* is the main point—not merely the coverage of content. The textbook is a resource for learning, not a secondary (or primary!) syllabus. And all activities that take place in the class have a purpose—they all fit into a cohesive structure with clearly identified goals and outcomes, which themselves have been hand selected for their value to the student in the long term.

The understanding-by-design model fits well with flipped learning because both are profoundly *student-centered* approaches to course design and instruction. In both backward design and flipped learning, we build the class around the notion of constructing what Ken Bain (2011) in his book *What the Best College Teachers Do* calls a "critical learning environment" where students have many rich opportunities for deep learning and self-reflection.

Although backward design by itself would be an excellent starting point for designing a flipped learning environment, the main reason we bring it up is to motivate another model for course design that marries the best ideas from backward design with a structured and intentional approach to building a course that applies particularly well to flipped learning: the "design for significant learning" model of Dee Fink.

Dee Fink's Design for Significant Learning

Closely related in spirit to backward design is the framework of *design for significant learning* proposed by Dee Fink (2013) in his book *Creating Significant Learning Experiences: An Integrated Approach to Designing College Courses*. An abbreviated workbook appeared under the title *A Self-Directed*

Guide to Designing Courses for Significant Learning (Fink 2003) and is freely available online.

The key concept of Fink's model that differentiates it from backward design is the idea of *integration*. In Fink's model, college courses have three major components: the *learning goals*, the *feedback and assessment mechanisms*, and the *teaching and learning activities*. Fink's model for course design stresses that these three components should be integrated throughout the course.

Fink's Model

Fink's model for designing an integrated course involves 12 steps:

1. *Identifying important situational factors.* These include the demographics of the students enrolled in the course, any special instructional challenges that the course may pose, the context into which the course fits in the larger curriculum, expectations that students and the larger professional community place on the course, and characteristics of the instructor.

2. *Identifying important learning goals.* As with backward design, we want to identify what students should know, understand, and be able to do both during and after the course. Fink breaks learning goals down further into *foundational knowledge, application, integration, human dimension, caring,* and *learning how to learn* goals. We are generally familiar with the first two kinds of goals but less so with the remaining four. An "integration" goal is one involving connections between and among ideas, people, and "realms of life." "Human dimension" goals involve learning about oneself and about others. "Caring" goals are those that involve developing new feelings, interests, and values about the subject. Finally, "learning how to learn" goals are those in which students learn how to be better learners, how to inquire about a subject, and how to become self-directing—in short, the goals of self-regulated learning that we discussed in chapter 2. For Fink, *significant learning* refers to the kind of learning that occurs at the nexus of all of these learning goals.

3. *Formulating appropriate feedback and assessment procedures.* Here "appropriate" means not only for the level of students and the course but also in the sense of whether the assessment promotes significant learning. For example, an assessment model that consists only of a handful of simple multiple-choice exams that cover only basic factual information is not likely to be considered an appropriate feedback and assessment procedure in itself. Instead, multiple-choice assessments could be part of a larger "appropriate" system that promotes significant learning; and some forms of well-constructed multiple-choice assessments have been shown

to evaluate higher levels of thinking rather effectively (e.g., see Huntley, Engelbrecht, and Harding 2011).

4. *Selecting effective teaching and learning activities.* In chapter 2 we saw that a preponderance of research evidence—on top of a mass of anecdotal experience—suggests that *active learning* is a highly effective paradigm for teaching and learning activities in the university. We also saw that this is a broad term that encompasses many distinct kinds of activities, with plenty of room for instructors to use different techniques to suit their styles, their students, and the content. Fink outlines active learning in considerable detail to include activities aimed at *experiences, information and ideas,* and *reflective dialogue.*

5. *Making sure that the primary components (in steps 1–4) are integrated.* In Fink's self-directed guide, this takes the form of a list of questions to answer, such as *How well are the situational factors included in the decisions about learning goals?* and *Are there any extraneous activities that do not serve any major learning goal?* The idea is that all the main parts of the course should support each other with no unproductive redundancy.

6. *Creating a thematic structure for the course.* Determine how major themes, topics, or concepts of the course will unfold throughout the semester. Fink recommends splitting the course into four to seven segments focusing on key issues or thematic blocks on which the course will focus, arranging these blocks into a logical sequence, and then determining how much class time to spend on each one.

7. *Selecting or creating a teaching strategy.* Fink distinguishes between a teaching *technique,* which is a single, discrete, specific activity related to instruction (e.g., lecture, peer instruction, or working problems in groups), and a teaching *strategy,* which refers to a set of learning activities done in a particular sequence that creates accumulating energy as students work toward a learning goal. Importantly for our purposes, Fink proposes an alternating sequence of in-class and out-of-class activities arranged in what he calls a "castle-top" diagram (see Figure 4.1). For flipped learning, the castle-top diagram becomes a focal point of the course design, as we will explore momentarily.

8. *Integrating the course structure and instructional strategy to create an overall scheme of learning activities.* Because a teaching strategy involves a sequence of learning activities, the design process clearly requires making that sequence fit within the course structure from step 6. Each major thematic block of the course has its own sequence of learning activities, so the end product of this step can be visualized as a sequence of castle-top diagrams that facilitates the creation of a weekly schedule and promotes

both the integration of learning activities and their development over time.

9. *Developing the grading system.* Having identified the major characteristics and goals of the course and having designed the thematic structure and activities for the course in an integrated way, the next step in the process is to develop a grading system that "reflects the full range of learning goals and activities" (Fink 2003, p. 31) but that is as simple and minimal as possible, realizing that not everything needs to be graded.

10. *Debugging possible problems.* Repeatedly ask the question, *What could go wrong?* Determine contingency plans for solving these problems in advance.

11. *Writing the course syllabus.* Fink (2003) describes it as "letting students know what you are planning" (p. 32). The syllabus should provide general information on the course, goals for the course, the structure and sequence of class activities planned in steps 6 through 8, the grading system from step 9, and course policies (possibly influenced by step 10).

12. *Planning an evaluation of the course and teaching.* Along with the usual end-of-semester course evaluations, the instructor needs to gather data in informal midsemester evaluations on how the course is going as well as plan for using the data gathered from course evaluations (both formal and informal).

Steps 1 through 5 are considered the "beginning phase" of course design, steps 6 through 8 the "intermediate phase," and steps 9 through 12 the "final phase." The preceding is merely an outline of the 12-step model that can be found in full in Fink's book or in the shorter workbook; we will not give all the details here but rather merely summarize and point readers to Fink's works for more.

Fink's 12-step model for course design provides a richly detailed method for building a course that takes the whole learning environment into consideration and provides an integrated and focused design as a result. Using this model is no guarantee that significant learning will happen or that students will be happy, but the use of a model like Fink's will help instructors create learning environments where significant learning is more likely to happen than if the course is simply put together with little forethought.

Figure 4.1. Fink castle-top diagram.

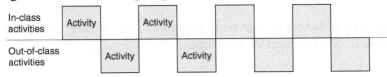

How the Significant Learning Model Adapts to Flipped Learning

The Fink model is intended to apply to any course whatsoever and is agnostic with respect to flipped learning. In fact, given that Fink's original book was published in 2003, it's doubtful that flipped learning was on the radar screen when the method was developed. However, we focus on Fink's process because it is well known and supported. There are annual workshops offered worldwide, for instance, and a website (http://designlearning.org) featuring examples of courses designed using this method and online resources for applying it to one's own courses. But particularly, this design method is well suited for designing courses around flipped learning principles.

Let's take a look at each of the steps in Fink's model and see how each applies to flipped learning specifically. In a flipped learning environment, many of the points of Fink's model stay the same, but some contain new factors to consider or particular adaptations to flipped learning.

Step 1: Situational Factors

Flipped learning requires that we consider situational factors that are especially important to a flipped learning environment but that may not be as applicable to a traditional course model:

- If we are using online video to support work in the individual space, then do students have 24/7 access to computers or tablets that will allow them to view it? Do students have ready access to a high-speed Internet connection for video streaming?
- If the course is face-to-face or hybrid (not fully online), is the meeting space well suited for active learning? Or, for example, does it have stadium-style fixed seating that would make forming small groups harder than if the desks could be moved?
- Are there aspects of the learners' life situations that would particularly interfere with flipped learning activities—for example, odd or busy work or family schedules that would make the individual space problematic? Do learners have preconceived notions about how the course should be taught, and could this lead to conflict later on when introducing flipped learning? Are there aspects of the learners' backgrounds that might make the independent learning experiences in the individual space harder than usual—for example, weaknesses in prerequisite knowledge or a lack of experience with self-regulation?

These sorts of factors need to be incorporated into this step, along with all the other factors common to any course.

Step 2: Learning Goals

In considering the learning goals for the course, refer to the taxonomy of six *types* of learning goals in this method (see Figure 4.2). Flipped learning courses still benefit from having goals selected from across this spectrum, but a particular focus of flipped learning is the development of self-regulated learning skills. Therefore, an emphasis on the *human dimension, caring,* and *learning how to learn* goals is important and taps into the potential that flipped learning provides. For example, a course goal of being able to extract relevant information from a video and demonstrating the ability to learn independently from it would be a flipped learning–specific course goal that would fit into the *learning how to learn* category and could be assessed on an almost daily basis. Self-regulation is a hallmark of the flipped learning environment because it can be so regularly practiced and assessed; therefore, it make sense to include goals specific to self-regulation in this step.

Figure 4.2. Fink learning goals.

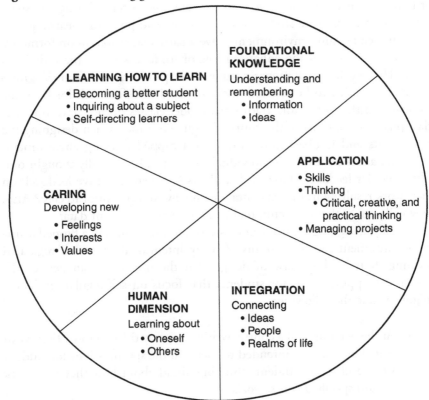

Step 3: Feedback and Assessment Procedures
Fink draws a distinction between educative assessment and auditive assessment. The latter refers to assessments whose sole purpose is to audit students' learning and provide the basis for a grade—that is, *auditive assessment* simply catalogues what students did right and did wrong. By contrast, *educative assessment* is intended to provide feedback to students that helps them learn and improve. Fink summarizes the main characteristics of educative assessment using the acronym FIDeLity: It should be frequent, immediate, discriminating (making clear the differences among poor, acceptable, and exceptional work), and loving (maintaining empathy in the way feedback is delivered). Particularly, there should be ample opportunities for students to self-assess.

What changes regarding assessment for flipped learning environments is the quantity and quality of *formative assessment* that can be given. Formative assessment (Scriven 1967) refers to assessments given to learners while a concept is still "forming," in order to gather data on student understanding and to make modifications to teaching and learning activities before instruction on the concept is over. Although every course should include a mixture of both formative and *summative* assessment (the latter referring to assessments given to measure student learning at the end point of a learning process), flipped learning environments have a particular emphasis on formative assessment because of the enhanced role of student work in the individual space. That work, which prepares students for productive work in the group space, is intended to be assessed and converted into feedback for both the student and the instructor. Traditional-model classes do not have this pre-class phase at the heart of the course design. Therefore, when designing the assessments and feedback procedures for a flipped learning environment, formative assessment for the individual space must be carefully thought out. This includes feedback. How will students be given educative feedback on their work resulting from first contact with new concepts prior to class? Also, how will you, as the instructor, make use of these assessment data?

Finally, designing feedback and assessment procedures in a flipped learning environment can be a means of being intentional about self-regulated learning. It is in this phase of design that the instructor can devise self-assessment opportunities for students that focus on self-regulation. These might include the following:

- At the beginning of a course, writing an essay titled "How I Earned an A in This Course" intended to focus on the specifications for student work and to get students thinking ahead about how they will work toward specified course goals

- Engaging in a self-assessment of course knowledge and skills and/or their existing self-regulation skills
- Having students do reflective writing on assigned readings and video, focusing on their cognitive processes during the reading and viewing process
- Spending the first five minutes of class time (assuming a face-to-face meeting) summarizing their individual space work and what was easy, hard, or surprising for them
- Writing one-minute papers at the end of a group meeting to summarize the main points of the class

These and many other ideas for formative assessment that is both educative and strongly focused on self-regulated learning are detailed in Nilson (2013).

Step 4: Teaching and Learning Activities

Fink stresses the importance of active learning in the selection of teaching and learning activities in this step, and this does not change when thinking about a flipped learning environment versus a traditional environment. The *holistic* view of active learning that Fink proposes—a fusion of experience, reflective dialogue, and information (see Figure 4.2)—still applies. However, for flipped learning environments the concept of active work in the individual space takes on an enlarged importance. Here, activities in the area of "information and ideas" typically take place in the individual space. In a flipped learning environment, during these individual space activities students are coming into contact with new concepts for the first time *through structured activities*. We don't want to simply give students a book or video and tell them to read or watch it; we give students *structure* to guide them through the process, extract usable information from those sources, and then incorporate that information into coherent schema by way of structured exercises and activities. We also want to have the results of this individual space activity in hand when we come to the group space, so assessment is important. All of this means that teaching and learning activities that are intended for the individual space—a context whose quality is unique to a flipped learning environment—require more structure and care than in a traditional class.

Step 5: Integrating Steps 1 Through 4

For flipped learning environments, not much changes in this step. We still ask the same kinds of questions that Fink's model asks for any course:

- How well do our choices about learning goals, feedback, assessment, and learning activities reflect the realities of the situational factors of the course? What potential conflicts might arise?

- How well do the assessment procedures (especially the formative assessments) for a flipped learning environment address the full range of learning goals? Do the plans for feedback provide students information about their progress on all of the learning goals?
- Do the learning activities that have been selected (including those intended to bolster self-regulated learning skills) support all the learning goals?
- How well does the feedback given to students prepare them for understanding the assessment criteria and for the assessments themselves?

Step 6: Course Structure

The differences in this step for flipped learning versus traditional environments are once again minimal. Here we still want to identify the main thematic blocks of a course and arrange them into a logical sequence. This step focuses more on the *content* of a course and its main thematic questions than it does the specific methodology for instruction or the learning environment.

Step 7: Instructional Strategy

Here, by contrast, is perhaps the most visible adaptation of this model for flipped learning. Fink (2003) describes an "instructional strategy" as

> a set of learning activities, arranged in a particular sequence so that the energy for learning increases and accumulates as students go through the sequence. This usually requires, among other things, that you set up some activities that (a) get students ready or prepared for later work, (b) give them opportunities to practice—with prompt feedback—doing whatever it is you want them to learn to do, (c) assess the quality of their performance, and (d) allow them to reflect on their learning. (p. 27)

Fink then illustrates this sequence of alternating in-class and out-of-class activities using what he terms a *castle-top diagram* (Figure 4.3).

The cells inside each of the squares of this diagram are to be filled in with activities of varied forms, all building upon each other. Note that in the diagram the first cell is an *in-class activity*. For flipped learning, this diagram is literally flipped. Figure 4.4 shows what the flipped learning castle-top diagram would look like, along with a slight shift in terminology to fit better with our definitions.

A flipped learning environment begins with first contact for students with new concepts, and this takes place "out of class" or in the individual

Figure 4.3. Fink castle-top diagram.

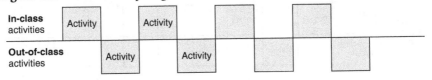

Figure 4.4. Flipped Fink castle-top diagram.

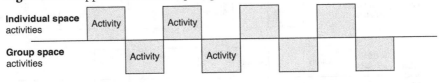

space. This is followed by work in the group space and then by work in the individual space that builds upon the group space, and so on. What we might use in each of those cells for activities is the topic of chapters 5 and 6.

Step 8: Overall Scheme of Learning Activities

Constructing an overall scheme of learning activities in which the various activities and instructional strategies fit into a coherent structure is not very different for flipped learning than it is for a traditional class—only the instructional strategy has really changed. In Fink, the overall scheme is illustrated as a sequence of castle-top diagrams, as shown in Figure 4.5. For flipped learning, the castle-tops are flipped, as shown in Figure 4.6.

Step 9: Grading Scheme

As Fink points out, a grading system should reflect the full range of activities and learning goals in a course, but one does not have to grade everything. In a flipped learning environment, there are two layers of activity that instructors need to consider in the grading system: the work that students do in the individual space to prepare for group space and the work that students do in the group space. For example, if a flipped learning environment requires students to watch a video online with embedded quizzes, should those quizzes be graded or should they merely be self-checks, with higher-stakes assessment saved for group space work? If graded, then on what basis, and what is a reasonable rubric for awarding grades? The same kinds of questions can be asked about group work in class: Should it be graded? If so, should you grade on points, on the basis of completeness and effort, through peer grading, or what? The answers to these questions vary with the instructor, course, and students.

Figure 4.5. Fink course structure—traditional.

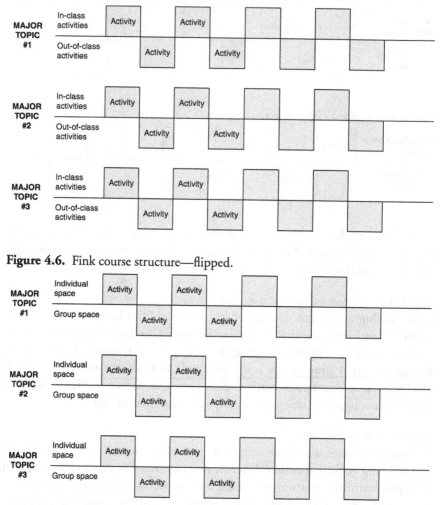

Figure 4.6. Fink course structure—flipped.

Step 10: What Could Go Wrong?
This is the step in which we look for potential problems with the course—loopholes, schedule conflicts, places where students might "hack" the course policies, and so on. Flipped learning courses have at least as many of these potential problems as traditional courses, and there are new issues raised as well because of the flipped structure:

- *Will students be able to access the technology used in the course?* This is a concern for all classes that use technology, but given that flipped learning environments often use technology in ways that are central and inextricable from the learning process (e.g., using online video for individual space preparation activities) the question of access to technology takes on an enhanced importance. Here, too, we need to think about *accessibility*; for example, if you use online video and it is not closed-captioned, how will learners with hearing impairments participate? Consultation with the accessibility officer for the institution is an excellent idea when designing a flipped learning course (or any course) to get a heads-up on potential accessibility issues.

- *How do we get students to do the individual space activities, and what happens if they come to class without having done them?* These two related questions are without doubt the most commonly asked questions one hears when discussing flipped learning, and rightly so, because the success at the heart of flipped learning—namely, the group space activities—is predicated on thorough student preparation. Traditionally structured classes must also deal with issues of student preparation, but the lack of preparation is not as potentially disastrous in a traditional class as it is in a flipped environment. These questions have to be addressed and plans made before the first day of class.

- *How do we convince students that a flipped learning environment is beneficial for them? And how will I know if it really is beneficial for them?* In other words, what is the plan for getting students to "buy in" to the flipped learning environment and showing them that they are learning in this environment?

- *How do I convince my colleagues and superiors that flipped learning is benefiting students?* This concern might be unique to flipped learning. In a traditional class, one typically doesn't worry if the teaching strategy is being perceived as ineffective, lazy, or weird by one's colleagues. But in many cases, as I have worked with professors in a range of institutions, there has been concern about the flipped learning environment, not necessarily from students but from deans and department chairs who are worried that the professor is not "really teaching" or that he or she is taking too much time away from research to engage in unproven pedagogical innovations. In some cases this concern—which we have seen and will see is nothing to worry about—extends to other constituencies. (For example, I once had a parent contact my university's institutional research board to complain that by using flipped learning I was "experimenting" on her child without authorization from the institutional research board!) What is the plan for handling possible concerns of this nature?

In chapter 8, we will take up some of the most common student concerns about flipped learning and discuss how to plan for these and turn them into teachable moments for our students.

Step 11: Writing the Syllabus
Writing the syllabus for a flipped learning course is not a significantly greater task than for a traditionally structured course. However, because many students find flipped learning to be a new and possibly disorienting experience, it is especially important to be clear about two aspects of the course:

1. *The expectations for students and for the instructor.* The syllabus should contain clear language about what students are expected to do and what they are *not* expected to do as part of the flipped learning environment, along with the complementary expectations for the instructor. For example, the syllabus should make it clear that students are expected to complete all preclass activities, and it should clearly state how those activities will be assessed and (perhaps more importantly) how they will be used in the class. Time estimates for how long it should take to complete preclass activities are very helpful as well. Also, letting students know that they are *not* responsible for learning all the material in a section, or attaining complete mastery over all the material in an activity, helps take the pressure off students as they learn independently.
2. *The schedule for when things are to be done.* Although this pertains to logistical information such as deadlines, having clear deadlines in a single place can help students get and stay oriented in a flipped learning environment. It is especially important to be clear about when work that is to be done in the individual space is due, because typically we want this work to be submitted prior to class meetings.

Step 12: Getting Evaluation Data
In any course, it is important not to wait until the end of the semester to get evaluative feedback from your students on how the course is going. Just as giving regular formative assessment to students allows you as the instructor to know where students are learning, where they are struggling, and how best to intervene, getting regular formative feedback from students lets you "take the temperature" of the class and know what is working and what should be improved before it becomes a crisis that cannot be addressed. Getting informal evaluation information from students about your teaching and the course can be as simple as giving a paper form to students to fill out in class, or an online form to be done by a deadline, asking basic

questions such as "What aspects of the course help your learning?" and "What aspects of the course could be changed to improve your learning?" More complex surveys could be given as well, even "practice versions" of the end-of-term course evaluations. Student feedback can also be obtained through student interviews or focus groups. Many university teaching centers will conduct small group interventions in which a staff member from the center will come and conduct a group interview with the class on their learning experiences (with the faculty member absent, of course) and then analyze and report the results. Getting regular feedback on students' learning experiences is especially important in a flipped learning environment to have actionable information about student perceptions of flipped learning and to snuff out potential problems before they snowball into serious issues.

Seven Steps to Flipped Learning Design: An Overview

In this chapter, we've seen the importance of careful course design and looked at one model of course design. We've also seen how it can help facilitate the planning of a flipped learning course. This discussion has up to this point been at the macro level, considering only the superstructure of a course. In the next few chapters, we will dive into the micro level where a course is actually put together and an individual lesson mapped out. These considerations fill in some of the gaps in the larger picture of course design. For example, in mapping out the instructional strategy for a flipped learning course, we know we want a sequence of learning activities that alternates from the individual to group spaces and builds on itself, but what will students actually *do*? What will you, the instructor, actually do?

The details of planning a flipped learning course can be mysterious and disorienting to instructors. What does one do with all that freed-up time in class? And how does one create individual space activities that are likely to get done? On a bigger scale, how does an instructor make this entire practice something that doesn't consume all the available time in a person's life?

Flipped learning is all about providing structure, and to provide some structure around the professional practice of teaching in a flipped learning environment, we introduce here a seven-step process for building a single instructional unit in a flipped learning environment. This process is a distillation of a workflow that I, personally, have developed over the course of several years of implementing flipped learning in my classes. It should be adapted to each person's specific needs, but I have found it to be a reliable framework for designing learning experiences that are true to the flipped learning philosophy and put students first in the process.

1. Come up with a brief but comprehensive list of learning objectives for your lesson.
2. Remix the learning objectives so that they appear in order of cognitive complexity.
3. Create a rough design of the group space activity you intend students to do.
4. Go back to the learning objectives list and split it into basic and advanced objectives.
5. Finish the design of the group space activity.
6. Design and construct the individual space activity.
7. Design and construct any post–group space activities you intended students to do.

In chapter 5, we will look at steps 1 through 4, which focus on *setting up* activities for individual and group space work. In chapter 6, we will look at steps 5 through 7, which concern *designing and carrying out* those activities. By the end of chapter 6, we will have a workflow that can be used on a daily basis to guide the effective preparation of flipped lessons.

What may be surprising or counterintuitive in this process is that it is not linear. That is, we don't start with the design of the individual space activities, then design the group space activities, and finally design the activities to follow the group space. There is some jumping around as we outline learning objectives and next the *group space* activity, followed by a jump backward to design the individual space activity, then jump forward and finish the group space activity, and next back again to finish the individual space activity, and finally jumping rather far ahead to design post–group space activities. So the order in which students encounter these objectives and activities is *not* the order in which we create them.

Why all the jumping around? It's because *the heart of flipped learning is the group space activity*, and the totality of the flipped lesson ought to be planned with this central experience in mind. Therefore, although we need to specify learning objectives before designing the group space activity, we need a solid sense of what the group space activity is going to entail to properly design the individual space and post–group space activities. Without that knowledge, we're likely to give more than is necessary for students to do before the group space activity rather than giving them an activity that includes *just enough* to "launch" the group space activity, and we won't have the best possible sense of where to start our post–group space activities or where to go with them.

5

DESIGNING FLIPPED LEARNING EXPERIENCES, PART 1: BUILDING THE FRAMEWORK FOR A LESSON

I n the last chapter, we looked at course design and how the 12-step framework proposed by Dee Fink can serve as a guide for building a course that uses flipped learning. Course design frameworks are intended to build the course at the global, or macro, level by thinking about situational factors, coursewide learning objectives, teaching strategies, and how all of these various components fit together to make an integrated, coherent learning environment for students. What was *not* discussed in depth previously is just exactly how to create the day-to-day learning activities that fit into the larger picture of the instructional strategy of a flipped learning course. In this chapter and in the next, we "zoom in" to this level of detail and discuss how this can be done.

At the end of the last chapter we presented a seven-step framework for designing an individual lesson for a flipped learning environment:

1. Come up with a brief but comprehensive list of learning objectives for your lesson.
2. Remix the learning objectives so that they appear in order of cognitive complexity.
3. Create a rough design of the group space activity you intend students to do.
4. Go back to the learning objectives list and split it into basic and advanced objectives.
5. Finish the design of the group space activity.

6. Design and construct the individual space activity.
7. Design and construct any post–group space activities you intend students to do.

I encourage you to approach these two chapters like a workbook. If you have a course that uses flipped learning, or one in which you would like to start using flipped learning, find a *single lesson* from that course and bring it to these two chapters. By working through the seven steps as they are presented here, you can give a traditionally structured lesson a "flipped makeover" and change it to one that uses flipped learning; if the lesson is already flipped, you can compare your workflow to the one suggested by the seven steps and possibly make improvements.

We noted earlier that these seven steps are a nonlinear process—the order in which we build the lesson is not the order in which students experience it—because the group space activity is what drives the rest of the lesson. In turn, the learning objectives that we set up for students in the lesson help determine what students should be doing. So, in this chapter, we'll begin by focusing on what we do with learning objectives, next discuss briefly some issues involving group space activities, and then circle back and focus on a framework for constructing effective individual space activities. As you bring the sample lesson to this chapter and the next, you'll see each of the seven steps broken into three parts: an introduction and overview that describes the general idea of the step, a section of *activities* that you can do to implement the step, and then a section of *questions and answers* that I have frequently received about that step as I have worked with many college instructors in the process of converting their courses into flipped learning experiences.

How do we set up a learning environment that takes place outside of our direct observation, in the students' individual spaces, in which students can successfully engage with new concepts for the first time through independent learning experiences? The stakes for this question are fairly high, not just because the success of the group space activities depends on it, but because in flipped learning we are not just teaching *content* but also critical self-regulated learning skills that the individual space activities can build, if we design them properly. In our process, it all begins with learning objectives.

The Centrality of Learning Objectives

Before we begin the seven-step process, it will be helpful to reflect on the importance of the starting point in that process, which is the identification of *learning objectives* for students. In the course design process, we took time to identify large, macro-level learning outcomes for the *course*. Here we want to think about learning objectives for a single lesson. If course-level objectives are like the view from the top of a skyscraper, lesson-level objectives are like the view from the first or second floor—they point the way through the immediate learning activities that students will traverse and provide a concrete set of tasks that students should be able to do once the lesson is done.

Why bother to write out these objectives at all if we have already articulated the course-level objectives? For one thing, learning objectives on the lesson level are often much more specific than those for a course. For example, a calculus course will have broad objectives:

> Given a real-world phenomenon and a question about its "change behavior," use the concepts of calculus to set up a computation that will provide insight about this behavior and help answer the question.

(In fact, this is a course-level objective for my online calculus class.) This is an appropriate broad objective for the course, but it doesn't include much detail, nor is it supposed to. The lesson-level objectives will spell out in much more detail what this course-level objective *looks like* in context. For example, a lesson-level objective connected to this course-level objective might be "Set up and solve an applied optimization problem." The course-level objectives (listed in the syllabus, according to our course design model) spell out in broad terms for students what they will be able to do upon successful completion of the course. The lesson-level objectives—probably too numerous to include in a syllabus, as there may be between 5 and 10 of these per lesson, times dozens of lessons throughout the course—flesh out the details and let both the student and the instructor know the extent to which the course-level objectives are being attained.

Another reason to have clearly articulated lesson-level learning objectives is that they give students a standard for knowing whether their day-to-day learning tasks on the "ground floor" level are effective. The importance of having objectives for learning really goes without saying. An archer's arrow is more likely to hit the center of a clearly defined target than it is to hit a target that is concealed and has no identifying marks. A doctor is more likely to treat an illness effectively with a diagnosis than without a diagnosis and is more likely to make a correct diagnosis with accurate catalogues of symptoms than without. Although it is possible to overemphasize learning objectives in a learning process (Torrance 2007), it is simply common sense that learning is more effective with learning objectives than without.

However, despite the self-evident benefit of learning objectives, there are reasons for using them, and those benefits are borne out by research. First, clearly articulated learning objectives can help students identify different kinds of knowledge involved in learning a subject, such as the differences between declarative and procedural knowledge, which can help students differentiate between "knowing the material" in the sense of simple factual recall versus "knowing the material" by being able to apply basic facts to solve problems (Eberly Center for Teaching Excellence 2003). Second, clear learning objectives set up a kind of checklist for students to use for their individual practice; for example, studies have shown that learners with specific goals when learning from a text paid more attention to the parts of the text that harmonized with those goals, which led to more effective learning (Rothkopf and Billington 1979). Third, having clear learning objectives helps to ensure that, on the one hand, the level of support given to novice learners is enough and, on the other, that the level of direct instruction given to more advanced learners is not too much. A meta-analysis of 70 different studies on guidance in learning (Clark 1989) suggests that some learners will not only learn less in a subject without explicit guidance but also actually *lose* learning that had previously taken place, although another study (Kalyuga, Ayres, Chandler, and Sweller. 2003) shows that too much direction can harm learners who are more advanced.

Additionally, all of the benefits we have mentioned so far of having explicit, clear learning objectives aid the formation of self-regulated learning skills and behaviors. A key condition of self-regulated learning (Pintrich 2004) is the presence of clear standards by which a learner can judge whether his learning processes are adequate, so that there can be some rational basis for continuing or making changes. Ultimately, a self-regulating learner can (and does) generate his *own* learning objectives when faced with a novel learning task. However, our students have typically not fully arrived at this stage yet; providing learning objectives for "ground-level" tasks in individual lessons provides modeling in how to create these for oneself.

With the understanding that learning objectives are, generally speaking, good for learning, we have a strong basis for starting our lesson-planning process.

Step 1: Determine the Learning Objectives for the Lesson

Teaching and learning are complex tasks, and it's difficult to know how well any student is doing without a clear idea of what the end should look like. In our course design process, we asked two questions about learning goals at the coursewide level:

> What are students supposed to learn? What (in my professional opinion) constitutes acceptable evidence that they have learned it?

On the level of an individual lesson, the answers to these questions are what we call *learning objectives*. They vary in their specificity depending on the context. At the course level, learning outcomes are broad and general. But at the lesson level, when we "zoom in" on the course, they become more specific instances of the course-level objectives.

No matter what the level of "zooming" is, though, learning objectives work best when they are *concrete* and *unambiguous* and somehow *measurable*. It's helpful to phrase learning objectives as *tasks* that a student performs and the instructor assesses to determine whether the performance is acceptable in the instructor's best professional judgment. Learning objectives should not only be unambiguous but also action oriented:

- *Unambiguous.* Students should be able to tell clearly what they should be able to do, and how *they*, the students, will know if they have learned something. Importantly, the instructor should assess students' work, and the students themselves should learn to assess their own work. Learning objectives do not need to avoid jargon, necessarily; in fact, students need to learn how to parse the language of a subject as determined by an expert. So if "Set up and solve an applied optimization problem" leaves students wondering what an "applied optimization problem" is, their first stop along the road to meeting that objective is to find out. However, what an objective *does* need to avoid is needlessly complicated or imprecise wording that adds to the "extrinsic load" that we discussed in chapter 2.
- *Action oriented.* Objectives should only refer to actions we can actually measure rather than internal states of mind or other nonmeasurable abstractions. As a consequence, words like *know* or *understand* or *appreciate* should not be part of a lesson-level learning objective. We obviously want students to know and understand and appreciate the important concepts of the course; but the question is, *How will a student know and how will you as the instructor know whether the student knows/appreciates/understands that concept?* Determine what, in your best professional judgment, could a student do to convince you that she "knows" or "understands" something. What action or actions, when performed to your satisfaction, will you accept as evidence? *That action* is the real learning objective. Once you determine the action, write out the learning objective using an action verb.

Note that when we say learning objectives should be "measurable," we do not necessarily mean they should be *quantifiable*. Many aspects of learning defy quantification, and attempts to fit a layer of quantification over student learning often result in a factory-like environment where the focus is diverted from significant learning experiences to statistically significant test outcomes. This is usually undesirable. However, *measuring* student learning can be done without turning the course into a series of tests. In fact, we do this all the time when we evaluate student writing, oral presentations, or projects—student work that does not naturally admit numerical measures. All we want for our objectives is clarity as to exactly what criteria are going to be evaluated, so we and our students can have a common language for understanding whether the work meets professional standards or not. And what we want to avoid are objectives that cannot be measured, quantifiably or otherwise, which is what we have when we use terms like *appreciate* that refer to internal states of being.

As an example, suppose a learning objective for a lesson in an American history course is given as follows:

Understand the causes of the U.S. entry into World War I.

Certainly this is an important thing to know for this course. But the ambiguity needs to be worked out. What exactly do we mean by "understand" here, and what evidence will you accept that a student "understands"? The word could mean any of the following:

- List at least five specific reasons given in your readings for the U.S. entry into World War I.
- Outline a sequence of historical events that led the United States to enter World War I.
- Explain how social and political events in the United States between 1900 and 1910 led to the U.S. entry into World War I.
- Categorize some commonly given reasons for the U.S. entry into World War I as political, social, and economic and explain your reasoning.
- Create a plausible "alternate history" of the United States in which one of the events leading to the U.S. entry into World War I didn't happen.
- Debate the legitimacy of one or more of the causes of the U.S. entry into World War I with another classmate and summarize the other person's argument.

These tasks are in *increasing order of cognitive complexity*. Listing facts from a textbook is a less complex task than outlining, which is less complex than explaining events in context, and so on. Successful completion of any one of them could be considered evidence that the student "understands," but they are all very different tasks, and without explicit cues as to what *you* consider to be understanding, it will be very difficult for students to provide the evidence of understanding that you deem necessary. In fact, as we noted earlier, many students when asked what it means to "understand" a subject will describe only the lowest-level tasks such as listing and outlining. By framing these tasks as action verbs tuned to the right level of cognitive complexity, you are helping students to work at the level you desire.

It's possible as well that when a learning objective phrased with "know" or "understand" is really analyzed in terms of what specific tasks you want students to perform you really want students to do several tasks in succession. Using the World War I example, once the "understand" objective is unpacked, it might become apparent that you want students to list reasons *and* outline them *and* categorize them *and* debate them. Using specific actions verbs therefore disambiguates what you want students to do, and this helps everyone.

Finally, notice again that some of these objectives are quantifiable (e.g., the first objective) whereas some are hard to quantify, but all of them are *measurable* if we use a well-constructed list of criteria for evaluation and grading. In fact, these objectives are the jumping-off point for grading.

Learning objectives need other characteristics as well:

- *Comprehensive.* Everything of importance in the lesson should be addressed by a combination of learning objectives (if not by its own learning objective). In other words, if something is important in the course and you feel students need to know it, write a learning objective for it, or else determine how a combination of existing learning objectives will provide you with the evidence you need.
- *Minimal.* At the same time, not everything in a lesson needs its own learning objective. In fact, we want to eliminate redundancies in learning objectives to make the cognitive load on students as low as possible (but no lower!). There's no point in having five learning objectives that all say essentially the same thing, or a single learning objective that is really just a combination of two or more other objectives.

Carrying Out Step 1

Here, as in each of the steps we will describe, we give an activity you can do to build that particular part of the lesson. For example, the following activity can help to develop the learning objectives for your lesson.

Carefully examine the unit or lesson you have chosen and decide on a list of three to eight learning objectives that meet the criteria noted previously and write them out. Remember to use action verbs, write clearly (because the student is the audience here), and make them comprehensive yet minimal. You may need to make choices about what material to cover and what to leave out. Write those in a list in the space provided. *Just list these in the order in which they appear, or the order in which they occurred to you.* We may change that order in Step 2.

Hint: If you're using a textbook, sometimes it's helpful to simply read through the section in the book that your lesson will cover or even skim through the exercises. Between the text and the exercises you should have a fair idea of what the objectives should be according to the book. Then you can modify those using your own agenda for student learning.

If you need more space, or have more than eight objectives, just put them on a separate page.

1. Objective:
2. Objective:
3. Objective:
4. Objective:
5. Objective:
6. Objective:
7. Objective:
8. Objective:

Questions and Answers About Step 1

Q: *I'm having a hard time finding appropriate action verbs to use for my learning objectives that aren't* know, understand, *or* appreciate. *Is there a place I can go for hints?*

A: Yes, and it's called "the Internet." More specifically, a search engine query under "learning objective action verbs" will return thousands of examples of action verbs that might describe what you have in mind or in some cases inspire you to try something with students. Many of these lists use something called Bloom's taxonomy, which is a way of categorizing cognitive tasks by their level of complexity. We'll say much more about Bloom's taxonomy in Step 2.

Q: *How many learning objectives should a lesson have?*

A: Previously, it was suggested to come up with three to eight specific learning objectives for the lesson. This is just an arbitrary range of numbers. It's quite possible that a complex lesson, or a lesson for a class that has a long meeting time, could have a fairly long list of learning objectives. However it's also possible to make up too many objectives. Take a good look at your list and ask yourself the following questions: *Are some of these objectives not strictly necessary for my lesson, and therefore I can remove them without harming the academic rigor of my class? Is it possible to combine some of these objectives into one larger objective of which the smaller ones are instances? Am I trying to do too much in one class meeting, and should I see if I can carve out more time in a second session to cover all these objectives?* Conversely, it's possible that a lesson could have just one or two concrete learning objectives (but not likely). It's more likely that the learning objectives you have can, and possibly should, be split up into smaller ones that can and perhaps should be measured separately. For example, "Write the equation for a line" would be a pretty concrete and unambiguous-seeming objective for a basic algebra class. However, actually there are layers to this objective. Do we want students to write the equation for a line given just two points on the line? Do we want students to write the equation for a line given a point and the slope? Do we want students to write the equation in standard form and also in slope-intercept form? It would make sense in context to make this into *three* objectives, each more atomistic than the bigger objective.

Q: *I feel like learning objectives are too confining, and I want some space for students to explore and go off script. Do I really need to have learning objectives that are this specific?*

A: It's absolutely true that some of the best learning experiences we and our students experience are those that are unplanned and off script, the result of serendipity and teachable moments that happen without warning. Learning objectives can be written in a way that makes them confining, and the resulting intellectual claustrophobia can turn memorable opportunities for learning into a dreary process of ticking off boxes from a checklist. Nobody wants a class to turn into this.

At the same time, a course or lesson that is completely *unconstrained* runs the risk of being an unproductive free-for-all, especially for the most novice learners in our courses, who (as the research mentioned earlier shows) need guidance to learn. Where does one strike the balance?

Here is an analogy that might be useful. I live in Michigan and enjoy hiking in the many forest and beach areas that are nearby. All of these have trails, and all the trails have occasional trail markers. The purpose of the trail is both to guide me along the path that the creators of the park felt offered the maximum amount of enjoyment (the best views, the most challenging hill climbs, etc.) and to prevent me from straying into areas that need to remain apart from human activity (sensitive lakeshore dunes, etc.).

The purpose of the trail markers is both to tell me where the trail is and to differentiate one trail from others. Sometimes it's fun to stray off the trail and go "into the wild," but in order to do this, I have to know where I can do it without damaging the environment, and I have to know where the main trail is once I'm done, so that I can complete the hike without getting lost.

Now imagine a hiking trail that has meter-high guardrails on each side of the trail and DayGlo orange signs every five meters telling you, possibly in angry fonts, that *this is the trail and you are not supposed to get off of it.* That level of micromanagement of my hiking experience would render the entire enterprise thoroughly unenjoyable. At the same time, having *no* trail or an *insufficient* number of markers makes the hiking experience suboptimal, because I don't necessarily know where I am going, and even if I am familiar with the area, if I stray off the trail too much I might miss the breathtaking views that the trail was designed to show me.

The courses we teach are like the trails, and the learning objectives are the markers along the trail. We take care to design our courses (our trails) so that they show our students (the hikers) all the best things about what we are teaching (the place where we are hiking). The learning objectives are in place to serve as a guide to direct students to the path that offers the maximum amount of fun, challenge, and learning. Although it's sometimes okay to deviate from a lesson, the learning objectives are there to help us decide *where* and *when* this is okay—because it's not always okay—and where to get back on track once the diversion is over.

Carrying this analogy a step further: If courses are trails and learning objectives trail markers, that would make instructors the trail guides who lead groups of hikers, checking to make sure that each person is okay and proceeding well along the trail and offering perspective on what each hiker is experiencing. (And this is all we can do; we can't hike the trail *for* them.) But if the hikers have a guide, what need is there for trail markers? Well, there's no need at all, provided that the guide plans on being there for every hike that takes place in the future. But, of course, that's an absurd idea; what we *really* intend is for hikers to *not need human guides at all* but rather be able to pick up and go hiking when they want and follow a trail intelligently so that they can have a great experience on their own, without us in the picture. Hence, we need learning objectives in our lessons because we won't always be there in the future for our students; we want them to be able to navigate learning experiences without a human guide—even to set up their own "trail markers" in a future learning process—and still have a great experience.

So don't think of learning objectives as *constraints* or *scripts* but rather as *guideposts* that provide guidance and direction through the lessons that we teach.

Step 2: Put the Learning Objectives in Order of Complexity

When you were writing down the learning objectives in Step 1, it's possible that the order in which you listed them is not in order of cognitive complexity. For example, you might have listed the most complex learning objective first because it occupies most of the students' time, or because it's the one you remember first because it's historically the biggest stumbling block for students. But, in fact, there may be other learning objectives farther down the list that are more basic, or simpler.

Step 2 is about *putting the list of learning objectives, which are the result of a brainstorming process, into order in terms of cognitive complexity.* A useful framework for doing this is *Bloom's taxonomy* (Bloom, Krathwohl, and Masia 1956; revised and updated in Anderson, Krathwohl, and Bloom 2001). Bloom's taxonomy is often depicted as a pyramid, with the lowest levels corresponding to the simplest cognitive tasks, with the complexity of those tasks increasing as higher levels of the pyramid are accessed (see Figure 5.1). The verbs in the pyramid correspond roughly to the following kinds of processes (Anderson and Krathwohl, 2001):

- *Remembering*: Retrieval of relevant knowledge from memory
- *Understanding*: Determining the meaning of instructional messages
- *Applying*: Carrying out a procedure in a given situation
- *Analyzing*: Breaking material down into its component parts and discerning relationships between the parts and between the parts and the whole
- *Evaluating*: Making judgments based on established criteria
- *Creating*: Putting elements together to form a novel, coherent whole

Bloom's taxonomy is one of many hierarchical frameworks for cognition that can help "remix" the list of learning objectives we made in Step 1 so that they appear in *increasing order of complexity* rather than order of appearance. The reason we would want to do this will become a little clearer in Step 4, but the basic idea is that *we will eventually want to let students know what they should know how to do before coming into the group space, and this list of tasks is usually just a subset of the entire list of learning objectives.* To give students that "basic" subset, we will need to have a roughly linear ordering of the learning objectives to know where the basics end and the more advanced objectives begin.

Because we are depicting our learning objectives as *tasks* that have clearly stated action verbs, it is quite helpful to have a sense of what sorts of actions correspond with the different levels of Bloom's taxonomy. There are many such lists of Bloom's taxonomy verbs made up already. Table 5.1 shows an

Figure 5.1. Bloom's taxonomy pyramid.

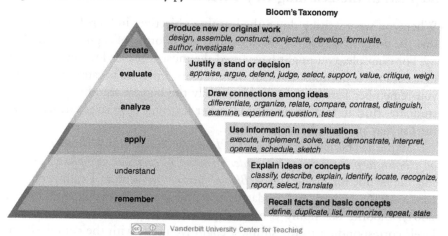

Source: Vanderbilt University Center for Teaching, Creative Commons License, https://www.flickr.com/photos/vandycft/29428436431

amalgamation of some of those lists. The list of verbs is neither exhaustive nor particularly well defined; it merely gives examples of some actions and where they might fall on Bloom's taxonomy. There could be variations. For example, the verb *describe* is given here as indicative of an *understanding* task; for example, a student could be asked to describe a chemical process as a way of making sense of the process. But the same verb, *describe,* could also be an *analyzing* task (e.g., if the student is asked to describe a relationship between one chemical process and another) or an *evaluating* task (e.g., if the student is asked to describe how a chemist's implementation of a chemical process in the lab follows safety procedures). As with most things, context is key.

We can use Bloom's taxonomy to determine how advanced our learning objectives are independently of the order in which we thought of them. For example, suppose that in planning out a lesson in algebra focusing on the quadratic formula we wrote down the objectives in the following order:

- State the quadratic formula.
- Use the quadratic formula to find the roots of a second-degree polynomial.
- Apply the quadratic formula to solve a real-world problem.
- State the conditions under which a second-degree polynomial will have two real roots, one repeated root, or two complex roots.

The fourth objective is an afterthought—it occurred to me after I had written down the other three. It's a legitimate objective but it wasn't one of the

TABLE 5.1
Common Verbs Associated With the Levels of Bloom's Taxonomy

Bloom's Taxonomy Level	Common Action Verbs for This Level
Remember	Define, state, identify, name, locate, recall, quote, match
Understand	Explain, classify, describe, predict, restate, translate, express
Apply	Solve, apply, modify, use, construct, prepare, produce, demonstrate
Analyze	Compare, contrast, distinguish, categorize, connect, differentiate, appraise
Evaluate	Reframe, criticize, summarize, defend, debate, argue, conclude
Create	Design, compose, conjecture, compile, construct, make, write, modify

main ones that I thought of. So there's a good chance it might be less complex than some of the other three that appear before it in the list.

Looking at the list of verbs, the first objective is pretty clearly a *remembering* task—this is merely asking the student to retrieve a formula from memory. (This doesn't make it *unimportant*—just low level.) The second objective is an objective about computation; it's about applying the basic formula to do a rote, mechanical computation. So this is an *applying* task, and a fairly low-level one at that. The third condition uses the word *solve*, which, in this context, means solving an equation; this is best categorized as an *applying* task again, albeit a more complex one than the second objective. Finally, the fourth objective says *state*, but what is meant here is that students should be able to take the basic formula and then use it to draw conclusions about mathematical expressions. That places it more in the realm of *applying* rather than *remembering*. Either way, this learning objective is at the middle of the pack in terms of complexity although it was the fourth item on the initial learning objectives list.

The point here is that Bloom's taxonomy provides a *framework* for thinking about how complex our learning objectives are, so we can sort the learning objectives in order of complexity, but it's not a formula that guarantees a perfect ordering. There are some professional judgment calls that you as an instructor and the resident content expert have to make. Also there is not a perfect one-to-one mapping from the verbs you use to Bloom's taxonomy; sometimes a verb you use (like *solve*) doesn't match with the same verb you see in a chart.

If this were my class, I would probably reorder the learning objectives by flipping the last two, giving the following final list of objectives in order from simple to complex:

- State the quadratic formula.
- Use the quadratic formula to find the roots of a second-degree polynomial.
- State the conditions under which a second-degree polynomial will have two real roots, one repeated root, or two complex roots.
- Apply the quadratic formula to solve a real-world problem.

I flipped the last two because I think, as a mathematician, that applying a formula to a real-world problem is harder for algebra students than applying it to find out information about an expression without a real-world context. But, again, this is a judgment call.

Carrying Out Step 2

Using one or more of the Bloom's taxonomy visualizations and lists of verbs (from those previously given or, better yet, from the Internet), reorder the learning objectives you wrote in Step 1 from *least complex* to *most complex*. It's okay if you feel like there is more than one way to do this; you are probably right. Some professional judgment will be necessary here.

1. Objective:
2. Objective:
3. Objective:
4. Objective:
5. Objective:
6. Objective:
7. Objective:
8. Objective:

Questions and Answers About Step 2

Q: *Does every lesson I plan need to have an instance from each of the six levels of Bloom's taxonomy? For example, is it okay to have a lesson made entirely of* remembering *tasks?*

A: This *can* happen sometimes. For example, there are courses in the health sciences for premedical and prenursing students that are entirely focused on medical terminology. Many of the lessons in those courses will focus on recall of terminology, so you might expect to see a lot of *remembering* tasks and not too many *evaluating* tasks. Conversely, some courses—for example, capstone courses in a major or service-learning courses—may have very few low-level tasks and focus instead mostly on higher-level tasks. However, good pedagogy generally speaking requires a balance of tasks across the cognitive spectrum. If you find yourself giving only low-level tasks, consider ways to introduce higher-level tasks in your course design (advice for all teaching, not just flipped learning).

Step 3: Outline the Group Space Activity

Although many treatments of, and questions about, flipped learning seem to revolve around the individual space—possibly because the strong emphasis on individual space makes flipped learning so distinctive and the individual space activities so problematic—the heart of the concept and its most important part is the group space. The whole point of flipped learning is to focus valuable class time, when students and instructor are together and can help each other, on tasks that are rigorous, creative, and challenging and therefore benefit the most from being together. (This is true even for online and hybrid courses where "class time" has a different meaning.) Those activities usually involve the items that are now in the bottom (more advanced) half of your remixed list of learning objectives. These objectives are at the heart of a university-level "understanding" of the subject, and therefore they are of utmost importance and deserve the lion's share of space and time.

The purpose of Step 3 is to have a rough idea of what students will do in class, so the preclass activity you design will be focused and free of redundancies and unnecessary work, which will in turn raise the probability of those activities being completed. You want to use class time to focus on the learning objectives you've identified at the "bottom" of the list—the hardest, most complex concepts students will need the most help understanding.

And here's the hard part about this step: *You will very likely not have enough time to address every single one of your objectives in class. In this step you will need to make a preliminary choice of which objectives you are not going to cover explicitly in class.* This is simply a practical fact about group space, or class time: There is not much of it, and we want to focus on giving students adequate amounts of time and space to explore the most difficult concepts when they can receive help the most readily. To pay the price for this, there are some objectives that students must be responsible for *before* they come to class (see Step 4).

So in this step you need to think about in-class activities that address the hardest elements of your learning objective list. This may be just a single objective! But if that one objective is so problematic that your students need to spend 45 laser-focused minutes on it, then so be it. (College students often struggle with focusing on one intellectual task for an extended period of time, so flipped learning design is helping them acquire and master this important self-regulation skill.)

Like any sort of accountability or assessment of individual space/preclass activity, this step is also intended to clarify how you will be spending time on other items in your class meeting. Activities may include

- beginning class with a brief entrance quiz over the reading and pre-class activity,
- beginning class with a Q&A over the reading and preclass activity (in small groups or as a class),
- having students present basic exercises (e.g., from a preclass activity) at the board for the rest of the class to discuss, or
- ending class with a self-regulated learning activity, such as a one-minute paper or exit ticket (Nilson 2013).

Because time is a scarce resource in class, you have to strike a careful balance between spending time on the main in-class activities and on these other, useful activities. For example, if you have a 50-minute class period, have designed an in-class activity that takes 40 minutes, and you want to spend 10 minutes on an entrance quiz with 10 minutes for discussion and then a one-minute paper at the end, the math just doesn't work out—something has to give. You get to decide what, and how.

As an example, let's go back to our hypothetical algebra class and its objectives:

- State the quadratic formula.
- Use the quadratic formula to find the roots of a second-degree polynomial.
- State the conditions under which a second-degree polynomial will have two real roots, one repeated root, or two complex roots.
- Apply the quadratic formula to solve a real-world problem.

Consider the following brainstormed plan for a 50-minute class session:

- First 10 minutes: Open Q&A on anything from the reading or video (with no predetermination).
- Next 25 minutes: A warm-up question asking them to write out the quadratic formula and then find the roots of two second-degree

polynomials. A follow-up question involving some real-world situation (with lots to choose from) in which we want to acquire some information that requires the quadratic formula—such as the classic problem of a projectile's equation of motion and determining when the projectile will hit the ground. An additional question could ask about determining when the roots of a polynomial are real or complex.
- Last 10 minutes: Debriefing and a one-minute paper to wrap things up.

There are 5 minutes missing from this outline to give some built-in slack time for the actual class. However, this is just an outline. I'll flesh it out later (in Step 5).

Carrying Out Step 3

Work out answers to the following questions:

- What are the *main objectives to address* from your list of learning objectives during in-class work? This should be a *relatively short list* of tasks that address the most complex items students need to learn, from which they will benefit by working together and with you present as the instructor to help on the spot.
- Generally speaking (fleshing out the details later), what will students *do* in class to show how well they are mastering the relevant learning objectives? (In other words, what's a rough outline of the tasks you are going to give to students?)
- In your best professional judgment, about how long will this take? (*Recommendation: If your in-class activity is taking up more than 70% of your contact time—for example, 35 out of 50 minutes—it needs to be shortened.*) Can some of it be done prior to class? Can some of it be moved to postclass? Can you give a simpler activity that still engages students at a high level?
- What *other* activities do you want students to do in class? How long will they take? When are they going to happen during the meeting? (And are all of these necessary or useful enough to justify spending class time on them?)

Questions and Answers About Step 3

Q: *What are some ways I can free up even more time in my class for active learning on the most difficult objectives?*

A: There may be several ways you can improve the efficiency of your class meeting by streamlining or eliminating things we often do in class out of habit:

- *Don't give course announcements in class.* Make class announcements via e-mail or your course's learning management system instead of taking up class time. At the very least, put up announcements on the board prior to class or in a handout, and then move on, after which the students are responsible.
- *Don't hand back papers in class.* Try prior to class time or by appointment in office hours. I recently realized that if I spent 10 seconds per student in a class of 30 students handing back papers that I would have spent 5 minutes transferring pieces of paper. How many times have you wished you had five more minutes to finish an activity?
- *Don't use paper at all.* Instead have students submit work electronically.

Step 4: Split Up the List of Learning Objectives

Our list of learning objectives has been ordered by cognitive complexity and a sense of what is going to happen in class. Now we move *backward* and look again at the objectives.

The list of learning objectives shows the tasks students should be able to do in order to provide evidence of mastery—*eventually*. The *timing* of that evidence matters, however. We don't need students to show they've mastered *every* learning objective *prior* to coming to class; that's unrealistic and creates excessive extrinsic cognitive load, and even if realistic and easy to accomplish would make our class obsolete!

So in this step we are going to do students a favor and specify what they need to be able to do through their individual space work, and what they will focus on doing during and after the group space activities. We do this by simply *splitting the list of learning objectives in two*—drawing a line that separates the individual space objectives from the group space objectives. We'll call those objectives *basic* and *advanced,* respectively.

Where this line is to be drawn is a function of your professional judgment. Look at your ordered list of learning objectives and ask two questions:

1. *What single item on my learning objectives list is the most advanced task I can reasonably expect a student to be fluent with through independent study?*
2. *What single item on my learning objectives list is the least advanced task that I plan on having students address through their active work in class?*

By answering these questions, you'll discover a line of demarcation. On one side of the line are learning objectives that are simple enough that students can gain basic fluency on their own through direct instruction and practice, in the individual space through structured first-contact activities. On the other side of the line are learning objectives that are advanced enough that students *might* be able to pick up basic fluency on their own, but they will need to do active work with other students in class to really begin to "get it."

Figure 5.2 illustrates this process. In the diagram, we have a number of learning objectives for the lesson—let's say *n* of them. In Step 2, we remixed these so that they now appear roughly in increasing order of cognitive complexity: Objective 1 is the simplest, Objective 2 is more complex than Objective 1, Objective 3 is more complex than either Objectives 1 or 2, and so on. Based on our professional judgment, we determine that somewhere down this ordered list—between Objective $k - 1$ and Objective k—is a cutoff point. Prior to that cutoff point, students can reasonably be expected to have productive encounters with those objectives in their individual space work before class (if we have a face-to-face course that meets on a regular basis). These are the *basic* objectives. After that cutoff point are the *advanced* objectives that are probably best left to be encountered during the group space. Objective $k - 1$ is the *most* complex of the basic objectives—the single most complex task that can be reasonably left up to the students to learn on their own in the individual space. Objective k is the *least* complex of the advanced objectives—the simplest task that will be encountered once students have acquired fluency with all the basic objectives. In this step, you find that line and then draw it.

Going back to the hypothetical algebra example, we had this ordered list of objectives:

- State the quadratic formula.
- Use the quadratic formula to find the roots of a second-degree polynomial.
- State the conditions under which a second-degree polynomial will have two real roots, one repeated root, or two complex roots.
- Apply the quadratic formula to solve a real-world problem.

What single item on my learning objectives list is the most advanced task I can reasonably expect a student to be fluent with through independent study? (This is "Objective $k - 1$" from Figure 5.2.) I think that this task would be the second one, using the quadratic formula to find the roots of a polynomial. Both it and the one before it are rote mechanical calculations that can be easily learned through direct instruction and practice, both of which can

Figure 5.2. Separating the list of learning objectives.

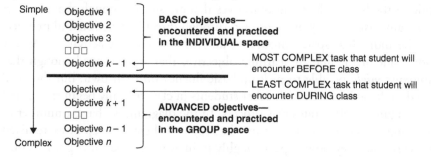

be provided through materials posted online (video, online homework, etc.). I don't necessarily expect students to *master* those skills before class (although some students will)—just get enough fluency to know more or less what they are doing.

What single item on my learning objectives list is the least advanced task that I plan on having students address through their active work in class? (This is "Objective *k*" from Figure 5.2.) I think that this would be the third item about applying the quadratic formula to classify the roots of a polynomial. This is almost simple enough to expect students to get some fluency on it before class, but I think it would work better as an in-class activity. This item becomes my line of demarcation:

Basic Objectives

- State the quadratic formula.
- Use the quadratic formula to find the roots of a second-degree polynomial.

Advanced Objectives

- State the conditions under which a second-degree polynomial will have two real roots, one repeated root, or two complex roots.
- Apply the quadratic formula to solve a real-world problem.

Eventually (Step 6) I am going to give these two connected lists to the students and make it clear that *students are expected to gain fluency only on the basic objectives* prior to class. Fluency on the advanced objectives prior to class would be awesome but not necessary; the advanced objectives merely set the agenda for what's happening in class.

Giving two lists of objectives tells students what they need to learn for class time: *You need to be reasonably fluent in stating the quadratic formula and using it to find the roots of a second-degree polynomial before you come to class; in other words, class activities will assume basic fluency on these.* It also tells them what they do *not* need to learn thoroughly for class time: *You will eventually need to show that you can state the conditions for roots of a quadratic polynomial and solve real-world problems with it; but not right this minute!* By telling students what they need to know for class *and* what they do *not* need to know for class, we lighten the cognitive load, model good self-regulation skills, improve the odds that preclass activities will be completed (more on this in Step 6), and set the agenda for the group space while communicating why students need to show up in the group space.

Carrying Out Step 4

Go back to your ordered list of learning objectives from Step 2 and draw a line that demarcates basic objectives from advanced objectives. Ask yourself, *Why am I drawing the line here?*

1. Objective:
2. Objective:
3. Objective:
4. Objective:
5. Objective:
6. Objective:
7. Objective:
8. Objective:

Questions and Answers About Step 4

Q: *What if I change my mind about where I want the line to go?*

A: This is okay. This is just a framework and not an exact science. Even in the algebra example, where the line goes is dependent on the particular group of students I'm working with; the line for a class in one semester could be different for a class in another semester. Doing flipped learning does require careful sensitivity to the abilities and needs of individual students and this feeds into the design process. Fortunately, flipped learning also allows you to form personal relationships with and talk to each student every day, so this is easier than in a traditionally structured course.

Q: *What if my line is at the very top of the list—that is, none of my objectives are simple enough to leave to students prior to class?*

A: Then you need to break down your learning objectives further and identify low-level tasks that you are taking for granted. For example, in the algebra example, suppose I only wrote down the last two objectives (which I moved into the advanced list). Thinking carefully about those objectives, I may realize that of course students should be able to use the quadratic formula in a basic way first—but that's such a low-level assumption that although it's necessary, it didn't occur to me. So I make this as a new objective and put it in the basic list. Same for stating the quadratic formula. Another possibility is that you may be underestimating your students' abilities to learn things on their own, or assuming they won't do the preclass work. Try not to go down that road.

What's Next?

By the end of Step 4, we've laid the groundwork for all the activities in the lesson we are about to teach—not only the learning objectives we want but also a sense of what students should be doing in their individual spaces and what we intend to do in the group space. Now it's time to design and make the activities that will form the learning environment for students—both individually and in a group. That is the focus of Steps 5 through 7.

6

DESIGNING FLIPPED LEARNING EXPERIENCES, PART 2: DESIGNING EFFECTIVE ACTIVITIES

In chapter 5 we examined a core idea in lesson planning, which is especially important in flipped learning design—the idea of *learning objectives* and how to rank them hierarchically in terms of cognitive complexity. Here at roughly the midpoint of the seven-step lesson-planning process, we have accomplished the following:

1. Established the learning objectives for the lesson in terms of clear, measurable tasks
2. Reordered the list of learning objectives so that the complexity of the tasks is roughly increasing
3. Finished a rough design of the group space activity that will form the centerpiece of the lesson
4. Decided which learning objectives are basic (to be done by students in their individual spaces) and which are advanced (to be done in the group space)

All four of these steps are intended to set up a strong foundation for the learning activities of the lesson. Those activities take place in three contexts: the individual space (or "before class" if the course is a face-to-face class); the group space (or "in class"); and the time and space that students spend *after* the group space, which could refer to a wide variety of tasks intended to shore up basic skills, extend the group space learning environment, or both.

In this chapter we will finish off our seven-step process by focusing on these three learning contexts, one at a time beginning with the group space activities.

Step 5: Finish the Design of the Group Space Activity

As we have mentioned before, the activity that takes place in the group space—whether this is a normal in-class meeting, a group video chat, or a time for group work on a discussion board in an asynchronous course—is at the heart of a course designed around flipped learning. It is here in the group space that we intend for students to engage with the concepts of the lesson that are the most complex, most perplexing, most difficult to navigate, and have the greatest potential for deep learning. Here students should *need* each other and the instructor, and the whole point of flipped learning is to make the satisfaction of that need as easy to attain as possible.

Having said this, flipped learning does not necessarily change the *kinds* of activities that serve this purpose in the group space. Effective active learning often does not look much different between flipped and unflipped course structures. Instead, what flipped learning gives students is the *time and space* to engage in those activities fully, without having to make time for a lecture and with initial preparations already thoroughly made (which we will discuss in Step 6). Sometimes, instructors who are new to flipped learning or who are curious about it ask, *What am I supposed to do with all the class time that is freed up by moving lectures out of the class space?* The best answer to this is *Do whatever it is you have always wanted to do, but didn't have the time.*

The Structure of Group Space

Group space itself has a structure—a beginning, a middle, and an end—that, if planned carefully, can greatly improve student learning. If we assume for the moment that we are thinking only of traditional, face-to-face courses, then that structure can be thought of as *the opening minutes of class, the middle of class*, and *the closing minutes of class*. Now that one has the full time of class to engage students in active learning, what should be done in each of these three stages of a class meeting?

The Opening Minutes

The opening minutes of a class are crucial for setting the stage for the group meeting both in terms of the tone that we set for the meeting and in terms of coming to an understanding of what was learned in the individual space (Lang n.d.). Instructors can use this initial 5 to 10 minutes of class to do some or all of the following:

- *Have students review, connect, and express what they have previously learned.* For example, an *entrance ticket* to class can have students focus their attention on the main points of the individual space activities and associated knowledge both for recall and to solicit questions for group discussion (Sheridan Center for Teaching and Learning n.d.).
- *Ask a compelling question.* Because much of the material we want students to learn takes the form of answers to questions (Willingham 2009), posing those questions at the beginning of class as a guide for the upcoming activity can help set students' frames of mind toward answering them.
- *Especially important for flipped learning courses, build in accountability for the individual space.* Students in a flipped learning environment will be working individually prior to class to get first exposure to new concepts and gain basic fluency in those concepts, according to the basic learning objectives that we picked out in Step 4. In Step 6 we will discuss a model for individual space activity, but no matter what model one uses, it's not a bad idea to ask students to be individually accountable for their work when they arrive at class. A simple example of accountability is a brief quiz over the main points of the individual space activity. Such a quiz could be given on paper, but it can also be given using classroom response systems or "clickers," which would provide instant feedback to the instructor about what students know and do not know from the individual space activity. Such feedback lets *students* know where they stand coming into class, and it lets the *instructor* know this as well so that last-second modifications to the lesson can be made (or the lesson can be completely thrown out!). Review and accountability could also be enhanced by giving students the answers to the preclass activities at the beginning of the class meeting and then using the beginning of class for students to discuss those answers and raise questions in small groups. Or individual students could be responsible for writing up and presenting a summary of the individual space learning activities to the rest of the class, using a rotating schedule for students to carry out this responsibility, or a student could be selected randomly for the day, which keeps all students on their toes.

The Middle Part

The middle section of a class is where most of the time resides, and it is where we focus the main work of the group space activity. This activity can look like almost anything: group work on application problems, laboratory-focused work in pairs, debates, service-learning—the list goes on. Flipped learning does not prescribe any specific activity for the group space; we only want the group space to do the following:

- *Be active.* We have already mentioned in chapter 2 how we now know that active learning leads to significant learning gains in students when compared to their counterparts taught in similar academic environments using less active techniques—for example, see Hake (1998) and Freeman and colleagues (2014). In order to reap the full benefits of the flipped learning environment, students need to be engaged in some form of active learning for as much of the group space as possible. Fortunately, "active learning" as described in the various studies that support it includes a broad spectrum of activities in which students are active in constructing their own meanings for the concepts being learned. For example, peer instruction (Mazur 1997) is a highly effective active learning technique particularly well suited for large lecture courses, whereas inquiry-based learning has been shown to have strongly positive effects with students in less populated courses—see, for example, Laursen, Hassi, Kogan, and Weston (2014) and Kogan and Laursen (2014).

- *Focus on advanced learning objectives.* The reason we split the list of learning objectives in two in Step 4 was to clearly delineate what students should learn on their own (with help) prior to class and what students will learn through active work during and following class. Therefore, we want the group space activities *not* to dwell overly on basic learning objectives and instead directly address the advanced learning objectives, or at least a subset of those. Let the preclass/individual space activity handle the basic objectives; class time, which is the scarcest and most valuable resource you and your students possess, needs to be focused on the advanced objectives, which are the ones that require the most resources.

- *Reach the students in their "zones of proximal development."* Lev Vygotsky formulated the concept of the *zone of proximal development* (ZPD) in his research on learning among children and defined it as "the domain of transitions that are accessible by the child" (Vygotsky, van der Veer, and Valsiner 1994, p. 211) and the area of "immature, but maturing processes" (Vygotsky 1998, p. 204). A learner's ZPD refers to the space of tasks that the learner *can* do with assistance, as opposed to those tasks that the learner can do easily without assistance and those that the learner cannot do with any amount of assistance. However, although the kinds of tasks that a learner can perform help to find where her ZPD resides, the concept of ZPD is about the *learner* and her state of intellectual development and not about the tasks themselves (Chaiklin 2003). To be sure, not all students will arrive at the group space activity with the same level of development. However, using the process we have described so far with its emphasis on basic and advanced objectives, instructors can set up a "target" ZPD for students by clearly indicating expectations for fluency prior to class. Ideally, students' ZPD will tend toward tasks that are indicated by the advanced learning objectives—they *can* do these tasks with assistance, which they will receive freely and in large quantities in the group space, and eventually they should be able to demonstrate mastery of these objectives independently *without* assistance. A well-designed group space activity hits students in their ZPDs: not so easy that the group space is unnecessary and not so difficult that the group space doesn't help.

The Closing Minutes

The closing few minutes of class are useful for activities that summarize, synthesize, and solicit questions. These can include one-minute papers, "muddiest point" activities, and others. Many of these activities promote metacognition and self-regulated learning by asking students to reflect on what they learned, difficulties they are encountering, and plans for what to do outside of class (Nilson 2013).

This three-part group structure can be adapted to fully online courses as well. Take, for example, an asynchronous online course that is structured into weekly modules. The individual space, which corresponds to the "preclass" time in a face-to-face course, can be the first two days of each module set aside for completion of an individual space activity (with the opportunity to discuss and ask questions along the way). The individual activity can be due at 11:59 p.m. of the second day of the module. The results from the individual space activity can be taken at face value as evidence of sufficient competence to begin the group space activities, or a discussion board activity can be set up for students to express what they learned on day three, mimicking the "first 10 minutes of class" experience for a face-to-face course. Then the group space activity can be a series of discussion questions to be addressed by the whole group or in small groups that report back to the whole group, analogous to small-group discussions and working groups in a face-to-face course. Then the module can be ended on the last day of the week with another short summative exercise similar to the exit ticket given in a face-to-face course.

The point is that "group space" is often automatically interpreted to mean "class time," but this is not necessarily the case. In-class meetings of a face-to-face course are an *instance* of group space but not the only one. Flipped learning design principles for group space activities apply no matter what the modality of the course.

Carrying Out Step 5

Questions to answer as you plan out the details of your group space activity should include the following:

- Is the activity aligned with the advanced learning objectives?
- Are there parts of the activity that seem too simple (i.e., would fit better in preclass activities), too advanced (i.e., would be better done after class), or redundant in a nonproductive way?
- Are the activities substantive, challenging, and appropriately pitched to the audience?
- Do you plan on grading the group space activity? If so, what does the rubric look like and how will students use the feedback to make improvements?
- Do the other activities for your class session (entrance quizzes, exit tickets, etc.) make sense in the overall context of the class session? Do they take up too much time?

Before moving on, and after answering these questions, make out a rough timetable for what will happen and when during your class session to make sure, if you teach a face-to-face course or are under a similar time constraint, that everything you have planned can be carried out comfortably in the time you have available.

Questions and Answers About Step 5

Q: *What happens if students come to class (the group space) and aren't prepared to work on my group space activity?*

A: This is, without a doubt, in a tie for first place as the most commonly asked question about flipped learning by practitioners (both new and seasoned) as well as those who are just curious. The other first-place winner is the related question *How do I make sure students do the individual space activities?* These two questions are opposite sides of the same coin. We will address the first one here, and the second one in Step 6.

First, we want to make sure that the group space activity isn't too advanced for students. If it turns out that it is, then you may not realize this until class time. In that case, you will need to improvise: Produce a simpler version of the same activity, create some connecting activities that bridge the individual space activities (based on the basic learning objectives) and the group space activity that you have, and so on. This is why the concept of the ZPD is so important. In a flipped learning environment, we instructors have to make educated guesses on the "center of mass" of the students' ZPDs based on their execution of basic learning objectives and design the group space activities accordingly. Getting this guesswork right is part science and part art (possibly part magic), and mostly it can be described as "craft." Perfecting that craft is part of being a professional educator; it takes practice to get it right consistently, and a framework like we have developed here helps one to practice well.

Second, underpreparation for group space has two dimensions. One dimension is the *extent* to which the class is unprepared; is it just one student, just a few, the whole class? The other dimension is the *degree* of underpreparation; is it only a few concepts that are being missed, widespread misconceptions about all the basic learning objectives, or somewhere in between? There could be another dimension added, which is *intent*. Are students underprepared *willfully* (i.e., they chose not to prepare) or did they simply lack the cognitive tools to complete the assignment? For now, we will leave the question of intent aside and focus on the aspects of underpreparation we can do something about. These two dimensions create four "quadrants of underpreparation" (see Figure 6.1).

In the "southwest" (bottom-left) quadrant we have underpreparation for the group space among a small number of students, and the degree of underpreparation is not great. For example, you might have two or three students who are still struggling with one item from the basic objectives list. If the class is in this quadrant, the instructor may not need to do anything other than communicate with those students throughout the group space. Often, a well-designed group space activity will provide scaffolding for students to clear up their misconceptions, and by the end of the group space they will have caught up. In a flipped learning environment, it is quite easy to maintain contact with those students (unless the class size is large) because of the time and space freed up from lecturing.

In the "northwest" (top-left) quadrant is the situation in which a few students have major misconceptions or issues with the material coming into the group space. Again, we will not include *intent* in the picture here, because once students show up to class unprepared, it's a moot point as to *why*; this can be addressed through ongoing communication, but in the moment, the students need to do something in the group space. The question is *what* they will do. If a small number of students have major gaps in their preparation, the instructor can put them in a separate group, or a separate space, and have them work in class on activities designed around the basic objectives while others work on the advanced material. For example, you might set up a "station" in your class—that is, a place for students to go if they need to review the basics or even watch the videos that they didn't watch. Students who demonstrate a strong lack of preparation can be sent there; others can opt to

Figure 6.1. Quadrants of underpreparation.

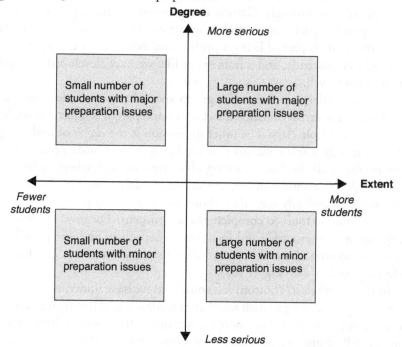

visit the "review station" if they feel the need. Students in this special space can still get the benefit of individual help from the instructor and from peers; they miss the benefits of working on the advanced objectives, but this is the price of not preparing.

Also crucial is that students need to have a way of asking questions and getting help during their individual space work so that the likelihood of underpreparation is minimized. One of the chief concerns brought up by students engaging in flipped learning environments for the first time is a per-ceived (possibly real) lack of support for their work outside of class. A simple discussion board where students can ask questions freely or anonymously can be enough; office hours (in person or online) or assigned study groups can also be beneficial. Students should be encouraged to ask questions and seek out help from all corners during their individual space through a multiplicity of channels. This way, if a small number of students arrives to class under-prepared, it will not be because they didn't have access to help prior to class.

In the "southeast" (bottom-right) quadrant is the classroom scenario in which a large number of students have a small number of problems, or a medium number of problems that are not severe in extent. In this case, the instructor can use the opening minutes of class to address this situa-tion through group discussion, clicker questions, or even direct instruction. Remember that direct instruction—lecture—is not *banned* from the class-room in a flipped learning environment; if it happens in the class during group space work, it is to be focused on specific questions that students have a stake in answering and not merely the default mode of instruction. Those opening 5 to 10 minutes provide a natural boundary on addressing student questions so that the lecture, if there is one, is limited and focused and does not take over the class. However, in many situations lecture might still be unnecessary, and through small-group discussions or peer instruction students can help each other in ways that instructors cannot.

Finally, in the "northeast" (top-right) quadrant is the "doomsday scenario" that often prompts the original question: *What do we do when large numbers of students come to the group space strongly underprepared?* My suggestion for triage in this situation has four parts:

1. Put away the group space activity you had planned and spend the class fielding specific questions from students about the material with which they struggled. Do this in a way that places the responsibility for ask-ing questions on the students. For example, get students into groups of three or four and have them generate specific questions that are then put on the board or projector, and then prioritized. *Do not accept requests that are not questions about specific items.* For example, "I didn't under-stand anything" is not a question and therefore not fair game from this impromptu Q&A session; neither is "Could you reteach section 3?" *Only specific, targeted questions are allowed and only those that are brought up by students.*

2. Then take your time to answer those questions in a succinct, clear way.

3. Before ending the class *make sure students are clear on the expectations being held for them, and if this situation happens again they will have to face consequences that could impact their grade in the course.* Set the boundaries in no uncertain terms. Ask students if they have questions about the boundaries; you might even have them sign a statement that affirms that they know what the boundaries are and agree to abide by them in the future.

4. Then make sure to end the class as planned, by taking the last few min-utes of class to have students engage in a metacognitive or self-regulation activity. A particular set of self-regulated learning questions you should ask might be the following: *Do you feel like you were unprepared for class? If so, why? Did you seek help from anyone before class? If so, what did you do,*

and why wasn't it helpful for you? If not, why not? What are your plans for preparing for the next class to ensure that you arrive sufficiently prepared to work? As for the group space activity, you can adjust the calendar to do it later, assign it as homework, or something else. *Please note: Under no circumstances should you reteach the material if you end up in the northeast quadrant.*

The first time a widespread pattern of serious underpreparation happens, the preceding steps turn the group space into something that addresses student questions (which is different from simply reteaching) and reaffirms the division of labor in the flipped learning model, and the air should be clear regarding how flipped learning works. The *second* time this happens, there have to be consequences for students, because they know the "rules" of flipped learning and are not taking sufficient steps to follow them. What you *do* in this scenario—a scenario that we should hasten to add is quite unlikely in my experience—is up to you, but if you reteach the material, then it sends the message to students that the flipped learning model is just an illusion, and if enough students underprepare enough, they'll get the traditional model. Setting clear boundaries with consequences for persistent violation is crucial for a successful flipped learning environment.

This sounds horrible, like we are refusing to do our jobs if this scenario happens. But in fact we are doing *precisely* our jobs when we set up rich learning environments for students and then ask that they prepare sufficiently to be productive in them; we are failing to be professionals if we let persistent, widespread underpreparation derail us from this important task into mere information transfer when we *know*, from decades of research, that this is not best for students.

However, please note that individual instructors bear significant responsibility here to make the expectations for students very clear from the beginning, to provide lots of support for students as they work in the individual space, and to design both individual and group space activities that are accessible to students. If we don't do these things, we have no basis for complaining about students' underpreparedness.

And this scenario further underscores the crucial importance of designing effective individual space activities, which we now discuss.

Step 6: Design and Construct the Individual Space Activity, Using the Guided Practice Model

Now we turn our attention to a crucial portion of the planning process: designing the activities that students will do in their individual spaces. As we have just discussed, although the group space activity is the heart of a flipped learning experience, the success of that activity is predicated on students learning enough *prior* to the experience to be productive when they get to the group space.

The primary purpose of the individual space activity is to "launch" the group space activity. We want to have students engage in just the right amount of learning prior to their group space experience. If we give too much for students to do (by giving redundant exercises, having them address learning objectives that aren't relevant, or giving work that is at too high a level to be manageable individually) then students will shut down. If we give too little work, or work that is too easy or simple, then students may complete it, but they will be unprepared for the group space. So we must proceed carefully and seek a balance.

We want to design an activity that is the following:

- *Minimal.* It should ask students to do no more than is necessary to demonstrate fluency on the basic learning objectives and prepare them to work well in class.
- *Simple.* The structure of the activity, and the student work contained in it, should be easy to understand and lead students to the learning activities along a clear path.
- *Engaging.* The work students are asked to do should spark their interest and encourage them to complete it.
- *Productive.* By doing the work in the preclass activity, students should be well prepared for the more challenging in-class activity coming up.
- *Failure-tolerant.* The preclass activity should be relatively forgiving, even welcoming, of initial mistakes. Mistakes and errors should not be a source of stress. Rather, they should be collected and used as learning data.

As I discussed in the preface, when I first started using flipped learning, it failed because my individual space work was not abiding by these principles. Over the years since then, I experimented and refined my approach until I arrived at a model that keeps these principles in mind and uses a simple and easy-to-follow workflow for class preparation. This model is what I call *Guided Practice.*

The Guided Practice model for individual space activities breaks up each individual space activity into five parts:

1. *Overview.* This is a short (one-paragraph) overview of the material students are about to encounter, with an emphasis on how it connects to

other things they have learned. This need not be text; a short video would suffice, or a mind map, or some other way of introducing the material and its connections to past content.

2. *Learning objectives.* Here we simply reproduce the split list of learning objectives, clearly labeled "Basic" and "Advanced," that we created in Step 4. We provide this list because one of the basic principles of self-regulated learning is that students are in possession of standards against which they can judge their progress as they learn. Eventually, in life, students will make up their own objectives. For now, we are training them to do so.

3. *Resources for learning.* This consists of a recommended "playlist" of items that will help students engage with the basic learning objectives productively and set themselves up for success in the exercises that are coming up. Here we list any text, video, multimedia, or other resources that would be helpful for these tasks.

4. *Exercises.* This section is the main area of activity for students. It consists of a small list of exercises that will instantiate the basic learning objectives—giving students the "practice" part of Guided Practice.

5. *Instructions for submitting work.* In the final section we give clear instructions on how to submit work. This is an important and often-overlooked step. Students in a flipped learning environment for the first time often feel disoriented, and clear instructions for turning their work in may seem like an obvious thing, but it goes a long way to helping students acclimate.

Following is an actual Guided Practice assignment used in an introductory calculus course. (No knowledge of calculus is necessary to understand it.) This Guided Practice assignment was completed before the beginning of a weeklong unit on the topic of instantaneous velocity and rate of change. This particular course happened to be an asynchronous online course, and the assignment was to be done during the first two days of the unit as part of students' individual space work. We begin with the overview (see Figure 6.2).

Next we have lists of learning objectives (see Figure 6.3). These two lists are the results of Steps 1, 2, and 4, which were done separately prior to writing up this assignment. But once those steps are done, the results are just imported into the document. Also, we have the "playlist" of learning resources. For this class, it includes a list of videos to watch and a reading assignment (see Figure 6.4).

This is the *default* set of learning resources, but students can choose to add to this list if they want, or use resources completely off the list. Students in the course are given the freedom to use whatever resources help them attain the learning objectives. And the way they work toward attainment of

Figure 6.2. Guided Practice: Overview.

Guided Practice for 1.8: The tangent line approximation

Overview

This section is a little different because we will be doing most of the work in your lab session with a computer. But this is appropriate since it's a very computationally oriented section. We will be looking at a common application of the derivative to making accurate predictions about a function, when we don't have complete information about the function. This is the basic idea behind such applications as weather forecasts, financial forecasting, laboratory estimates, and more. We know by now that the derivative $f'(a)$ at a point $x = a$ gives the slope of the tangent line to the graph of f at $x = a$. This tangent line is also called the **local linearization** of f at $x = a$, and we will learn how to compute local linearizations and use them to estimate values of a function.

Figure 6.3. Guided Practice: Learning objectives.

Learning Objectives

BASIC learning objectives

Each student will be responsible for learning and demonstrating proficiency in the following objectives PRIOR to the class meeting. **The entrance quiz for the class meeting will cover these objectives.**

- (*Algebra review*) Given the slope of a line and a point (not necessarily the *y*-intercept) on that line, state an equation for that line in *point-slope form* and in *slope-intercept form*.
- Given the value of the derivative of f at a point $x = a$ (i.e., given $f'[a]$), write the *equation of the tangent line* to the graph of f at $x = a$.
- Explain what is meant by the *local linearization* of a function f at the point $x = a$.
- Use a local linearization of a function at $x = a$ to approximate values of f near $x = a$.

ADVANCED learning objectives

The following objectives should be mastered by each student DURING and FOLLOWING the class session through active work and practice:

- Given a function f, find its local linearization at $x = a$.
- If $L(x)$ is the local linearization of a function $f(x)$ at $x = a$, and if b is some point near a, determine whether $L(b)$ is greater than, less than, or equal to $f(b)$ and explain.

---

those learning objectives is by working through the exercises that come next (see Figure 6.5).

Notice that the exercises are directly linked to the basic learning objectives. For example, one of the basic objectives was "Use a local linearization of a function at $x = a$ to approximate values of f near $x = a$," and among the

Figure 6.4. Guided Practice: Resources.

Resources

Reading: **Read Section 1.8, pages 71–77 in *Active Calculus*.** We will work some of the activities in class, but you may also work on them outside of class for further understanding.

Viewing: Watch the following videos at the MTH 201 YouTube Playlist. These have a total running time of 18 minutes, 34 seconds:

- Quick Review: The tangent line approximation **(2:18)**
- Calculating a tangent line **(5:42)**
- Using a tangent line **(3:27)**
- Using the local linearization **(7:07)**

Figure 6.5. Guided Practice: Exercises.

Exercises

These exercises can be done during or after your reading and video watching. They are intended to help you make examples of the concepts you are reading and viewing. Work these out on scratch paper, and then you will be asked to submit the results on a web form at the end.

1. A line has a slope equal to –3 and goes through the point (4, 6). State the equation of this line in point-slope form and then in slope-intercept form.
2. The function f has the following features: We know that $f(2) = -3$. State the equation of the tangent line to the graph of f at $x = 2$ in point-slope form and then in slope-intercept form.
3. The tangent line to the graph of f at $x = 2$ that you calculated in question 2 is called the local linearization of f at $x = 2$. Use the local linearization to predict the value of $f(2.1)$ and explain briefly what you did.
4. What specific mathematical questions do you have about the reading and viewing that you would like to discuss in class?

---

exercises is one that asks students to do exactly that. All of the terminology and rote procedures are given, with multiple examples, in the video playlist.

Therefore, by working through these Guided Practice exercises, students are getting *practice* on basic learning objectives that is *guided* by the structure of the assignment. Finally, students get clear directions on how to submit their work (see Figure 6.6).

The submission form here is a Google Form, which accepts input from a variety of question types and then puts the results into a spreadsheet, along with a time and date stamp. Before the group space activities begin, the instructor can scan through the responses to the Guided Practice assignments

Figure 6.6. Guided Practice: Submission instructions.

Turn-in instructions

Go to the web form located at the following link and type in your answers: http://bit.ly/14FjsHH

Responses are due **one hour before your section's class time**. If you do not have access to the Internet where you live, please let me know in advance and we will make alternative arrangements.

---

and look for patterns and misconceptions very easily and then make on-the-fly adjustments to the group space activities.

Here are two more Guided Practice activities from the same course:

1. Guided Practice for module on basic derivative computation: https://goo.gl/Z3LOMM
2. Guided Practice for module on applied optimization: https://goo.gl/IKQH52

Carrying Out Step 6

Much of the work in setting up a Guided Practice assignment for the lesson you have chosen has already been done if you have carried out Steps 1 through 5. Use the following procedure to guide your construction of this activity:

1. Write out an overview for your lesson, or give a mind map or similar means of introducing the new material and connecting it to previously learned materials.
2. Copy the split lists of learning objectives you made in Step 4.
3. Gather any text, video, or other resources for learning that you can find or make and include them in a list in your document. Remember not to make this too long, and encourage students to add resources that they find and exercise choice in what resources they use.
4. Write up a short list of exercises—"low-hanging fruit" that students can do that will lead them through successful engagement with the basic learning objectives.
5. Determine how students will submit their work, and give clear instructions on how to do this. If you have time, actually make up the form for submitting work and include a link to it.

You will also need to determine how these assignments will be distributed (on paper? on a learning management system? through e-mail?).

Questions and Answers About Step 6

Q: *Do I have to include video in the list of resources I give students?*

A: *No.* Online video is not a requirement for setting up an effective flipped learning environment. In fact, as we saw in an earlier chapter, the first pioneering instances of flipped learning predate the existence of online video as we know it by at least five years, sometimes as much as a decade. (YouTube didn't launch until 2005, five years after the seminal Lage, Platt, and Treglia article on the inverted classroom.) In a more contemporary example, Lorena Barba's MOOC on numerical methods (discussed earlier) contains just a single video for the whole course; students' initial work on a lesson came primarily from working with interactive code blocks (Barba n.d.). Video is an efficient way to provide lecture in an easily accessible way, but don't feel constrained to use it if you'd rather not.

Q: *If I choose to use video, is it better if I make my own instead of using those made by somebody else?*

A: There is some evidence to suggest that it would be better for students if they used videos made by you rather than someone else. One study (Rose 2009) showed that instructor-made videos fostered an enhanced sense of connection between the students and the instructor, thereby raising students' autonomous motivation, as we described in our earlier discussion of self-determination theory. Although the study did not address the differences between instructor-made and other video, presumably the feelings of connection between students and instructor would not be enhanced if the instructor is not in the video. Other studies (e.g., Fernandez, Simo, and Sallan 2009) corroborate this effect. On the other hand, according to a large-scale meta-analysis of studies on student use of video podcasts (Kay 2012), the chief reasons given by students for using video podcasts like the videos in a flipped learning environment were for learning-related purposes (preparing for class, taking better notes, etc.), for control (such as the ability to pause and replay), and to make up missed class. These reasons do not have an immediate connection to the person making the video. In brief, it's best if you as the instructor can make high-quality videos for students. But if this is impractical, students seem to get as much out of a high-quality video made by another person as they might if it was made by you, although they may miss out on enhanced feelings of connectedness and motivation.

Q: *So it's okay if I just curate rather than create video?*

A: Generally speaking, yes (although see the previous answer for a caveat). There is a growing number of very high-quality videos available freely online to use. However, that degree of quantity does not, unfortunately, correlate with quality. The more *video* about a certain subject that is posted to the Internet, the more *bad* video is posted—bad in terms of pedagogical value, sound or video quality, or goodness of fit to the way you are conducting your class. Curating video can save a lot of time over creating it yourself—unless you find yourself spending hours doing quality control on the video you are attempting to curate. It might be worth it to simply block out the time and learn how to make video yourself, and then do it. We will discuss this issue in more depth in chapter 8.

Q: *What should I include in the resource playlist?*

A: A mix of media is important for variety and to reach learners with different preferences; take a "both/and" approach rather than "either/or," including anything that looks helpful—video *and* text *and* audio *and* computer simulations *and* games and so on—and then let students choose freely from among the resources you've compiled.

Q: *How extensive should the Guided Practice be? How much work needs to take place?*

A: Again, the Guided Practice should be *just enough to launch the group space.* A reasonable rule of thumb is as follows: Think about what the lesson would look like if it were traditionally structured, with group space used for first contact with new concepts (by lecture, etc.) and the individual space used for homework and other activities. How much time would that traditional group space occupy? This is the target for the time requirement for the Guided Practice. In other words, we aim for close to a 1:1 swap of group space and individual space.

For example, if one of my calculus class meetings takes 50 minutes, then the total time requirement for the Guided Practice for the lesson that would have gone in that class meeting should be around 50 minutes combined, including time needed to watch video and do exercises, based on a reasonable estimate by you as the instructor. The sample Guided Practice shown earlier is for a weeklong unit, which in a face-to-face course would consist of three 50-minute meetings. Accordingly, the Guided Practice for this unit was built so that, in my best professional judgment, a student with no serious deficiencies in her background could complete it in under three hours.

What we want to avoid is using the flipped learning structure to "supersaturate" students with work, by swapping a 50-minute lecture session with 100 minutes of online video, for instance. This would have serious consequences for cognitive load and motivation.

Q: *The previous example used an Internet form to get student submissions. Is this necessary?*

A: Electronic submission is just a convenience, but it's used to facilitate what's really important about submissions of Guided Practice: *getting the submissions prior to the group space.* Why is it important to get the submissions prior to class, as opposed to at the beginning of class or later? It's because Guided Practice is formative assessment, used to guide us as much as it is to guide the students. It tells us what students know and what they don't know even before we engage in any group space activity, so that the "hot spots" are known, there are no surprises when we arrive at the group space, and we can make adjustments to our plans. We simply can't do this if we don't get the submissions prior to the group space.

Q: *How should I grade individual space activities like Guided Practice?*

A: I recommend that *Guided Practice assignments be graded on a one- or two-level rubric on the basis only of completeness, effort, and timeliness.* My own personal practice is that Guided Practices are graded pass/fail, with a "pass" being awarded if the work is turned in on time (11:59 p.m. of the evening before the class meeting), and each exercise on the assignment shows evidence of a good-faith effort to be right. *Actual correctness does not factor into the grade.* On the contrary, not all the questions asked even have a right answer. The only ways to earn a "fail" on a Guided Practice are to submit it late, leave one of the exercises blank, or give an answer to an exercise of the form "I don't know" or "I was confused." (If students are confused, they are expected to ask questions and then give an answer that reflects their best understanding at the moment—but they are not allowed to opt out of an exercise because they encountered difficulty.)

Keeping this kind of grading system for Guided Practice has several benefits. First, it's very easy to grade a lot of assigments all at once, because all you have to do is scan to look for late or insufficient submissions, mark those "fail" and then mark the rest "pass"; this frees you up to respond to students individually if they had difficulty. Second, it makes the assignment failure-tolerant for students, which is important for tasks involving learning something for the first time. If Guided Practices are relatively high stakes, then students are likely to encounter so much stress in completing them that they may not give their best efforts, or even worse they may cheat, and the data you get from the assignment are untrustworthy. Third, by not grading actual correctness, you get the raw, unfiltered best efforts of students and have data for your class meeting that are much more true to life.

Some are hesitant to grade work on something other than the basis of correctness and quality. You can factor this in to the grading system if you want. However, keep in mind that Guided Practice is a *formative* assessment, not a *summative* assessment—it is gauging student progress at the earliest point of development. So you can make an argument that this kind of assessment should be lightly graded, and then later you can hold very high standards for quality on the summative end.

Although a light touch is recommended on each *individual* Guided Practice, you can, however, make completion of Guided Practice a strong requirement for course grades. For example, in my calculus class, students must pass 12 out of 13 Guided Practices to be eligible for an A in the course, 10 out of 13 for a B, and 8 out of 13 for a C. Each individual assignment is simple to pass; repeated failures to do so will have severe effects on the course grade.

Q: *And now for the big question: How do I make sure students actually do the individual space activities?*

A: As mentioned earlier, this question is in a tie as the most asked question about flipped learning. Keep in mind that our students are adults in college, and unless we want to turn our classes into miniature surveillance states where students' every move is monitored, we cannot "make sure" they do anything. The best we can do is to create activities that they *want* to complete. To do this, we need to appeal to theoretical frameworks such as self-determination theory to understand what motivates students and cognitive load theory to understand how students manage work. The Guided Practice model is built with all of these considerations in mind.

The Guided Practice model is built on the premise of minimizing extrinsic load by giving a clear statement of the lesson under study, reducing cognitive load by clearly stating not only the learning objectives for the lesson but also which learning objectives are to be addressed prior to class and which do not need to be addressed for now, saving students the time and energy spent searching for learning resources by giving a well-constructed playlist of learning resources to save students the trouble of looking these up themselves (unless they want to), and giving a set of exercises that provides the "just enough" level of work. The Guided Practice model also aims to maximize the return on students' investment in time and energy by being tuned to the basic learning objectives and including nothing unnecessary for the individual space. By keeping cognitive load down to a minimum and making sure the germane load of the work is truly helpful, student motivation rises because it is neither merely busywork nor crushingly difficult, and in turn the likelihood of completion is raised.

The grading system described in the previous question—that is, grading Guided Practice on the basis of timeliness, completion, and effort only— also increases the likelihood of students completing and learning from the Guided Practice. Literally the only way not to get full credit on the assignment is to give less than a good-faith effort. Mistakes are not only okay but also valuable if made honestly. All one has to do is give a reasonable and reasonably complete attempt and turn it in on time. On the other hand, Guided Practice counts as a significant portion of the semester grade, so giving this consistent good-faith effort is essential. This sounds like extrinsic motivation, and it probably is, but it aims to be *autonomous* motivation and not *controlled* motivation. Students may not find completing a Guided Practice assignment intrinsically interesting for its own sake, but if it contains work that is "just enough" and tuned to important and clearly stated learning objectives—and if group space activities are consistently shown to require a solid understanding of the basic objectives that are addressed in the Guided Practice—then students will choose to complete the Guided Practice because they see that it is essential for learning the subject, and learning the subject is important for reasons that they believe in.

I have found in my own courses that very consistently about 90% of students complete the Guided Practice before every class with a pass grade. When I ask them about it, they say they complete them even though they can be hard work, because it's simple and risk free to give a good-faith effort, and because the rest of the class really does quite visibly use the results. Conversely, if individual space activities rely on controlled motivation (i.e., students do them because they are told to and not because they perceive any value in them personally) and have a large amount of extrinsic load, we shouldn't be surprised when students don't typically do them.

Step 7: Design and Construct Any Post–Group Space Activities

The work of learning the material in your lesson isn't done just because group space/class time is over. There could be learning objectives that take significant time and space to master, more time and space than are available in a class meeting. It's completely within the definition of *flipped learning* to have students do extended work to reach the uppermost levels of Bloom's taxonomy or to solidify the foundational ideas at the bottom of the taxonomy through postclass work—by any of a number of methods:

- Students might be tasked with completing a formal write-up of their in-class work to submit later as homework.

- Students might be given a postclass project that expands further on the objectives done in class.
- Students might be given a lab or service-learning assignment that applies the advanced objectives to something even higher up Bloom's taxonomy.
- Alternatively, students might be given more practice work that focuses on drill and mastery of the lower-level tasks on Bloom's taxonomy.

The possibilities are extensive here. However, as with any class and regardless of structure, post–group space activities afford a great chance to engage students in self-regulated learning activities such as the following:

- Reflecting back on their work in the group space and/or in the Guided Practice to identify methods of studying that worked well and methods that didn't work well
- Reflecting back on their motivation, affect, and behavior through a learning journal
- Making plans for how to spend the time in between group space activities
- Doing summative writing assignments to make connections between ideas and summarize what was done in the lesson

These correspond to Pintrich's "Phase 4" of self-regulated learning (reaction/reflection) over the lesson just completed and "Phase 1" (forethought/activity/planning) for what may be coming up (Pintrich 2004).

Carrying Out Step 7

- What advanced learning objectives from your list will need further attention after the in-class activity has been completed?
- What other learning objectives (basic or advanced) would benefit from further practice?
- What activities outside of class would provide continued engagement with the advanced learning objectives?
- What activities outside of class would provide further depth and breadth with basic learning objectives?
- Now make a list of activities to assign for postclass work. Estimate the time required for the average student to complete these activities.
- Write up the assignments you intend to give for postclass activity.
- Looking at the time estimates for the postclass activities and the time estimates for the preclass activities, determine whether your total time

requirements for out-of-class work average out to two to three times the amount of time spent in class. If it's more, then think of ways to trim back the size or extent of some of your activities.

Questions and Answers About Step 7

Q: *So, Step 7 seems no different from a traditionally structured course.*

A: In some ways that's right. Every course regardless of structure has these extended activities that take time and space not available to us in class. The big difference here in flipped learning is that we have devoted significant class time to drilling deeply into the advanced learning objectives, so every student has a reference point for those objectives as they move forward. For example, suppose students in our hypothetical algebra class from earlier were given a postclass assignment to go out and collect some data that have a roughly parabolic shape to them, find a formula that fits the data, and then use the quadratic formula to say something interesting about it. (Fitting a model to data would probably be an additional learning objective, or maybe this was an advanced objective from an earlier lesson.) If a student had trouble with the math, we could say, "Remember the activity we did in class that was similar to this? How did this work then?"

Q: *Is it possible that I could* not *focus class time on the most advanced objectives, and instead use a postclass activity for these and spend class time hitting sort of the "middle" of my objectives list?*

A: Using class time to cover most but not all of the advanced objectives and then saving the "most advanced" objectives for outside-class work *could* work well for students. But remember the point of flipped learning is to work on those most difficult tasks *while there is support readily available.* How the objectives are addressed is up to you, but do keep in mind that we want to put students in a position where they are not encountering new and advanced objectives when they are apart from a corresponding level of help and connection.

Summing Up

We've introduced a seven-step process for constructing a single lesson in a class that is structured on flipped learning principles:

1. Come up with a brief but comprehensive list of learning objectives for your lesson.

2. Remix the learning objectives so that they appear in order of cognitive complexity.
3. Create a rough design of the group space activity you intend students to do.
4. Go back to the learning objectives list and split it into basic and advanced objectives.
5. Finish the design of the group space activity.
6. Design and construct the individual space activity.
7. Design and construct any post–group space activities you intended students to do.

This is an outline that can be replicated over and over again for an entire semester's or quarter's worth of lessons. With practice, these steps will provide a comfortable rhythm that makes preparing flipped learning lessons predictable and familiar, if not easy.

This method fits into the overall course design model we borrowed from Dee Fink for planning out the overall scheme of learning activities in the course. Coupled with the other levels of Fink's design model, we now have a complete method for designing flipped learning environments at both the "macro" and "micro" levels, in terms of both the big-picture structure of the course and the day-to-day business of planning lessons.

However, neither Fink's course design model nor our seven steps nor the Guided Practice model are surefire guarantees for creating the ultimate flipped learning course. You will need to maintain the "P" in the early definition of *flipped learning* and be a professional educator, maintaining awareness of the needs of students and making adjustments when their needs and your constraints call for it. The best learning, after all, tends to happen *outside* the structures we build for it.

PART THREE

TEACHING AND LEARNING IN A FLIPPED LEARNING ENVIRONMENT

7

VARIATIONS ON A THEME

As we've learned about the history and theoretical bases for flipped learning and as we've seen how to design courses with flipped learning experiences in mind, one thing should be clear: *Flipped learning is not just one thing or one way of conducting a course*. Flipped learning, rather, is a "big tent" under which can fit many different disciplines, institutional types, student demographics, and even pedagogical methods. Flipped learning is at home just as much in the STEM disciplines as it is in the social sciences, humanities, fine arts, and preprofessional and vocational studies. It fits just as well with small classes as large classes, with introductory courses as with advanced seminars, with specialized niche courses as with broad general education courses. Flipped learning is a universal platform that can be used and adapted to practically any situation.

Even so, when we typically think about flipped learning, we tend to have a certain kind of environment in mind—namely, a class that meets face-to-face on a fixed schedule in a physical classroom and that *uses* high technology frequently and therefore has free *access* to high technology. Many descriptions of "the flipped classroom" take this particular situation as an assumption and build an entire pedagogical model around it.

However, we know that reality suggests differently.

First, more and more courses in colleges and universities are offered either partially or wholly online, often without face-to-face meetings, fixed schedules, or even physical classrooms in which they meet. One study of two-year colleges (Lokken, Womer, and Mullins 2012) shows that although overall enrollment at these institutions declined by 3.5% from fall 2013 to fall 2014, enrollment in online courses offered by two-year institutions increased by 4.68% in the same time period. Indeed, the increase in online enrollments at two-year institutions has been above 4% per year each year since 2009 and has been as high as 9% per year. This popularity of online courses is not just limited to two-year institutions. A 2012 report by the

National Center for Education Statistics (Ginder and Stearns 2012) shows that 21.8%—more than one in five—of all undergraduate students enrolled in Title IV four-year institutions in the United States are enrolled in at least one "distance education" course (which means at least some of the course is online). Among graduate students, this percentage is 24.3%. And these data are from 2014 and 2012; if the trends indicated in those studies have continued over the intervening years, the numbers of students enrolled in online courses will likely be higher, perhaps much more so. The data indicate that we can no longer assume that a college class necessarily looks like it did in yesteryear, meeting three times a week, at the same times of the day, in person in a fixed location.

Second, and on the other end of the spectrum, many educational environments cannot assume the availability of high technology such as easy access to modern computers or to broadband Internet. Many universities and colleges, especially those serving remote areas or impoverished regions, aren't able to provide the level of technological access to students (and many students won't have that access themselves) that one typically associates with flipped learning, with its use of online video and other technological amenities. By the same token, some instructors who are in situations where there is access to technology may choose not to incorporate high technology into their teaching, out of preference or because it may not make sense for the pedagogical activities they have planned. Either way, it is not a safe assumption to say that flipped learning *must* be couched in a context of high technology.

Third, regardless of the technological context, it may not be the case that instructors will choose to convert an *entire course* over to a flipped learning environment. Rather, an instructor may wish to use a kind of hybrid model, with some parts of the course using flipped learning and others keeping a traditional model. Our treatment of flipped learning, especially course design, has assumed that the entire course is going to be flipped, but this need not be the desired case.

In this chapter we will address how flipped learning can be implemented effectively in each of these variations on the basic theme.

Flipped Learning in Online and Hybrid Courses

As mentioned previously, the number of college students (in the United States, at least) is on the rise and has been so for several years now. Online courses pose a number of unique pedagogical questions, and as they become more commonplace, best practices for designing and conducting these courses to maximize the results for students will continue to evolve. There are many questions to answer about the design of effective online courses, and in this book we do not intend to address all of those. Other sources such as Michelle Miller's (2014) *Minds Online: Teaching Effectively with Technology* do an excellent job of taking the comprehensive view. Here we merely want to address whether it is possible to have a flipped learning environment in a course where there may not be any class meetings or any physical classroom.

First, we need to understand that "online" courses may take many different forms. The Online Learning Consortium, one of the leading organizations for providing professional development in online learning, categorizes courses in six different ways (Sener 2015):

1. *Traditional classroom courses.* Predominantly held in face-to-face meetings in fixed locations, the format of these meetings can vary, including lectures, workshops, and laboratories; computer usage may be involved. But the course *meets* and it does so in a physical place.

2. *Synchronous distributed courses.* Web-based technologies provide real-time instruction to students in a remote location. For example, a traditional classroom course that has a live video feed available to students at a job site would be a synchronous distributed course. It is "synchronous" because all students are engaging in the group space at the same time.

3. *Web-enhanced courses.* Online activity complements but does not reduce the number of class meetings. Many flipped learning environments that use a traditional classroom structure could be considered web-enhanced if there is a requirement for completing online activities such as watching video or engaging in computer simulations. Note that web-enhanced courses can use online activity to replace *activities* in a course, perhaps a significant percentage of them, but this category does not have any *meetings* replaced with online activity.

4. *Blended/hybrid classroom courses.* A significant percentage—often more than 20% but less than 100%—of traditional classroom meetings are replaced by online activities. For example, a class normally meeting on a Monday/Wednesday/Friday schedule that has its Monday meeting (or its Monday and Friday meetings) replaced by online activities would be considered blended or hybrid.

5. *Blended/hybrid online courses.* "Mirror image" of blended classroom courses. Here most course activity takes place online but some small amount of face-to-face classroom activity is required. For example, a course whose group space consists of participation in online discussion boards but then meets in a classroom once a month for testing would be a hybrid online course.

6. *Online courses.* At the far end of the spectrum, courses where 100% of the course activities take place online—both the individual space and the group space, using the nomenclature we've developed for flipped learning.

Note that there is yet another kind of online course—the MOOC. Although experiments with MOOCs date back to 2006 (Davidson 2013), MOOCs first entered the public consciousness through a course on artificial intelligence offered by Sebastian Thrun and Peter Norvig through Stanford University in 2011 (Ng and Widom 2014), which was opened for free to the general public and drew over 160,000 online registrants. Although the debate over the meaning of MOOCs for higher education at large still persists and MOOC offerings continue to expand, the interest among two- and four-year institutions for providing MOOCs remains somewhat low. In 2014, for example, it was found that 70% of community colleges in the United States have no plans to incorporate existing MOOC content into their traditional course offerings (up from 42% in 2012), and only 5% indicated that they are developing or offering MOOCs of their own. In 2015, just over 550 four-year universities offered MOOCs worldwide, a rather small amount compared to 2,765 Title IV degree-granting four-year institutions just in the United States as of 2008 (National Center for Education Statistics n.d.). Therefore, although the massive scale of MOOCs raises interesting questions for flipped learning and its notion of "group space," we will not include MOOCs in our discussion here due to their relative infrequency among rank-and-file faculty.

For many institutions, the exact definition of what is a *traditional* versus *hybrid* versus *online* course is determined by the institution, or a committee within the institution. For example, my home institution defines a *hybrid course* to be one that intends to replace at least 15%, but less than 100%, of the course meeting time (about six hours in a three-credit semester course) with online instruction; anything less than this is considered a traditional classroom. An online course meets 100% of the time online (although there may not be any synchronous meetings), and there is no distinction between hybrid classroom and hybrid online courses, or between traditional and web-enhanced courses as we saw defined by the Online Learning Consortium earlier.

If you are introducing significant amounts of online materials as part of a conversion to a flipped learning model in a course, it's important to check your institution's guidelines to see how these courses are classified, and also to be aware of any additional actions you may need to take. These institutional definitions of *online, hybrid,* and *traditional courses* could have significant implications for course development and for student registration. For example, some institutions may define a *hybrid course* to be one in which a certain percentage of the *course content* is delivered online, regardless of how the class meeting schedule is affected. Therefore, converting a traditional-model class into a flipped learning model, in which live lectures are replaced with online video that students are required to watch, could reclassify the course from "traditional" to "hybrid" and therefore could require the instructor to get approval from the college or university to run it. In other institutions, hybrid courses (however they are classifed) may have different tuition and fee structures for students, and students may be limited as to the number of hybrid or online courses they can take, so the possibility of a course inadvertently being reclassified as "hybrid" or "online" could have significant consequences for students.

But if you are teaching a class that is already classified as "hybrid" or "online," is it possible to introduce a flipped learning structure to that course? And if so, how?

Throughout this book, we have been careful not to privilege any one form of class structure when considering flipped learning design. In particular, we have avoided the use of the term *class time* to refer to flipped learning activities (as in "students get first contact with new concepts *before class*") because this presupposes the existence of a synchronous face-to-face meeting time and space. In other words, our definition of *flipped learning* has made room for online and hybrid courses from the ground up. All we need to adapt hybrid and online courses to a flipped learning model is to consider *individual space* and *group space* in those courses and what students will be doing in those spaces.

Hybrid Courses

In a hybrid course, whether "hybrid classroom" or "hybrid online," one approach to flipped learning is to use the face-to-face portion of the course as the group space, and everything else is the individual space. For example, if a hybrid course has 50% of its class meetings online, then the online portion of the course can be used for individual space activities such as working through Guided Practice, engaging in online homework, or working on writing assignments whereas the remaining face-to-face group meetings become the group space, much as they would in a traditional classroom course designed along flipped learning lines.

Although such a basic division of labor makes sense from a scheduling standpoint, students might be better served to have *more group space* in the course. After all, the group space is where we want students to engage in the most difficult and complex tasks in the course, while they have their classmates and an instructor present to lend a hand. The more of this group space experience we can give students, the better off their learning might be. It might also be the case that the precise scheduling of the hybrid course might have so few face-to-face meetings that we cannot rely on those meetings as the only time group space happens; for example, some hybrid courses meet only in alternate weeks, and some only for tests and exams (where the meeting is specifically set aside for something other than group space work).

To provide more group space experience to students in a hybrid course, part of the group space must be conducted online. This group space does not have to be *synchronous*—that is, with all students online at the same time so that they can interact in real time. Indeed, some hybrid courses and many fully online courses *cannot* have synchronous meetings because of the disparity of schedules among the students. Instead, effective online group spaces must be set up and maintained by the instructor (or the course assistants, if any). Effective online group space can be realized in a number of ways:

- *Discussion boards.* The standard way to establish student-student and student-instructor interaction in an online setting, and there are many resources available on how to conduct effective discussion board activity (Cornell University Center for Teaching Excellence n.d.; Rovai 2007).
- *Team-based chat tools.* Tools such as Slack (http://slack.com) are an alternative to discussion boards (Wan 2015). They combine the structure of a discussion board with the freeflowing real-time conversation of instant messaging, highly reminiscent of Internet Relay Chat (IRC) channels. In these environments, different channels are set up for different aspects of the course—for example, one channel for each assignment along with channels for ongoing discussion of the syllabus and for random talk among students—and students drop in and interact when needed. The chat takes place in real time but is saved as a searchable archive.
- *Audio-based interaction tools.* Tools such as VoiceThread (https://voicethread.com) provide an alternative to text-based tools like discussion boards or chat programs by allowing users to post media with a voice-over, and then others can leave comments in text, audio, or video to create asynchronous participation around a central group of readings, problems, or multimedia.

Some combination of these technological tools could also be used; indeed, many tools in one category are built to allow interaction with tools in another category. For example, content created in VoiceThread can be embedded on many online discussion forums by using basic HTML embed code that can be generated using VoiceThread.

Online Courses

Fully online courses present unique challenges to flipped learning, but those challenges are not insurmountable. It merely takes creativity in setting up the individual and group spaces and diligence in managing them.

Online courses that are *synchronous* (that have regularly scheduled group meetings online) offer a simple way of delineating individual space from group space: The group space can be the online meeting, and individual space can be everything else. Getting students to work together actively in an online synchronous setting can be tricky; the instructor is limited by the capabilities of the technology being used. For example, some web meeting tools such as WebEx (www.webex.com) have the capability of forming "breakout" rooms, allowing small groups to split off from an online meeting of a larger group and meet together online, then reform as a large group. This feature allows an online synchronous meeting to run very similarly to how a group meeting would run in a face-to-face class. But if the technology used doesn't allow breakout sessions, more creativity is required, the amount of which depends on the severity of the limitations. However, it's important to keep in mind that in flipped learning we still want to use the group space as a space for active learning; we have to resist the temptation to use it primarily for direct instruction despite any limitations in software.

Online courses that are *asynchronous* have no scheduled group meetings; students engage with the course on their own schedules, and there may be no single time when all students can be together online. In one sense, an asynchronous online course never meets; in another very real sense, it is *always* meeting—students could be accessing the course and encountering learning activities at any moment, and student group activities can happen spontaneously outside any instructor-mandated schedule. In such courses, the concepts of *group space* and *individual space* must be carefully defined and the expectations for those spaces made clear; additionally, enough flexibility needs to be maintained to allow students the freedom to adapt the course to their schedules (which is often the main reason students take online courses).

Regardless of whether the group space takes place online or face-to-face, the *purpose* of the group space in a flipped learning environment is still the same: It is to be used as a *dynamic, interactive learning environment where the educator guides students as they apply concepts and engage creatively in the subject matter*. To do this, the individual space must still be used for first contact with new concepts in the form of structured activity.

How might this look for the different kinds of online courses we have described? Let's look at two case studies from real courses, to see how flipped learning was implemented in different contexts.

The first of these consists of the hybrid courses taught by Mark Hale, associate professor of higher education at Dallas Baptist University, whom we first met in chapter 3. In addition to his many administrative duties, he teaches hybrid courses for graduate students, including Legal Issues and Finance in Higher Education and Philosophy of Higher Education. When Hale first decided to convert these courses into a flipped learning environment, the courses employed a schedule that alternated weeks between online and face-to-face work—fully online one week, then fully face-to-face the next. As we mentioned in chapter 3, Hale felt that this schedule wasn't serving students well; many students didn't prepare adequately in the online week for the activities that took place in the face-to-face meetings in the following week. So Hale changed the schedule so that the course met once a week face-to-face for 75 minutes, and the remaining activities during the same week were all online.

Hale used the 75-minute face-to-face meeting as the sole instance of group space in his course ("Quadrant 3" and "Quadrant 4" in his formulation that we discussed in chapter 3). All the online activities were considered "individual space"—there for students to gain meaningful first contact with new concepts individually, through guided and structured assignments.

Note that this formulation takes a significant portion—half, to be precise—of the meeting time of the class, which in a traditional classroom setting would likely be considered "group space," and turns it into all individual space. Therefore, in one sense, the class is "meeting" half as often. However, Hale found there was no drop-off in the quality or quantity of learning in the course even though there was only roughly half of the group space. Indeed, he reports:

> The response was overwhelmingly positive. My students were much more engaged with the material. Many requested additional flipped learning opportunities. Those that stayed on the schedule and completed the prep work did better in the class. It was easy to tell who had reviewed the course content prior to the group space meeting. At the outset of the class I shared the quadrant format and explained how the course would flow. I also explained that if they did not do the prep work (reading/course content/assessment, etc.) they would not be prepared to actively participate in the group space activities. This served as an incentive to arrive at group space ready to contribute. The group space time moved very quickly and required a tight schedule to cover the required material. It also required me

to have several different ideas about the activities and exercises I would use in class for a variety of possible needs, as I only had a limited amount of time to prep for the group space upon review of the session assessments. (personal e-mail communication, June 23, 2016)

In other words, aside from an accelerated pace, the students experienced deeper learning and a more positive experience in the flipped setting than in the traditional setting despite only having half as much group space. Hale's experience suggests that investing more time in well-designed individual space activities might make the group space much more efficient and fruitful.

Still, for those who might be nervous about taking away group space, alternative forms of group space could have been used in a hybrid course like Hale's. For example, a dedicated time frame (say, a 12-hour period following the submission of an individual space activity) could be set up during which students are directed to a discussion board or team-chat environment to debate a question and then report back to the whole group. This is "group space" even though students may not be together at the same time in the same place—indeed, the students could well be thousands of miles apart—because the *work* is being done collaboratively.

The other case study to examine is a fully online course. This course is actually my own, an online version of Grand Valley State University's standard Calculus 1 course. In an ordinary face-to-face setting, the course meets in four 50-minute segments each week for 14 weeks, with one day per week in a 50-minute lab setting in which students are working on collaborative, technology-focused activities. In 2015, a section of the course was designed as a fully online, asynchronous course that was offered during a 12-week summer term. Being asynchronous, there were no class meetings at all and no fixed location. (Indeed, the students in the course tended to be widely dispersed geographically.)

The course was broken into 12 "modules," each focused around a topical question in the course (e.g., *How do we calculate change?* and *How do we find the best value of a function?*). Each module lasted exactly one week, defined to run from 12:01 a.m. Monday to 11:59 p.m. the following Sunday. The weekly structure was further broken down as follows:

- The first two days of the week (Monday, Tuesday) were set aside to be focused solely on individual space work. Students were given a Guided Practice for the module. This typically covered two sections of material—a fairly significant amount, so students were expected to spend the first two days of the module in individual space, doing the reading and viewing and responding to the exercises. There was also online homework for each module, which students were free to attempt during this two-day individual space period. Also each week, a different group of students was put in charge of managing the class's online discussion board; each member of this "Discussion Team" was given a different "Problem of the Week" that probed deeper into the concepts of the module. Each student on the Discussion Team was tasked with writing up a proposed solution to his Problem of the Week and posting it to a private discussion-team-only group on the discussion board, where the other team members and I would look it over for errors and make suggestions. The Guided Practice was always due at 11:59 p.m. on Tuesday nights, and the student solutions for the Problems of the Week were to be included in a public post on the discussion board by 8:00 a.m. Wednesday morning.

- On Wednesdays, the week shifted from individual space work to group space work. Students were expected to work out their own solutions to the Problems of the Week, compare their work with the student solutions, and ask questions about that work in follow-up areas on the discussion board. This ongoing discussion often took place over four to five days; it was the class's version of having students go to the board and work out problems for class discussion. Another form of group space work was ongoing discussion of online homework problems, which students were free to address on the discussion board.

In a face-to-face format using flipped learning (which I have also taught), each meeting would cover roughly one-third of a "module" in the online class, and students would be completing a Guided Practice of one-third the length before each meeting. During class, students would be working on problems very similar to the Problems of the Week and presenting their work to each other. In the online course, students did roughly the same *things* but in different groupings—with two entire days spent in individual space and then five days spent in asynchronous group space, contributing to and reflecting on the discussion as their schedule permitted.

There was also a postclass phase in the online course with students completing short "miniprojects" (which replaced the in-class lab session) throughout the week and creating personal videos in which they worked through past online homework problems at a whiteboard.

This online structure for calculus doesn't seek to replicate the in-class experience; this seems impossible without having actual meeting times, which we in fact were not allowed to have (in order to accommodate all students regardless of schedule). Instead, it refactored the individual space from three separated periods (before each class meeting) into one larger block, and then repurposed the rest of the week for free-flowing ongoing group space work.

In this discussion of online and hybrid courses, we mainly wish to emphasize that flipped learning works here just as it works in face-to-face courses, and one does not need a classroom or class meetings to have a "flipped classroom." In fact, the growing prevalence of hybrid and online courses provides ample reason to migrate away from the term *flipped classroom* and focus on the *learning* that students do regardless of the physical context. The only thing that has to be kept in mind is individual and group space, and how these will be used in the ways that flipped learning suggests.

Flipped Learning in a Low-Tech Setting

In the previous section on hybrid and online courses, we pointed out a common stereotype of flipped learning environments—namely, that they require a classroom and class meetings. A similar stereotype has to do with technology. Many descriptions of flipped learning presuppose that high technology—including such technologies as high-speed Internet, online video, personal devices capable of accessing streaming video, and classroom technologies like classroom response devices—is omnipresent and readily available. In fact, one recent study attempting to do a comprehensive meta-analysis of flipped learning courses actually *excludes* courses from the study if they do not use online video, indicating that a course cannot be considered "flipped" if online video is not used (Lowell Bishop and Verleger 2013). The seemingly inextricable relationship between flipped learning and technology should cause us to ask, *Can flipped learning be implemented where there is little to no high technology available?*

In addition to addressing the technological stereotype of flipped learning courses, this question addresses flipped learning in several pedagogical scenarios that are quite common in higher education:

- Some instructors have technology available to them (and so do their students), but for personal or pedagogical reasons choose not to use it.
- Some colleges and universities may not have the physical infrastructure or financial resources to afford technologies such as high-speed Internet, video streaming, or classroom response devices. Or the technology may be *present* but *access* to it is limited. For example, a university I once visited in a developing nation had exactly one computer lab on campus, which was enclosed in a locked, barred room only open a few hours a day out of concerns that the equipment would be stolen.

- Some *institutions* may have access to high technology, but its *students* do not. Colleges and universities that serve impoverished communities encounter this scenario all too frequently.

We do not wish flipped learning to be a pedagogical model available only to those in a position of privilege. Flipped learning can benefit *all* students (indeed, this is what sets it apart from proto-versions of flipped learning such as the Oxford model), and therefore it's worth considering whether flipped learning can be accomplished in a technologically minimalist setting.

Fortunately, it appears that although flipped learning does benefit from a rich technological context, high technology is not necessary to implement it. As with online and hybrid courses, all we need to keep in mind is how we want to organize individual space and group space, and how to use them in accordance with flipped learning principles.

In a low-tech course, the individual space is still to be used as an opportunity for students to gain first contact with new concepts through structured activities. "Direct instruction" in this setting often takes the form of recorded lectures. If the instructor chooses to keep lectures as the primary form of direct instruction, those lectures do not have to be converted to recorded video. They could just as easily be made available as audio recordings and then placed online or made available to students through physical media such as flash drives, CDs, or even audio cassettes. There are advantages to using audio instead of video: Digital audio recordings are smaller in size, require less bandwidth for streaming or downloading; and regardless of format, audio can be played back on a variety of inexpensive devices. Replacing video lectures with audio lectures plus printed outlines or lecture questions would be a lower-tech alternative. However, lectures need not be used at all! Direct instruction can easily take the form of readings (online or physical) that are structured through a Guided Practice assignment "layered" onto the readings, in which students engage with portions of the text, guided by clearly stated learning objectives and exercises that help students gain the insights they need for the group space.

It should be noted here, again, that simply giving students a block of readings to complete before class and then expecting productive discussion in class is not likely to result in flipped learning, because of the lack of structure given to students as they encounter new ideas for the first time. In order to help students truly prepare for the group space, and in order to help them develop the habits of self-regulated learning we have discussed, structure is key—whether it comes from Guided Practice or some other form of structure you provide.

The individual space assignments (Guided Practice or something else) are often distributed to students online, through a learning management system. If the students or the institution have extremely limited access to such a system or the technology it requires, assignments can simply be given out on paper at the end of a class period before it is due. As far as submitting those assignments goes, students can do them on paper and bring them to class on the day they are due. However, note that submitting the Guided Practice work *on the day of the group space* makes it difficult to quickly assess student learning from the individual space and make adjustments to the group space; it's much better if students can submit this work *prior* to class somehow, through e-mail or through placing it in a physical inbox.

For group space activities, technology is not so much of an issue unless you choose a pedagogical model that relies on it. Peer instruction, which we have discussed earlier, typically is such a model, because it uses classroom response devices ("clickers") to gather student votes on conceptual questions. However, even here there are lower-tech alternatives. The lowest-tech alternative is to have students use colored index cards to indicate their choices in a multiple-choice question (blue for "1," red for "2," etc.), and hold them up on the instructor's command with their eyes shut so as not to see other students' votes; or have students write their responses in large font on pieces of paper that are held up. A slightly higher-tech version of this is the "plicker," a sort of reverse-clicker method where students are given printed pieces of paper to hold up as their responses to a multiple-choice question with each response on a different printed page with a QR code on it, and the instructor scans the room with a tablet or smartphone using a specialized app that scans the papers and tallies the results (https://plickers .com). Even a pedagogical method as traditionally technology heavy as peer instruction can be carried out, albeit with less efficiency, with lower tech or no tech at all.

As a case study in flipped learning with minimalist technology, we consider the literature courses of Haerin (Helen) Shin at Vanderbilt University. In Shin's course, students do the readings for the class *in class* rather than before, in the form of communal "close readings" (Shin 2015). Shin chooses very short texts for her group space activities, such as the 155-word short story "On Exactitude in Science" by Jorge Luis Borges; with such a short text, the students read together in class and pore over each word and phrase in an intensive discussion. This stands in marked contrast to the traditional model of literature courses, flipped or otherwise, in which students do all readings before class and then discuss in class; Shin uses her model of close reading to capture the spontaneity and synergy of a group of people reading something together for the first time, at the same time. And this requires no technology whatsoever.

So although technology does tend to make flipped learning easier to implement, it's not necessary.

"Partially Flipped" Course Design

As a final variation on the basic theme of flipped learning, we will consider the question of *whether flipped learning can be done as part, but not all, of a course.* That is, we will now consider whether it's possible to have a course partly consisting of a traditional model, with the group space being used for first contact with new concepts and for direct instruction and the individual space being used for further exploration; other parts of the course are the opposite. We will call this a "partially flipped" design.

Before we address this, let's first consider why such a design might be attractive to instructors. Often, instructors consider a partially flipped design because they are interested in flipped learning but not ready to commit to designing an entire course around it. They want to test-drive flipped learning on a limited trial basis and see how it goes, and perhaps they want to have an exit strategy in case students become uncomfortable with the flipped environment. Other times, a partially flipped design is being used because it makes more pedagogical sense for the course being taught than a fully flipped design—for example, if the course has a significant amount of material that requires direct instruction and this direct instruction is impractical to deliver via recorded video or other media. In still other contexts, a partially flipped design might be chosen because the instructor intends to "phase in" flipped learning over the course of a semester, with the first few weeks traditional but gradually introducing more and more flipping throughout the term until the course is fully flipped by the last few weeks of the term.

Whatever the reason, any attempt to use this model should be done with care. The main potential issue here is *student expectations* and the reception of mixed signals about the student's role in the course.

When students come into a course, they come with preconceptions about their roles and the instructor's role. Overwhelmingly often, the preconception is that *the instructor transmits knowledge and I receive it.* Witness how often student course evaluations respond to active learning by saying, "The instructor didn't teach." The default setting for students' perceived role in the class is that they are there to listen and take notes during lecture, and then go do homework between classes (that will look very similar to the lectures). Students may not enjoy this role, but it is familiar and safe. As we will discuss in chapter 8, introducing flipped learning radically reforms the roles of student and instructor in the class, and although the benefits are great, this change takes considerable time and effort to internalize.

The problem with a partially flipped design is that students are made to jump back and forth between the preconceived roles in the course and the new roles defined by flipped learning. Many students begin to wonder what the "rules" are for the course; many will enter the flipped lessons of the course and either not take them seriously because they know that lecture will come back soon enough, or else they will be confused about whether they are supposed to prepare for class or not. The jump to a flipped learning environment can be so great a conceptual leap for many students that it is better to go "all in" and have a single, consistent set of expectations—no matter how uncomfortable—for students to follow for the entire course. Although the adjustment can be hard, it's easier when they are completely immersed in the environment.

That said, there are ways to implement a partially flipped design that avoid this complication. In particular, a partially flipped design can be used to introduce flipped learning gradually to a class, in such a way that the initial meetings of the course are completely traditional in format, and gradually more flipped learning activities are introduced until the course operates entirely under a flipped learning model in the latter part of the course. This approach follows the concept of *gradual release of responsibility* (GRR), an idea first introduced in literacy training by David Pearson and Margaret Gallagher (1983) and expanded by Douglas Fisher and Nancy Frey (2013). Instruction in the GRR model follows four distinct phases:

1. *Focused lesson.* Instruction begins with a time for direct instruction in which the teacher demonstrates or models what she is thinking about a particular concept.
2. *Guided instruction.* Next, the instructor meets with students in groups with the purpose of having them begin to take over some of the responsibility for their work, while providing ready guidance during the process.
3. *Collaborative learning.* Then students work in heterogeneous groups, still with guidance available from the instructor but with more responsibility; students are often required to produce evidence of their individual progress independently of the progress of the group.
4. *Independent tasks.* Finally, students are given tasks that require completely independent work.

The GRR model is clearly very similar to the flipped learning model, and the two fit together well. In a partially flipped model, the GRR approach can be applied as follows:

- In the beginning of the semester, the focused lesson and guided instruction phases can take place entirely during class, with collaborative learning filling in any time left over; then the remaining collaborative learning tasks along with independent tasks are relegated to individual space. (This is just the traditional model of course design.)

- Then, at some point early in the semester, the focused lesson portion and some or all of the guided instruction phases can be moved to individual space, and the time liberated from the group space can be used for additional guided instruction along with collaborative learning and independent tasks.
- Over the course of the semester, more and more of the guided instruction can be shifted to the individual space, until eventually all of it is. This places more and more of the focus of the group space on collaborative learning and independent tasks, until by (say) the final third of the semester all of the focused lesson and guided instruction phases are in individual space and the group space is entirely focused on collaborative learning and independent tasks—which is the flipped learning model.

The idea is that the course *starts* traditional and *ends* flipped, and partially flipped design is employed to gradually release responsibility to students.

This is the approach taken by Jennifer Ebbler, who teaches classics at the University of Texas at Austin. She decided to redesign her Introduction to Ancient Rome course, a general education course taken by around 300 students at a time, to a flipped learning model to attempt to increase student engagement and achievement. Her first iteration, which she dubbed "Rome 1.0," used a fully flipped design throughout the semester. She encountered significant resistance from students under this model for various reasons, to the point where students even created an "I Hate the Flipped Classroom" Facebook group to protest the course. Undeterred, Ebbler reconsidered some elements of the design of her course, and in "Rome 2.0" offered the following year, she took a "gradual release of responsibility" approach:

- The beginning of the course was done in a purely traditional model, with in-class lectures and homework and writing assignments done in the individual space.
- Each week after the first week, Ebbler began to put more and more of the lectures online and had students watch them before class, and then used class time for active learning tasks including clicker questions, large-group discussions, debates, and role-playing activities.
- By the middle of the semester, *all* of the lectures were online and *all* of the group space was used for active learning.

Using this model, Ebbler encountered *no* significant resistance from students, and students' performance on standard exams and quizzes rose significantly. Ebbler's experience suggests that a partially flipped design that is used to phase in flipped learning can be the best model for certain audiences.

If a gradual phase-in of flipped learning design doesn't fit the needs of the course, another way to use partial flipping is by identifying a regularly recurring portion of the course and have that portion *always* use a flipped learning design. For example:

- If a course meets four hours per week and one of those hours is a laboratory or recitation section, then that one hour naturally lends itself to intensive collaborative activity (indeed, it would suffer if it were used for direct instruction). That one hour is a perfect candidate for flipped learning and can be designed for that once a week. This one-hour section has a Guided Practice assignment attached to it in which students might meet a particular kind of problem or discussion question for the first time, and students will be expected to become fluent with basic learning objectives related to that new concept, and then spend the entire group space for this one meeting in active learning work.
- If the course has regularly recurring timed exams, then review days for those exams can be structured using flipped learning. Students would complete structured assignments that introduce review problems that may be new to the students but use concepts they have learned previously; then they spend the entire review session in active collaborative work.
- The instructor can simply designate one day a week to follow a flipped learning design—for example, "Flipped Fridays." In this way, students learn the expectations for that once-a-week meeting, and following the "rules" for flipped learning comes a little easier.

From personal experience, I still believe that complete immersion in a flipped learning environment is best for students—making sure that instructors also extend themselves generously to give support as students work—but it's possible to implement flipped learning partially, or gradually, in ways that can be quite effective if the situation calls for it.

What's Next

You might have noticed that in some of the descriptions of variations on flipped learning, some elephants in the room have made their presence

known: Specifically, we've mentioned the possibility of students showing resistance, displeasure, even outright revolt against the flipped learning
model. If you are an instructor curious about flipped learning, particularly if
you are not protected by tenure, the possibility of mass student displeasure
at this model can't be very reassuring. Or if you are an experienced user of
flipped learning, perhaps you have experienced this yourself and are wondering if, and how, it can be avoided. In the next chapter, we will take up this
and other thorny questions about living with flipped learning and making it
a sustainable career practice.

8

LIVING AND WORKING
WITH FLIPPED LEARNING

Throughout this book, we have examined flipped learning from the standpoint of using it in our classes. What is flipped learning? Where did it arise, and what teaching and learning problems was it invented to solve? What is the theoretical basis for flipped learning, and what does current research say about it? How do we design a course around flipped learning, and how can we plan a lesson using flipped learning principles? All of these questions are pertinent for any instructor curious about flipped learning, or interested in improving practice.

But there are other questions about flipped learning that are just as pertinent that don't involve course design, theoretical frameworks, or even pedagogy. They pertain instead to the fact that instructors are *professionals* who have to maintain progress and success across a variety of professional areas in order to advance in their jobs, as well as *human beings* with personal reasons for being interested in flipped learning and teaching in general alongside personal desires to be happy and productive in their life and work. When instructors ask these kinds of questions, they take many forms, such as:

- If I try out flipped learning, will my students hate it, and will I have to deal with a toxic student-professor relationship the entire semester?
- If I use flipped learning, will I be endangering my chances at tenure or reappointment?
- If I use flipped learning in my courses, will this take so much time that I won't be able to work on anything else, or have a life?

This chapter is intended to discuss *these* kinds of questions.

In doing so, we are not only bringing the book to a conclusion but also bringing it full circle. In the preface, we learned how flipped learning, despite all good intentions, can be done poorly, which leads to stressful situations in the classroom. Any instructor who truly cares about teaching and about students will take such failures personally to some degree. "Flipped failure" is not only an experience I have had with my own classes but also an experience shared by many instructors I have met—and a point of worry for many others who are curious about flipped learning but are uncertain about the environment it will create. We can't fully eliminate the possibility for negative experiences with flipped learning or any kind of pedagogy without taking the human element fully out of teaching. But we can minimize these contingencies and work to make the use of flipped learning the cornerstone of a productive and student-centered approach to our work. As we end this book, we're going to look at some practices that can create a positive, enjoyable, and productive environment for both instructors and students.

What Is the Ideal Outcome of a Flipped Learning Environment?

As one thinks about flipped learning, it is almost impossible to avoid thinking about the worst-case scenarios, or what could go wrong. Indeed, some instructors will dwell on those worst-case outcomes and decide not to use flipped learning because of them. It is not entirely bad to think about what could go wrong, to the extent that it makes us think about *planning* for those worst-case scenarios and being ready for them, which we will consider in due course in this chapter. But, before we discuss what could go *wrong*, it is important to think about what could go *right*.

If you have read through the rest of this book, or if you have a reasonable idea of what flipped learning is and how you might implement it in your courses, stop right now and take five minutes to write down a paragraph that describes what the *ideal outcome* of using flipped learning would be for your students. What would they be doing? What would they be able to do? What kind of learning environment would your class be, day in and day out? What would be *great* about it? What positive impacts would it have on the lives of your students, not only during the semester but also years from now?

Take five minutes and answer those questions, optimistically and with a best-case scenario in mind, and write down your thoughts.

You might write something like this:

> Ever since installing flipped learning as the basic model for my teaching in this course, the course has been transformed. Students no longer come to class and expect me both to keep them awake and to spoon-feed them. Instead, they take charge of their own learning; they show up to class, if not 100% fluent on basic learning objectives then at least fluent enough

to have questions in which they are invested; they pursue those questions vigorously with their classmates; and they participate in high-level cognitive activities with full engagement. It gets downright *loud* in my class sometimes because there is so much activity, and all that activity is purposeful. Outside of class, students are learning slowly but surely to self-regulate their learning—they no longer ask me to reteach the material but rather if I have any suggestions for good YouTube resources where they can teach themselves. I still see some of the same struggles and misconceptions as always, but now they are *good* struggles, *honest* struggles where the students are really aware of what they know and what they don't know and are doing what they can to close the gap. In class, I am no longer *talking at* students but *working with* students—working *with* them and not *against* them. The adversarial relationship that I used to have with students in this class is now more like a client/consultant relationship, where my clients (the students) are working with me (the consultant) to cocreate something that they want, that is of equal value to both. Once the class is done, the students may forget some of the fine points of the content of the class but they *won't* forget how to learn on their own, or be responsible with their time, or how to give and receive help, or how to take initiative to pose and pursue questions that matter to them. And the biggest change of all? I'm finally *happy* with this course—and *because* of it.

An environment where students are happy, productive, and growing into the lifelong learners we want them to be—and in which we are happy, productive, and successful as a result—is the ideal we all wish to have. The trick is managing the inevitable nonideal situations that will come up in the process.

Common Issues for Students With Flipped Learning

Although flipped learning is enjoying an increasing prevalence in higher education as well as primary and secondary education, it is still quite likely that the vast majority of a student's educational experience has been in the traditional model, where the teacher lectures during class and students do homework outside of class. As a result, it's likely that if you use flipped learning in your class, it will be the first flipped learning environment students will have ever seen. (Unfortunately, many instructors who do use flipped learning don't necessarily do it particularly effectively, and so what few experiences students may have with flipped learning might be strongly negative.)

Because students have made it through 12 years of primary and secondary education mostly by "doing school" in the traditional manner, changing to a flipped learning model will probably pose a threat to them. Students' uneasiness with this change can manifest itself in "push-back" against flipped learning, which will sound like complaints but are really more expressions of uncertainty about what they are doing. If misunderstood or handled poorly, this push-back can lead to tension and dissension in the classroom and a strongly negative outcome for everyone involved. But if we listen and act with students' best interests in mind, these expressions can turn into power-ful moments of learning, not only about the subject at hand but also about the lifelong learning and self-regulation skills that students need. Flipped learning tends to bring these issues to the surface, which is ultimately a good thing; we shouldn't view this as conflict but rather as an opportunity to teach.

The following sections deal with some common issues that students raise with flipped learning, especially if they are new to this environment, along with some conversations about learning that we can have with students as a result. Remember that these are issues, not necessarily complaints, despite appearances to the contrary. Almost always there is a grain of truth in them and a call for us to listen carefully and reexamine what we've designed for the course to make sure all students are included and supported.

Issue 1: "You're Not Teaching the Class"

The Issue

One of the first things that students notice in a flipped learning environment is the drastically different role of lecture when compared with the traditional learning environment, especially in the group space. Flipped learning does not *eliminate* lecture necessarily; insofar as lecture is a part of the course, flipped learning puts it in a context where its strengths as an instructional method benefit students the most. And that context, we claim, is in the *individual* space, where students can pace themselves, take breaks, watch in small study groups, pause and replay, and take the lecture in on their own terms and schedules. Still, although this seems reasonable, many students still experience a deep-seated discomfort with not having class time or group space focused on lectures.

Why is this? It seems mainly because students' academic backgrounds overwhelmingly use the traditional model, in which direct instruction is the purpose of the group space. This is how students have "done school" for many years. If students' primary contact with the teacher is in the group space, which is spent on direct instruction, then naturally students will see the primary *function* of the teacher as being a lecturer. Hence, students come to equate "teaching" with "lecturing," and so when a teacher isn't lec-turing in the group space, the teacher isn't *teaching*.

This observation might call into question whether students know good teaching when they see it. Interestingly, research into students' perceptions of what constitutes "excellent" or "effective" teaching suggests that they do. Studies focusing on student perceptions of the characteristics of effective teaching report remarkably consistent results that aren't completely out of sync with our own ideas about good teaching. One study (Onwuegbuzie et al. 2007) examined the responses of 912 undergraduate and graduate students from different academic majors at a U.S. university and revealed nine characteristics associated by those students with effective teaching: being student-centered, knowledgeable about the subject area, professional, enthusiastic, effective at communication, accessible, competent at instruction, fair and respectful, and consistent with providing adequate performance feedback. This list is in order of decreasing endorsement levels; "student-centered" is the most endorsed characteristic by this sample, with about 59% of respondents giving this as a response. Other studies, such as those by Witcher and Onwuegbuzie (1999), Spencer and Schmelkin (2002), and Greimel-Fuhrmann and Geyer (2003), reach broadly similar conclusions, with the predominant characteristic of a "good teacher" as being one who is *student-centered*—a concept whose descriptions include such terms as *friendly*, *patient*, and *fair* and characterized by awareness of and responsiveness to student needs.

So when students argue that "you're not teaching the class," it *might* mean that they believe lecturing is teaching and vice versa. But it might also signal a belief that by not delivering direct instruction directly to the student, the professor is failing on one of the characteristics identified previously. For example, if the professor isn't spending class time working out problems on the board but rather letting students wrestle with the problems themselves, students might perceive this as not being "student-centered" or perhaps not being willing to communicate with students, or even not being competent as an instructor—when in reality, the opposite of all these might be the case.

The Conversation

Concerns that students have about "not teaching the class" can be turned into conversations about the roles of professor and student in higher education and the nature of excellent teaching. Specifically, we can ask students two questions:

1. *What are our respective roles as instructor and student?* The relationship between student and professor in higher education is markedly different from the relationship in primary and secondary schools. In college, the student is presumably being prepared to function independently as an adult. The student *is* an adult (unless the student is an advanced high school student taking college classes). Therefore, the relationship is not transactional, where students pay money to receive a "good" from the

professor; nor is it parental, where the professor takes the role of caretaker and authority figure in the lives of the students. Rather, the relationship is like that of a client and a consultant, where the client seeks the help of the consultant and the two cocreate something of equal value to each: the client's education. The relationship has changed and therefore the instruction is going to change, and it is a relationship based on mutual work toward a common goal in which the consultant helps, but the client also pitches in.

2. *What sort of knowledge and skills are expected of you when you reach the working world?* In a university setting, unlike in a primary or secondary school setting, we are not just acquiring information about content but preparing for careers and life situations in which the content is shifting and not only the problems that the students will be called upon to solve but also the tools used to solve them may not have been invented yet. In this kind of reality, students don't just need content or information transferred from one place to the next. In flipped learning, dealing with this issue is an opportunity to explain why the method of teaching that you are adopting is suited to the kinds of "mental muscles" that students need to build.

Issue 2: "I'm Having to Teach Myself the Subject"

The Issue

When students work in their individual space in a flipped learning environment, they are responsible for having meaningful first contact with new concepts and attaining some progress on a list of basic learning objectives. Being in individual space, the student is often working alone on these tasks, and this, coupled with the emphasis on active learning over direct instruction during the group space, can lead some students to believe they are "teaching themselves the subject." This perception is rooted in several beliefs about teaching and learning that appear to be common among college students:

- *The belief that the role of the teacher is to provide direct instruction on new concepts.* Certainly this is one possible aspect of the role of a college professor, and it should be noted that flipped learning does not remove this role from professors, because professors can provide direct instruction both in the individual space and even (in limited quantities) in the group space. However, the general belief is that learning happens because the student listens well and takes notes during a lecture that happens during a group meeting, with assistance from doing homework occasionally, and any other mode of instruction is merely the instructor "not teaching" as we discussed previously. In particular, asking the student to gain some basic fluency with a new concept in her individual space is not perceived as another way to learn but rather a dereliction of duty on the part of the instructor, a subcontracting of the basic job of teaching to the student.

- *The belief that the student is incapable of having meaningful first contact with new concepts outside of live direct instruction.* Many students simply lack the belief that they are personally capable of understanding new concepts through individual work—they *can't* learn without someone lecturing to them first. So when they are asked to do so, not only is it perceived as a shirking of professional duties by the instructor but also it is asking them (the students) to do the impossible. This belief can arise from many different sources: past difficulties with the subject, legitimate issues of preparation on prerequisite material, learning disabilities, being told in the past that they are not smart enough to do well in the subject, a lack of personal investment in the subject, or just simply because in their past classroom experiences (which, again, are likely to be predominantly traditionally structured) the students have never been *asked* to learn something in this context.

- *The belief that any learning that is expected outside direct instruction in the group space is inappropriate.* Even if a student doesn't subscribe to the first two beliefs—that is, the student believes that the teacher can do more to assist learning than by providing direct instruction and that the learner has the ability to learn on her own—there may still be the belief that the student *shouldn't have to* learn on her own, that self-teaching in college happens not because this is an intentional part of the college experience but because the teacher is shirking his duties. "If the teacher were doing his job," it may be said, "I wouldn't have to learn outside of class."

Also embedded in this issue is a potential concern about support structures in the course. Some students may not share in the preceding beliefs, but if they perceive that they are not being supported in their individual work—that they are being "pushed into the deep end" or "hung out to dry"—then they will feel as though they are not merely working individually but are on their own.

The Conversation
This concern, if raised by a student, has to have a response, because it strikes at the heart of the mission of higher education and a positive belief structure about students.

We need to think carefully in this situation about whether our support structures for students as they work are sufficient. Is there a perception that students are on their own and cannot count on asking for or receiving quality help when they are working individually? If so, is there any basis for that claim? Asking the students directly is the best approach; then listen carefully and act on any reasonable means of improving support for students.

We should also ask students some pointed questions about teaching and learning:

- What do you think are the roles of the professor and the student in this class? And don't just say, "The teacher has to teach"; what does "teaching" mean?
- Do you believe that it's *possible* to learn some new things individually, or does this learning happen *only* in class?
- Do you believe that it's *appropriate* to be asked to learn some new things individually?

All of these questions can start some interesting and productive conversations among students when this issue arises. But it's also useful to determine the answers to these questions *before* the issue arises. In my own classes, I couch these questions in an activity, adapted from Dana Ernst of Northern Arizona University (Ernst 2015), given on the first day of class to "set the stage" for shared beliefs about teaching and learning. In this activity, students are asked the following series of questions:

- What are the goals of a university education?
- How does a person learn something new?
- What do you reasonably expect to remember from your courses in 20 years?

Students think about these questions one at a time, first to develop an individual answer, and then in conversation with a small group; afterward the small groups report back to the whole class. The responses students give, despite the diversity of the students and the courses in which they are enrolled, tend to be remarkably consistent semester after semester. Students often identify "being prepared for a career" as a primary goal of a university education, but when pressed about what it means to be "prepared for a career," invariably *the ability to learn and pick up new skills on one's own* is one of the top responses, often overwhelmingly the most common. When asked about how a person learns something new, invariably students mention *trial and error*—experimenting, trying things out, and identifying and learning from failure—as the primary way. Very rarely will students say that a person learns something new only by listening to a lecture. When asked about what they can reasonably expect to remember from their courses in 20 years, the list includes items such as *experiences, failures, processes,* and *workflows* that have been hammered out through trial and error and personal experience, and *items of course content that they use to create beneficial constructs in a real-world setting*—all things that connote *figuring something out on one's own.*

From this conversation it is often quite natural to point out that not only have students themselves identified learning on one's own as a major goal of a university education but also that the primary way to learn something new and to make it stick for the long term is to figure it out on one's own. Therefore, it's appropriate to make self-teaching a major feature of the class—not only appropriate but also necessary, if it is as important as students say. Students themselves truly believe that learning on one's own is important and appropriate; this activity helps to get that into the open and provides us, the professors, with an opportunity to explain how the flipped structure of the course will give students valuable practice in doing so, in a safe environment where there is lots of support. So rather than *refute* the idea that students are teaching themselves in a flipped learning environment, professors should *embrace* this idea and explain how this is making students' college experience more valuable.

At the same time, we should also explain how students are not expected to "teach themselves" the *entire* course—hence the break between basic and advanced learning objectives as outlined in the earlier discussion on Guided Practice. The basic objectives are the ones that students should be self-teaching with guidance; the advanced objectives are for the entire class to learn together—quite the opposite of "teaching oneself."

Issue 3: "I Learn Best When I Am Lectured To"

The Issue
This point is raised sometimes by students in a flipped learning environment when they believe that the mode of instruction—which in flipped learning is focused, in the group space, on active learning and not as much on lecture—is at odds with their "learning style." It can be difficult to discern what a student really means when saying this. On the one hand, "learning styles" do exist and are the subject of considerable attention in the research literature (e.g., Kolb 1981). In fact, we saw in chapter 2 that one of the original formulations of flipped learning was made specifically to address differences in learning styles. On the other hand, it's questionable whether a student who voices concern about learning styles is referring to the concept studied

by psychologists. It seems equally likely that the student could just be saying that active learning isn't as easy as lecture, and the resulting cognitive load is taken to be a sign that the instruction doesn't "fit my learning style."

Many times when students raise this issue, it's not raised as a complaint. Rather, it's a concern based on an interpretation that the increased cognitive load associated with flipped learning, with its emphasis on individual efforts at learning new concepts and diminished role of direct instruction, means that flipped learning doesn't "work as well" for them as traditional instruction. This concern is quite natural; when we perform the same task in two different ways and one of those ways presents more resistance and requires more effort than the other, it makes sense to conclude that the way that causes less resistance "fits" us better and that we ought to be doing it that way. The concern can become a serious student-instructor issue if it isn't addressed because it can appear that we are deliberately making students do things "the hard way" unnecessarily. It is like saying that riding a unicycle doesn't "work as well" as riding a bicycle, which in turn doesn't "work as well" as driving a car—the belief is that all three vehicles are designed to do the same thing, so the "best" approach is to use the vehicle that incurs the least amount of effort. That this analogy is based on a fallacious premise—namely, that all three vehicles exist solely to get from point A to point B—may not occur to the person holding it.

The Conversation

The conversation that we should have with students who express this concern is about what *learning* means and what goals we have for learning in a college class, and hence what goals we have for different kinds of instruction. Some students believe that "learning" a subject amounts merely to accumulating factual knowledge about the subject and being able to perform very simple tasks related to those facts. Of course, we have bigger goals for learning—and in many cases, students share those goals. In order to reach the higher levels of Bloom's taxonomy and really *learn* a subject, something more than a transferral of information needs to take place, and this requires methods that go beyond just lecturing. Those methods entail more cognitive load; but it doesn't mean they don't "work as well" as other methods. It just means they are moving beyond surface learning to something deeper, and this necessarily requires more effort and produces more resistance. (Unless we are designing our pedagogy poorly and introducing excessive *extraneous load*; this possibility is a constant call to examine our course designs critically.)

An activity that I frequently do with students to illustrate the role of direct instruction in learning is the following: I simply ask students, *What are the most important three to five things you have ever learned how to do in your life?* Students are allowed to think of anything, not necessarily school related. After a few minutes of reflection, they share their lists. Many of them contain skills and tasks that are truly essential for viable personhood, such as going to the bathroom on one's own, being able to feed oneself, speaking one's native language, being able to walk, and so on. Once the results have been discussed, students are asked, *How did you learn these things?* Of course, the role of direct instruction is minimal, if present at all, in most of these critically important tasks. One can be shown how to do any of these things, but the actual learning of them involves moving past the lecture, and more effort and resistance is encountered naturally in the process. But this doesn't mean that the process doesn't "work as well" as direct instruction or lecture.

The point of the exercise is to show students that they have an amazing, innate human ability to learn things on their own. Sadly, this fact seems to become less and less apparent to students the longer they remain in school. I have encountered many students who frankly believe that they are *incapable* of learning on their own, largely due to a "learned helplessness" that comes from over a decade of institutionalized instruction that tells them so by making the "learning process" fundamentally centered around an instructor, rather than around the learner. In flipped learning, what we are trying to do is not banish direct instruction but put it at the service of the learner, to support her efforts in becoming an independent and self-regulating learner. It's worth the time to tell students this explicitly.

Issue 4: "It Takes Too Much Time Outside of Class"

The Issue

In a traditionally structured course, students encounter new concepts in the group space and then use the individual space for further work such as homework and writing assignments. When this structure is flipped, many students find the initial encounter with new concepts to be tremendously time-consuming. I have had students report that they spend six to eight hours preparing for one single 50-minute class session. Assuming the student isn't exaggerating, that's far too much time spent on class preparation. Something had gone wrong, either with the student's preparation activities or with the assignment that I gave to implement that preparation (or both).

To address this issue, first consider that the student may *not* be exaggerating by saying that he or she spends many hours preparing for a single class. Is it possible that we've designed the individual space activities less than optimally? To answer this question it is helpful to have a framework for how much time individual space activities like Guided Practice should take, possibly using the following rule of thumb: *The Guided Practice for a single*

50-minute lesson should take no more than 75 minutes if done by a student who has adequately understood the prerequisite material.

This time frame *includes the running time of the videos assigned and the estimated time to complete reading assignments.* So, for example, a Guided Practice for a 50-minute class session might contain 15 minutes' worth of video to watch, followed by exercises that will take 30 minutes or so to complete once the videos have been completed. The remainder of the time might be dedicated to reading or rewatching portions of the videos or asking questions.

This time frame accords with the common rule of thumb that college students should spend two to three hours outside of class working for every one hour in class. For a 50-minute session, this amounts to 100 to 150 minutes; the 75-minute time frame is therefore assuming that about half the time outside of class should be spent preparing for class. The other half is spent on postclass activities; because we are shifting some of the items of work that would traditionally be "homework" back into the group space instead of individual space, we are "buying" that time outside of class for students to prepare.

This time frame can feel quite limiting—and *limitation* is the point. The purpose of the flipped learning environment is not *to create more work for students*; it's to put student work in the context that helps students the most. So we must avoid what has been called the "course-and-a-half syndrome" (Sabourin 2014), in which all the work of a traditionally structured class is retained while more work is added on by using the individual space as an "overflow." By sticking to the rule of thumb that the time spent in the individual space should be not much more than the time that would have been spent on those activities in the group space of a traditionally structured course, we keep away from the course-and-a-half phenomenon while also staying close to the core concepts of flipped learning. Keeping the individual space activity limited keeps it minimal and focused. The boundaries help us clarify what the basic learning objectives are versus the advanced objectives, and they prevent us from assigning work that isn't necessary.

If we have this framework in place and are reasonably sure that our individual space activities would—if done by a student who is adequately prepared on the prerequisite material—be completed in that time frame, then this issue might be a combination of several issues:

- *The individual space activity might need more structure.* When we mention "adequate preparation on prerequisite material," we are referring only to whether or not the student has attained the learning objectives for that material. It is possible that a student might be adequately prepared, but because the student is a novice learner, she lacks experience with bringing her knowledge to bear on new tasks.

- *The student might be engaging in unproductive study habits.* If the student isn't using time well then she or he will tend to use more of it. This could come in the form of unproductive reading habits whereby students spend time reading but not closely or for comprehension, so that when it's time to do exercises, the knowledge isn't there. A similar shortcoming can be found with video—just because students watch lots of videos these days, it doesn't mean that the student can watch a lecture recorded to a video and get the information out of it that he needs. Or the student might not be taking initiative to seek help or alternative resources if he is stuck on something, which is a key self-regulated learning behavior. All of these habits add significantly to the time it takes to complete individual space work, even if the student is "adequately prepared on prerequisite material."
- *The student might be engaging in perfectionist practices on individual space work.* We have previously recommended that Guided Practice and other individual space work be graded on the basis of completeness, effort, and timeliness—not on correctness—so that we get honest, actionable learning data from students. Students, then, can *try* to be right, but if getting a response exactly right requires hours of study and practice, then we can accept work that isn't fully correct but shows where the student stands in a formative state. This tolerance for incorrectness also makes it far more possible for the work to be completed within the limited time frame suggested previously. However, students—who are used to being graded on correctness—can be quick to forget that for Guided Practice it's okay not to be right sometimes, and they end up spending hours trying to make the submission perfect. Perfectionism is a hard habit for college students to break if they have fallen into it.
- *The student might be spending a normal, expected amount of time on individual space work, but it's more time than she or he is used to spending outside of class.* The standard "exchange rate" for time spent outside of class in higher education tends to center around two to three hours of purposeful work on a class for every hour spent in the class meeting. This is partially the basis for the time frame given previously (that the Guided Practice for a 50-minute lesson should take about 75 minutes to complete), because the individual space activity plus postclass activities plus miscellaneous activities like attending office hours will come out to about 100 to 150 minutes for one 50-minute lesson. This is a standard expectation, and in my experience the vast majority of students never spend anywhere close to this amount of time on their classes. A recent report found that the average U.S.

college student spends only 17 hours per week on all of their classes combined (Pierre 2014), which is far short of the 30 to 45 hours a week that would be expected if a student carried a 15-credit course load. Therefore, a typical college student entering a flipped learning environment in which the individual space work has been carefully calibrated and designed will experience a much higher demand on time outside of class. This will feel like "too much time," but only because the student has typically not spent *enough* time outside of class previously. Said differently, flipped learning doesn't require an unreasonable amount of time outside of class; it requires the *expected* amount of time outside of class, and actually *requires* it.

The Conversation

As mentioned previously, we should be careful to calibrate individual space activities so that they are structured and do not inherently take excessive amounts of time. The Guided Practice model has this structure built in, so that students should have an easier time navigating the work. Insofar as the activity can be further minimized without losing instructional value, we should do so, and always be on the lookout for ways to streamline the work we assign. If the "too much time" issue comes up among students, this is the first thing to check.

Once we are reasonably satisfied that the assignment is as lean as we can make it, we have to ask some questions of students:

- *What are you doing when you do this work?* That is, what are the habits and practices that you engage in when doing the Guided Practice or other individual space activity? In asking this question of students, we are helping them learn how to self-regulate by leading them through Pintrich's phases of self-regulation (Pintrich 2004), which we discussed in chapter 2. An exploration of this question gets students to engage especially in metacognition and the specific phases of forethought and planning and of reaction and reflection. It also gives us insights on how to diagnose poor or unproductive habits. Asking this question is just part of the job of being a professional educator.
- *How much time spent outside of class on a collage course is appropriate?* This addresses the final issue noted previously, that students frequently underestimate how much time is appropriate for spending outside of class on a college course. Whether the "two to three hours outside of class" rule is *truly appropriate* is an interesting conversation to have with students.

These conversations are highly valuable to students as they move along the path toward becoming effective self-regulating learners. Traditionally structured courses rarely bring these to the surface; flipped learning provides regular opportunities to do so.

Issue 5: "I Don't Have a Way to Ask Questions Before Class"

The Issue
In a live lecture, as one might get in a traditionally structured class, there is at least the perception that a student can stop the lecture at any moment and ask for clarification or further insight. In a flipped learning environment, where direct instruction is relocated to the individual space and students are responsible for first contact with new concepts, there is frequently an equal and opposite perception that no such intervention can be made because students are working individually. Students often feel that they have no way to get help when they are learning the new concepts in the individual space.

On this issue, unfortunately, the students might be exactly right. If Guided Practice or other individual space activities are set up for students to encounter new concepts individually, but the channels for interacting with others and getting help are not present or hard to access, then students really *don't* have a way to ask questions or seek help, and this is not the situation in which we'd like to place students. Students are encountering new concepts in the *individual space* but we don't want students to be *on their own* while they are learning. The intention with flipped learning is for students to develop skills with self-teaching and self-regulated learning—which includes taking initiative to seek help from experts and friends if needed. There should be varied and robust opportunities for students to ask questions, seek clarification, and collaborate with others while they are working in their individual spaces, and our syllabi should make it clear that it is okay to ask for help on individual space work. (The boundaries for acceptable collaboration should also be clearly spelled out in your academic integrity policy in the syllabus; but there should be *some* way for students to ask questions during this phase, even if those questions may be addressed only to you.)

The Conversation
When this issue arises, there are two sets of questions that we need to ask, one to our students and one to ourselves.

1. We should ask ourselves, *Am I providing enough ways for students to ask questions and seek help while learning individually? Are the students sufficiently aware of these resources? And are there ways to improve those channels*

or add more? It is almost certain that *some* channels for students to ask questions in the individual space are already in place. At the very least, students should have the old standbys of office hours and e-mail. But the channels you have set up may not be sufficient for student needs. For example, office hours may not be feasible for students who live off campus when they have a question in their individual space work; e-mail requests for help might not have a quick enough response to be useful. Sometimes student expectations for help are unrealistic—for example, if a student wants to get a response to an e-mail sent at 1:00 a.m. within the hour. But it's also worth a little self-examination to consider whether we could respond faster to e-mail in general. Also it's worth considering whether additional collaboration tools can be added to the course that would provide more channels for question-asking. For example, in addition to e-mail and office hours, an electronic discussion board can be added, not with the intent of grading any of the responses but simply as a way of throwing out questions at any point so that the entire class can read and respond. Or instead of a discussion board, a channel on a team-based communications tool like Slack could be set up; or a single-purpose chat room using Gitter (https://gitter.im) or IRC could be created instead of, or in addition to, a discussion board. If your institution has a tutoring center for your subject, you could investigate letting students ask questions on individual space work there. The idea here is that if students are perceiving that they "can't ask questions" while working in the individual space, we need to take that perception seriously and look into ways of providing more channels that work better for students.

2. We should ask students, *What improvements or additions could we include to make it easier for you to ask questions?* Of course, it's possible that students may simply not be aware that they can ask questions through existing channels. If so, then this question will focus them on those channels and help them become aware. If they *are* aware of the opportunities to ask questions, then this question will help them clarify their issue, which is not that they "can't ask questions" but rather they *can* ask questions but the existing channels aren't working optimally for them. If students can isolate what is not working for them, then we can begin to address those issues. If not, it's possible that students simply aren't using the existing channels as they were intended to be used, and this provides a point of instruction.

In asking these questions, we communicate to students that we take the ability to ask questions seriously, and we communicate that we are open to making changes to the course infrastructure in ways that will make it easier and more helpful to ask questions. In return, this places the onus for *using* those channels on the student.

We should emphasize that one thing that does get lost in a flipped learning environment is the expectation of *instant* responses in a lecture if the lecture is taking place during the individual space. However, there is a purpose for this: Instead of getting that instant response, it's expected that the student will pause to formulate her *own* responses or to puzzle through something that was said or written *on her own*, before having the professor swoop in to resolve the difficulty. This is a feature, not a bug, and it helps to build individual thinking skills and self-regulation.

How to Handle the Nonideal

You might look at this list of issues, or imagine others that aren't listed, and feel dread. We do not seek or desire conflict with students. We hope for productive and enjoyable professional relationships with our students. So we naturally feel apprehensive about anything we do that might incite conflict, even outright rebellion, among students. And, to be honest, in my experience, every flipped learning class I have ever taught has had at least one student who rebels against the model, early and often and usually quite strenuously. Conflict with students in a flipped learning environment is more likely than in a traditional environment because of the radical way the "rules" of learning have been altered.

However, these conflicts happen not because we are deliberately making students mad (at least they *shouldn't* happen because of this) but rather because students are encountering a paradigm shift in the way their university education is being conducted. No longer are they allowed to be passive bystanders in their education; no longer are they allowed to put aside their work for the class in between the meeting dates; no longer is the course a game to be played. Students deep down *want* classes like this, despite what they sometimes say. The conflict that arises is often a coping mechanism that indicates a struggle to transition to the new model. Therefore, these conflicts ought to be seen as opportunities for important conversations about teaching and learning that *ought* to be happening in *all* of the students' courses.

Turning these conflicts into meaningful learning experiences requires that we exhibit some of the best characteristics of effective teaching—namely, the following:

- *Stay positive and student-centered.* We mentioned earlier that among several studies conducted to isolate what college students perceive as the key properties of effective teaching most have to do with personal characteristics of the instructor. Those traits include being student-centered, acting in a professional way, demonstrating enthusiasm, and being fair and respectful. When conflicts arise in any student-instructor interaction, the instructor must "turn up" these traits and avoid anything that leads in the wrong direction. For example, don't go to social media to vent your frustrations with students when they don't "buy in" to flipped learning; don't show up to class angry; don't become disinterested and just "phone in" the rest of the semester. Instead, celebrate student successes ("Look at what you were able to learn without having a lecture in class!"); praise work that is well done while giving positive, constructive, caring feedback on what needs correction; greet students with a smile and interact with them in a way that projects interest and caring.

- *Stress the benefits and find shared goals.* Throughout this book we have provided research reviews and case studies that stress the benefits of flipped learning. You can, and should, pass some of these along to students to stress that the course is conducted in the way you have designed specifically to make it as easy as possible to attain the kinds of deep, long-lasting learning that students need for viability in the professional world and in life. As the "setting the stage" first-day exercise mentioned earlier illustrates, many times students share goals for learning that strongly overlap with ours; they realize that surface learning will not give them the edge they need to secure the job they want and that the goal of university learning is not merely acquisition of basic knowledge but rather the kinds of intellectual skills that outlive the final exam. If you can shift the narrative from student frustrations with flipped learning and onto the shared goals for education that you and your students have, flipped learning will be much more palatable.

An exercise that Christine Rener, professor of chemistry at Grand Valley State University, does with her class on the first day establishes some of these shared goals. While discussing the syllabus, she poses a choice to her students. She mentions that they have enough time in class to conduct class in one of two ways. Either class can be focused on a lecture that covers the basic ideas, and then students will be responsible for working on their own to deepen their understanding through homework and other work, or she can arrange for lectures to be made available online, have students watch them before class, and then focus class time on working on the homework and other work that deepens their understanding. *But there is not enough time in class to do both,* so students have a choice of which way class should be done. She then lets students vote on which of the two formats they want and promises to abide by the results of the vote. It's a gutsy move, because she has planned the course out using a flipped learning model. However, every time she has done this, students overwhelmingly have voted for the flipped model (without knowing that it is called by that name). Students therefore have *chosen* to use the flipped model because they have identified it as preferable for their learning goals, and at any point in the semester, she can return back to the fact that *students voted to do class this way* and remind them why.

- *Clarify expectations and provide generous support.* Along with finding shared goals, having shared expectations that are clearly communicated can defuse conflict. Many times students may balk at the flipped learning model because they perceive that they will have to "teach themselves the subject" when, in reality, the self-teaching should be limited to a subset of learning objectives that have been identified as ones they can handle individually, and instruction on the subject will include some self-teaching but also plenty of direct instruction, one-on-one tutorial, and group work. Students aren't expected to become experts on the whole subject themselves, and once this expectation is clarified, many students breathe a sigh of relief and are on board. One very common misconception about flipped learning is that the student will be completely on his or her own; by providing generous levels of support, including office hours but also in-class support and electronic and asynchronous channels such as discussion boards, you can dispel that misconception and earn students' trust.

- *Communicate early, often, and personally.* The most important thing an instructor can do in any teaching situation is communicate with students about their experiences and get their feedback. A flipped learning design offers an unparalleled opportunity to do this; in a small enough class you may be able to have conversations with every student every day. It is exceedingly easy in a flipped learning environment to pull up a chair, either physically or virtually, next to a student and ask, "How is the course going for you so far?" In addition to person-to-person communication, give *informal course evaluations* regularly in which students have the opportunity (anonymously, if it helps) to leave their thoughts about what is going well and what can be improved in the course so far. Online tools for making and collecting surveys, such as Google Forms or Survey Monkey, are so easy and accessible today that making and giving informal course evaluations is trivial. You can, for example, give an informal evaluation at the end of the second, fourth, and eighth week of a 14-week semester to allow students to "speak" their minds. This provides usable data for you and communicates to students that their voices matter and can effect change.

- *Listen to students and be open to change.* If we are to communicate with students, we have to listen to what they say, even if a great deal of it is negative. Not all of the negative comments we receive are mindless complaints; very many of them are truthful, substantive, and informative about how we can improve our courses without sacrificing the flipped learning environment.

The issues and potential sources of conflict we have identified here are not restricted just to students. Colleagues and administrators can have the same issues as students, and for the same reasons—sometimes because students report their experiences to them, and they are trying to look out for students' interests.

Advice for the Nontenured

Nontenured faculty—both those who are tenure track but still working toward tenure and those not on the tenure track at all, including adjunct and contingent faculty—will understandably question the value of risking major student conflicts without tenure in place as a protection. The pretenured faculty on the tenure track may see flipped learning as something that has to wait until tenure is earned, so that student conflicts won't damage their career prospects. Adjunct and contingent faculty may perceive that the risk isn't worth the reward—that although flipped learning seems to benefit students in many ways, the time and energy it takes to implement plus the potential for catastrophic student conflicts, unmitigated by the protections of tenure or multiyear appointments, is not commensurate with those benefits.

These misgivings are understandable. But they shouldn't stand in the way of doing what's right for students. Instead, they should indicate that nontenured faculty should "proceed with caution" regarding flipped learning, with the following advice.

First, faculty who are considering flipped learning should plan carefully what they want to do in their courses once they are flipped, and take their time flipping. When a faculty member learns about flipped learning and then *immediately* goes to implement it in courses starting a month from now, the results are usually less than optimal. Instead, take your time. If you are interested, pick a course that you are going to teach one year from now. Then *gradually* go through the course design process for designing or redesigning it with a flipped learning model. Giving yourself a year will allow you time to design the entire structure of the course, create or curate any materials you wish to use (especially online video), and learn about best practices. You can try out flipped learning using the "partially flipped" model discussed in the previous chapter. If six months is a more desirable time frame, then this is definitely possible. But *don't* leap directly into flipped learning if you are uncomfortable with the possible consequences. Use the time to read and plan.

Second, once a reasonable plan for a flipped learning course is in place, nontenured faculty would benefit from discussing the plans with a superior, like a department chair or dean. Inform that person what you are thinking about doing and what your plan is, and ask for advice or input on the design and how this might play out on your professional record. This refers to not only potential student conflicts but also potential benefits. For example, some faculty might be surprised to find out that their academic dean has been thinking about flipped learning for a long time and would like one of her faculty to get around to actually *doing* it. Perhaps there are funding sources or reassigned time opportunities for faculty who are willing to take risks. Whatever the case, keep your superiors informed.

Third, remember the characteristics of excellent teaching we mentioned previously and practice them often while teaching in a flipped learning environment. Be sure to *communicate with students early and often* about their experiences and *listen to them and be open to change*. Very many student conflicts can be resolved or headed off just by letting students know that you are listening and that their voices matter.

Fourth, if there remains a concern about the potential effects of student conflicts on tenure or reappointment coming from the flipped learning model, check your institution's or department's criteria for tenure or reappointment to see exactly what might be scrutinized in the tenure or reappointment process. For example, some institutions allow faculty in their tenure and promotion materials to include measures of student learning in addition to student course evaluations as evidence of teaching effectiveness; if this is true for your institution, then you can administer assessments that can show student learning in a more objective setting than a course evaluation, and we have already mentioned that flipped learning tends to produce this kind of evidence.

Here we give a special word to those faculty at institutions where tenure, promotion, or reappointment are based primarily on research productivity rather than on effective teaching. In these situations, there can be a concern that too much time spent on experimenting with new teaching techniques will hurt one's productivity in research—or cause a *perception* from other faculty that too much time is being spent on teaching and not enough on research. If you are in that situation, it can be rough, because the assumption may be in place that *any* time taken away from something else and added to research activity will improve the quantity and quality of the research that's produced. This is false, but it is a belief often ensconced among elite institutions and considered unassailable. To implement flipped learning without running afoul of concerns about research productivity, the faculty member will have to take care to document and make the case that research productivity wasn't harmed by using flipped learning; the faculty member also has to make a case that not only was research productivity not harmed but also that either student learning and student satisfaction with the courses significantly improved or if it did not significantly improve the faculty member has isolated the causes and made changes to the teaching. In short, faculty at research-intensive universities need not shy away from using flipped learning but rather need to be constantly collecting data on teaching effectiveness and also producing research at least at the level of a faculty member who is *not* teaching with flipped learning. This is difficult, but definitely not impossible, and it makes the faculty member a much more well-rounded professional.

Fifth and finally, realize that in most institutions tenure is not a reward for those who avoid risks. Rather, it is a reward for demonstrating excellence across the faculty member's entire professional spectrum and an indicator of that faculty member's long-term value to the institution. Faculty who avoid taking educated risks that could improve their work might get tenure, but faculty who *do* take risks and demonstrate successful results—or at least the ability to engage in "productive failure" by learning from mistakes and making corrections—almost always get tenure. The same can be said for reappointment to nontenure-track positions.

In brief, don't let the lack of tenure be a deterrent for trying things in the classroom that have a high probability of being the right thing for students. Just proceed carefully, plan well, communicate with and listen to your students, and keep students' best interests in mind.

Managing Time and Work

Another issue that often becomes a concern for faculty who are interested in flipped learning is the time commitment involved. Faculty overwork is a real concern in the professoriate today, and in the interest of learning how to say no to more work than we can handle, any new pedagogical approach that appears to require lots of investment in time and energy (to say nothing of the potential for student dissatisfaction) can, and possibly should, understandably be viewed with skepticism.

In my experience and in that of other faculty members using flipped learning, at least some of these concerns about time commitments are fully justified. Many parts of designing and conducting a flipped learning–oriented course require a significant time commitment. First, many courses will need to be redesigned from a traditional model, and this takes work, as we have seen. Second, creating a repository of learning resources for students to use in their individual space work can take a tremendous amount of time, especially if the instructor wants to use online video that she has created. Third, grading could potentially take more time, depending on how the instructor chooses to handle the increased volume of formative assessment that flipped learning tends to create.

Let's expand on the second point about creating learning resources. Very often, the learning resources used for flipped learning courses are videos; this is, at least, the popular conception of learning resources for students in their individual space work. There are two ways to approach video in a flipped learning environment: You can *create* them yourself, or you can *curate* them by pulling already made video from different sources. (You can also do a little of each.) However, both methods are time-consuming. Creating a video involves learning the technological tools for video creation; those tools are improving every day in terms of cost and ease of use, but it is still an investment in time to learn them. Then, once basic fluency in the tools is obtained, it takes skill, practice, and a heaping portion of learning from mistakes in order to make good instructional video. Curating video already made might seem like the solution here, but this too takes time—sometimes just as much time and energy as making video yourself, because it involves sifting through the mountains of video available online to find examples that fit your class (and finding a good fit doesn't always happen) and then stitching together the short list of video for a given topic to make a coherent whole. Many instructors who go this route end up creating some or all of the video content themselves.

Designing a course using flipped learning is going to be a time investment, just like most things worth doing. We shouldn't let this fact, on its own, dissuade us from using flipped learning, any more than we should let concerns about potential student conflicts or tenure and reappointment issues dissuade us. Rather, just as in those other situations, we should proceed carefully and work smartly.

The items that require the greatest time commitment in flipped learning are items that are done "up front," *before* the class actually runs (or, at least, they *can* be done prior to the course launch): designing the course structure and instructional strategy, creating or curating the learning resources, designing the grading system, and so on. This is actually good news, because you can manage this workload by *giving yourself lead time* in creating a flipped learning course. Earlier in this chapter we mentioned a "one-year plan" for designing or redesigning a course to use flipped learning. This was advice to pretenured faculty, to encourage a "slow and steady" approach to flipped learning rather than a hasty jump to something new. But it is also good advice to anyone developing a flipped learning course for the first time, because the amount of time needed to create resources and design a course structure is manageable if spread out over six months to a year, whereas it can be a crushing burden to try this just weeks before the start of the semester. The best way to manage time is to give yourself more of it, and because flipped learning course construction is "front loaded" in this way, starting six months to a year out from the actual launch of the course gives you that time.

Another way to manage time is to *think creatively about learning resources.* These often include video in a flipped learning course, but not always, and to reiterate a point we have made earlier, *flipped learning does not require the use of video at all.* If creating video for students isn't a realistic possibility for you, then think about curating video that is already in existence. But also consider other forms of learning resources such as the following:

- *Printed and electronic textbooks.* The printed textbook is still in many ways the ideal medium for storing and transmitting information, and when paired with well-constructed exercises (e.g., exercises you might make in a Guided Practice assignment), they can be a source of direct instruction. Electronic textbooks are a particularly useful modern variant, as they are often cheap or free and can be accessed on students' devices or on the web. Tools exist today to allow collaborative annotation of electronic texts, such as Perusall (https://perusall.com) and Hypothes.is (https://hypothes.is) to turn reading into an asynchronous text-focused social discussion.
- *Websites, including blogs and longform social media.* Like print and electronic textbooks, websites—including blogs and long-form social media sites such as Medium (https://medium.com) or Quora (www .quora.com)—can provide information and insight just like a lecture can.
- *Audio resources and podcasts.* Audio resources such as radio shows and podcasts can provide access to new concepts as well, while providing the perspective of others as one might find in a well-constructed lecture. In fact, some audio resources *are* lectures in the form of audio recordings (possibly with transcriptions).

- *Games and simulations.* One way to model the "first contact with new concepts" idea is to focus individual space not on listening to a lecture or reading a text but on interacting with a model or simulation, generating observations and questions, and then coming to the group space with those questions and observations to share. Flipped learning with simulations has been used with particular effectiveness in the biomedical and health sciences, especially in developing clinical skills—for example, Bristol (2014), Critz and Knight (2013), Herreid and Schiller (2013), and Lasater (2007).

As we mentioned in chapter 6, it can be helpful to make learning resources *varied* and to give students options for how they can learn new information. It doesn't have to be all video; it doesn't have to be video at all. Using learning resources that are not video, for example, by finding and selecting a good textbook and then augmenting it with good support activities, can have just as much learning value for students and take up far less time to prepare.

Yet another way to manage time, as well as promote your personal sanity, is to *work with partners*. Rather than going it alone in creating a flipped learning environment, team up with colleagues at your institution—or at other institutions—and work together. For example, the redesign of a single course in a department can be done by several faculty members in the department who teach the course. This spreads the work out (making 90 course videos isn't so bad when divided up among five people, for instance), promotes a diversity of pedagogical ideas, and provides a ready social network for mutual support once the course runs. Faculty in different departments can also band together as a group to convert different courses; insights from one discipline can often be helpful in another, and the social network support is still there for when the course begins. Students, too, are often more likely to accept the flipped learning model as normal when they realize that several professors are using it, as opposed to just one "lone ranger." Even faculty across different institutions can work together and communicate with each other through social media.

Finally, perhaps the best way to manage time is to *use a trusted and intuitive workflow* for the day-to-day operations of a flipped learning course. We have attempted to provide this workflow in the seven-step process we described in earlier chapters. The moving parts of designing a flipped learning lesson, which is something instructors have to do day in and day out, become intuitive and natural when put into a system and schedule that can be internalized.

Although there can be a significant time and energy investment on the *front* end of running a flipped learning course, this investment can be managed well using the preceding advice. Additionally, there is a significant payoff on the *back* end of this process once the course has been put together and is actually running. Once the course has been constructed and the materials have been created, both can be reused almost indefinitely with little degradation in the quality of student learning. Unlike lecture notes, which get "stale" quickly upon repeated use, a reused group space activity is likely to generate new results every time it's used with a new group. Once an arsenal of learning resources, Guided Practice activities, and group space exercises has been made for a course, it will need only occasional maintenance over time, so if you teach a course on a regular basis—including faculty whose job is to teach several sections of the same course every semester—flipped learning designs can result in substantial decreases in workload once the initial cost of setup has been paid.

In general, flipped learning does not necessarily require more time than a traditional setup. The time is merely distributed differently, with flipped learning requiring more time and effort during the initial design and construction phase of a course than the traditional model. But then as the course runs, flipped learning requires less time and attention on "prep work" than traditional courses do; the time instead is spent interacting with students, which ultimately helps both the students and the professor more. But even the time that is required while the course is running can be managed by using a consistent and internalized workflow, like the seven-step method.

Flipped Learning and the Rest of Your Career: Scholarship

In this chapter, we've discussed how to make the practice of flipped learning an integrated and sustainable part of a well-balanced career in the professoriate. Most of our discussion has centered around how to make flipped learning a central part of our *teaching* responsibilities and how to be happy with flipped learning on a day-to-day basis. But there are other responsibilities that many faculty bear—namely, *scholarship* and *service*. As a final point about living and working with flipped learning, let's look at how the practice of flipped learning can bolster faculty work in these two areas.

Before we dive in, a word on scholarship and service expectations. The typical tenure-track faculty member at an American college or university is expected to engage in teaching *and* scholarship *and* service (to one's department, college, university, and outside the university). Often these expectations are written into the requirements for tenure or promotion and remain in place after tenure. However, not all faculty are typical. Contingent and adjunct faculty, for example, generally have no responsibilities for either scholarship or service; long-term but nontenure-track faculty as well as faculty at two-year institutions may have expectations for service but not scholarship; those who teach as part of a postdoctoral program have strong expectations for scholarship but not service. Therefore, what we discuss in this section may not apply equally to everyone.

However, if you are one of these "atypical" faculty members with lower-than-usual expectations for either scholarship or service, take what we discuss here as an invitation. The scholarship we describe needs experienced practitioners to share their work and their discoveries. The service opportunities we describe need them to share their expertise. Even if scholarship or service is not strongly expected, these are still valuable—not to mention enjoyable—areas of faculty work, of great use to higher education and students everywhere.

Scholarship is a term that often is synonymous with *research*, but *scholarship* has a broader meaning. In his classic book *Scholarship Reconsidered* (Boyer 1990), Ernest Boyer proposes a fourfold model of the work of the professoriate based on the following kinds of scholarship: *scholarship of discovery*, *scholarship of integration*, *scholarship of application*, and *scholarship of teaching*. The typical areas of research done by university faculty, where new frontiers are explored within the faculty member's domain area of expertise, are usually categorized as "discovery" or "application." Interdisciplinary scholarship is generally considered "integration."

Less well understood by many faculty is the *scholarship of teaching*. This refers to a scholarly approach to the notions of teaching and learning in which rigorous methodology is brought to bear on what happens in the college classroom. The scholarship of teaching, which is now called the *scholarship of teaching and learning* (SoTL for short—pronounced "SOH-tull"), coined by Randy Bass (1999) in his seminal article "The Scholarship of Teaching: What's the Problem"—investigates questions about university teaching and learning in a way that "begins with intellectual curiosity, is conducted deliberately and systematically, is grounded in an analysis of some evidence, and results in findings shared with peers to be reviewed and to expand a knowledge base" (Chick n.d.). We usually distinguish the *scholarship of teaching and learning* from "scholarly teaching," the latter indicating teaching practices that are *informed by* research whereas the former *is* that research, done using rigorous methodology to find out new things or answer new questions about how students learn and how professors can teach.

Since 1990, SoTL has grown into an active and vitally important part of the landscape of higher education. Today, dozens of peer-reviewed SoTL journals are published, and numerous professional organizations and conferences exist to further SoTL research and disseminate its findings. SoTL has grown into a distinct academic discipline, both generally and as a subdiscipline within academic subjects. And as we discussed in an earlier chapter, it is fertile ground for scholarly work about flipped learning.

If you are using flipped learning in your classes at any level, there is a strong chance that you can turn your experiences into SoTL research that can be published in a peer-reviewed journal, thereby contributing to the body of knowledge of what we know about teaching and learning and contributing to your overall professional portfolio in the form of legitimate, peer-reviewed research. In particular, SoTL research can be a part of the overall research program for any faculty member, particularly those in institutions that have expectations for scholarly production.

So how does one *do* SoTL? The basic framework for SoTL research looks very much like that of any methodologically rigorous investigation.

Like any research, we start with a *question* or an *observation* that we would like to know more about. Flipped learning is bursting with questions and observations. You have probably had many of them just in reading this book. For example, one might have a question about the videos used in a flipped learning environment:

> Are students more likely to complete Guided Practice assignments if the videos used are made by the instructor versus another person?

An observation from a flipped learning environment might be the following:

> My students are completing the Guided Practice assignments, but they still don't seem fully prepared for the group space work.

Pat Hutchings (2000) created a means of categorizing different kinds of SoTL questions:

- *What works?* Questions of this form ask whether a particular method or item used in instruction is effective in learning.
- *What is?* Questions of this form seek to determine the characteristics of student work or behavior—what is really going on when students perform a particular task.
- *What could be?* Questions of this form cast a vision for what *could* be done in teaching or learning.

Then, after formulating the basic form of a question, we try to narrow and focus the question and perhaps determine what the *real* question actually is. For example, in the question *Are students more likely to complete Guided Practice assignments if the videos used are made by the instructor versus another person?* there is at least one *What is?* question implicitly made—namely, *At what rate are students generally completing Guided Practice assignments?* There could also be a *What works?* question in the form of *Are videos made by me more effective at raising completion rates on Guided Practice than videos made by another person?*

Likewise observations like *My students are completing the Guided Practice assignments, but they still don't seem fully prepared for the group space work* should be converted into questions to investigate. For example, from this observation, several questions might arise:

- Are students really completing the Guided Practice? What are the completion rates throughout the class?
- What are students actually doing when they work the Guided Practice? Is it possible, for example, that students are finding responses to exercises from an online source and not answering questions themselves? Are they watching all the videos and doing the reading? Are they engaging in good viewing or reading practices when they do this?
- Would adding a layer of accountability at the beginning of class, like a quiz over the Guided Practice, be effective in improving the preparation level (and not just the completion rates) of the class?

We sometimes have to use our specific domain knowledge to sharpen some of these questions. For example, in mathematics, "reading the book" is a much different task than reading a text in another discipline, and questions about whether students are engaging in "effective reading practices" take on additional nuances when applied to the reading of mathematical texts.

Next, we do a search through the literature to see what is already known about the question. For example, in a literature search on the questions about students not being fully prepared for group space work, one might come across literature about *knowledge activation*—for example, articles such as Baumert and colleagues' (2010) for general purposes, or discipline-specific ones like Baranes, Perry, and Stigler's (1989). This might lead you to think that the missing link between completion of Guided Practice and effective group space work is a knowledge activation step. This leads to another *What works?* question: *Would adding a knowledge activation activity between the beginning of class and the start of the group space activities result in more effective group work?* Other results from the literature might show what others have discovered in related questions.

After doing a literature review, it's time to determine how we are going to collect evidence that will shed light on the question and its answers. That evidence can be quantitative or qualitative, or a mixture of both. The means of gathering evidence in SoTL is incredibly varied. Some studies involve control and experimental groups like classic scientific studies; some are purely observational or involve interviews; some involve surveys; some involve the deployment of quantitative instruments that gather numerical data about student learning; some are a mixture of all these; some are none of these. Some are more exotic, using functional MRI machines or devices that track eye movements to detect physiological patterns in students as they engage in a learning task. In this small space, we won't attempt to list all the possibilities. Rather, we emphasize only that many different methods for gathering evidence—and many definitions of *evidence*—are in existence, and it reinforces the importance of a thorough literature review because the more we look at existing SoTL studies, the more methodologies we see. One reasonable piece of starting advice is to find a study whose core questions resemble those of your study, scrutinize the design of that study, and then take a similar approach.

At this point, the basic framework of a SoTL research project has been constructed, and it's ready to be conducted—except for one very important task, which is getting approval from your institution's institutional research board (IRB), which certifies research proposals that involve human subjects. (The exact name of this committee can vary from campus to campus.) Although we often think of studies involving human subjects as those in medical trials or psychological experiments, SoTL research almost always involves working with live students—therefore, human subjects. To do SoTL, then, we are legally obligated to seek certification from the IRB that our proposed study minimizes, as much as possible, the possibility of "harm" to our subjects.

This concept of "harm" doesn't refer merely to physical harm but also includes psychological harm, harm to one's academic record, and harm to one's privacy. For example, suppose we are conducting a study to see if giving oral exams through the course of a semester improves performance on the final exam; a control group receives traditional written exams throughout the semester, an experimental group receives oral exams, and both groups get the same traditional written final exam, and we compare the results. Several questions about harm arise:

- How do we know that the oral exams aren't simply harder than the written exams, and therefore students in the experimental group will end up with worse grades? How do we minimize the harm to a student's GPA (and potential employability later) from having been in the study?

- If a student is assigned to the experimental group randomly, what happens if that student is not a native English speaker, or has a learning disability, or otherwise has a condition that makes it harder to take oral exams than written exams? Will such students be able to opt out of the study? (On the other hand, if we let students self-select the group to which they belong, will we be certain that any results in the data will be mainly attributable to the experiment and not because students who prefer oral exams selected the oral exam group?)
- If we use the final exam grades as data in the study, how do we ensure that it will be impossible to determine students' identities from their data?
- Is the use of final exam data in violation of Family Educational Rights and Privacy Act (FERPA)?

These and other questions must be accounted for as part of the review process that takes place usually within the university, through the IRB. This process can look different in different places, but the one thing all SoTL researchers should know is that *it takes time*. Therefore, time for IRB review has to be built into the timeline for actually completing a SoTL study. For example, if you come up with an idea for a SoTL study in the fall semester, running that study in the spring semester may not be realistic, because it might take several weeks to get IRB approval.

The details of the process vary within institutions and can vary significantly among different countries where national laws protecting student privacy differ. Therefore, we will not go into the details here; you should contact your university's IRB for an overview of the process and information on what must be submitted, and how. For now, just realize that getting IRB approval is an essential part of SoTL research and a means of protecting students against unethical practices.

Once the SoTL study is designed and approved, the study needs to be carried out according to plan and the data need to be tabulated and stored. The specifics of this part of the process are at least as varied as the ways of designing the study. Quantitative studies involve performing statistical analyses; qualitative studies involve finding patterns in verbal responses from interviews and surveys by "coding" the responses and then categorizing results according to the coding. Then, once the data are processed, they must be analyzed to draw out any information that might be present that have something to say about the original research questions.

Here we want to be careful to take a critical and scientific approach to the data we collect and the information contained in the data. If we are proponents of flipped learning, it can be very easy to interpret the results of a flipped learning SoTL study in a positive light simply because we have a positive view of flipped learning. We should avoid such bias; if a well-designed study produces results that indicate flipped learning didn't perform in a way that benefits students, be honest about it, and interpret the data as truthfully as possible—and then think about possible confounding variables that you didn't consider, or ways to ask the original questions in a way that more accurately pursues the idea you had in mind. In the course of doing a SoTL project, it's quite likely that the attempt to answer one question will raise many other questions. In this way, research in SoTL is self-generating. The more we look into questions about teaching and learning, the more there is to look into. And so as we finish up one project, others are waiting in the wings.

Then, having analyzed the data, we write it up into a presentable form and submit it for peer review. As we mentioned earlier, SoTL-specific journals are numerous, including the following prominent examples:

- *Active Learning in Higher Education*
- *International Journal for the Scholarship of Teaching and Learning*
- *International Journal of Teaching and Learning in Higher Education*
- *The Journal on Excellence in College Teaching*
- *The Journal of Scholarship of Teaching and Learning*
- *Teaching & Learning Inquiry*

There are dozens of other such journals in print (or online), both for general SoTL work and for teaching and learning research done within a particular discipline. Additionally, many journals that are not themselves devoted to SoTL will often publish research on teaching and learning issues.

In addition to journals, conferences devoted to SoTL—many of which accept conference papers through a peer-review process, making them more valuable to a tenure and promotion portfolio—are conducted all over the world several times a year. Some of the biggest such conferences include the Teaching Professor Conference and its spin-off, the Teaching Professor Technology Conference; the Lilly Conference on College Teaching, which has a central national meeting and several regional meetings each year; and the annual conference of the International Society for the Scholarship of Teaching and Learning.

The sheer quantity of peer-reviewed journals and national and international conferences presents numerous opportunities to parlay one's experience with flipped learning into significant, career-building scholarship. But, if one is to do SoTL research and make it part of one's scholarly program, it still remains to make the case that SoTL really is research. Sadly, SoTL research is not universally seen as legitimate as scholarship in one's discipline. This seems to be more due to bias than to a command of the facts. Some scholars, for example, view the inherent messiness of SoTL research as an indicator that the research findings are untrustworthy. But such a view ignores many years and innumerable research papers in the social sciences, whose methodology is similar to that of SoTL; just because a research study doesn't have the same level of precision and control as a physics experiment at CERN or a Food and Drug Administration (FDA) clinical drug trial does not mean the findings are untrustworthy. What's important is whether the research questions are clear, the methods well designed and properly chosen, the data collected as scientifically as possible, and the results well interpreted. And we, as SoTL researchers, have to be realistic about the limitations of those results and be careful not to design shoddy studies in the first place.

But make no mistake—SoTL is real research and valid scholarship that has just as valid a claim in the scholarly life of the professoriate as disciplinary research.

Flipped Learning and the Rest of Your Career: Service

The practice of flipped learning provides avenues not only for significant scholarship but also for significant service to one's department, university, and professional community. We end this chapter with a brief description of one way of providing service to others, and that is through disseminating our experiences through conference talks and workshops.

For as long as there has been flipped learning, there have been workshops about flipped learning. As we saw earlier in this book, Wesley Baker, who was one of the originators (if not *the* originator) of flipped learning in higher education, started to give workshops to his colleagues at other small liberal arts colleges almost as soon as he started to use flipped learning in his classes. And the success of Jon Bergman and Aaron Sams in popularizing flipped learning among primary and secondary educators in the United States came not so much from their seminal 2012 book but from the extensive schedule of professional development workshops given in the time between their first experiments with flipped learning and the publication of that book. There seems to be something about flipped learning that lends itself extremely well to helping others learn about it.

You might be one of only a few on your campus doing flipped learning. This can be a challenge, because flipped learning is easier to do with a community of practice in place, but this challenge also presents an opportunity for service, because you can be the catalyst for that community at your institution.

Doing so can be exceedingly simple. If your institution has a *teaching and learning center*—a central office that assists faculty in teaching—check with them to see if you can be of service somehow in communicating your experiences with other faculty and if there might be other faculty who have expressed an interest in flipped learning. Some teaching and learning centers provide faculty workshops or seminars on pedagogical issues, and your experiences would set you up well to lead one. Sometimes, more extensive *faculty learning communities* are in place where faculty with similar interests come together for a semester or a year and engage in monthly reading and discussion times on a single topic; flipped learning can be your topic and you can be the leader. If your campus does *not* have a teaching and learning center, you can ask the person in charge of instruction at your institution (usually a dean) or ask around at a department or all faculty meeting.

In many different ways, you can serve colleagues at your institution by offering to share your experiences and be a resource for others. Studies show that the number-one barrier for faculty to adopt "evidence-based" teaching practices, including flipped learning, is the absence of a local person who has used that practice and can be a go-to, "right down the hall" resource for questions and informal discussion (Henderson and Dancy 2007). With your experience teaching with flipped learning, you can be that "person down the hall" who can provide support to others.

On a more extended level, conference talks that share experiences and results can serve the broader higher education community as flipped learning takes hold. These are talks not at the level of a peer-reviewed SoTL study but rather of a more expository nature. They do not have the same kind of rigor that a SoTL study has, but they are valuable in their own way by providing perspective and a chance for others to see flipped learning instantiated in real life, with real students and a real professor. Many disciplinary conferences have presentation sessions not only for "discovery"-type scholarship but also for teaching presentations, and these fit well in those venues. Many times, a well-presented talk on flipped learning can result in an invitation to visit another campus to give a workshop or a longer talk to faculty at that institution. So by giving simple conference talks, an entire chain reaction of service can result that indirectly benefits the education of hundreds or even thousands of students.

In Brief

Whereas the first chapters of this book have set up the theory and philosophy of flipped learning and then the nuts and bolts of practicing it, in this chapter we've tried to see how flipped learning is not a crazy experiment but a legitimate, even normative form of course design and instruction with which you can live happily every day of your career. Like anything new to you, it does not come without expense or risk. However, both the expense and the risks are manageable, and the potential benefits for you and your students are great. The practice of flipped learning not only holds the promise of making teaching more effective and more fun but also leads naturally to avenues of productivity in scholarship and service that can benefit your career in ways that simply sticking with the status quo do not.

In short, flipped learning is a sustainable practice. It can become a part of your career and provide a basis for satisfaction and productivity for years to come. It's worth using and worth perfecting.

APPENDIX

Glossary of Techniques and Tools

Throughout this book, we've referenced not only general concepts for successful flipped learning experiences but also specific teaching techniques and tools for making it happen. Some of these tools and techniques may be quite familiar—others, not so much. In this appendix, we list many of the tools and techniques mentioned throughout the book, in alphabetical order, along with three pieces of information about them: *What is it*, which describes the tool or technique; *what's it for*, describing potential uses for student learning in a flipped learning environment; and *to learn more*, with links to more information.

Classroom Response Systems (Clickers)

- *What it is*: Classroom response systems, more commonly called *clickers*, refer to a variety of technological tools that allow students to respond to instructor questions by voting. Originally, clickers were small, handheld devices with numeric keypads. When one of the buttons was pressed, the clicker produced radio signals that transmitted information about which button was pressed. In other words, the device allowed students to submit a vote in the form of a number from zero to nine. Those signals are received by a special receiver that tallies the votes and produces the results. Typically, students have the clickers and the instructor has the receiver. Today, physical clicker devices are still used but software versions are increasingly prevalent. These are web-based applications that allow students to vote using a web browser on a smartphone, tablet, or computer. Among the advantages of software-based systems are the ability to use the system on devices students may already own, and the ability to ask question types other than multiple choice. For example, most of the software-based systems described in this appendix allow not only multiple-choice questions but also *multiple-selection* (select all responses that meet a criteria) questions, questions involving text input, and questions whose responses involve graphics.

- *What it's for*: Classroom response systems are typically used for in-class work, and they lend themselves well to group space activities in a flipped learning environment, particularly in large classes. For example, during group space (after students have learned the basics of new concepts during their individual space sessions), an instructor can structure a group discussion by presenting difficult conceptual questions to students for voting using their classroom response system. The voting process allows each student to have a voice (rather than only those who raise their hands or otherwise contribute to the class), the system software makes collection and visualization of student votes simple, and the results of the votes can be used to power group discussions or other active learning. In particular, *peer instruction,* mentioned in chapter 2 and described later, is a well-established use of classroom response systems in a flipped learning environment with proven results. Classroom voting is also an effective way to gather assessment data during the first few minutes of class about student work from the preclass assignments and promote accountability for completing it.
- *To learn more*: The most comprehensive resource on the use of classroom response systems is Derek Bruff's (2009) *Teaching With Classroom Response Systems: Creating Active Learning Environments,* which contains a wide variety of use cases in many different disciplines and instructional situations. The following are links to some of the major manufacturers and developers:

  o Physical clicker devices: Turning Point (www.turningtechnologies .com), iClicker (www1.iclicker.com)
  o Software-based systems: Learning Catalytics (https://learning catalytics.com), PollEverywhere (http://polleverywhere.com), Top Hat (https://tophat.com)

Entrance/Exit Tickets

- *What it is*: Entrance tickets are short activities for students to do upon arrival at a group space session (e.g., class meeting) in which they are presented with one or more short prompts and then asked to respond to those prompts. The responses give instructors a brief dose of formative assessment on student knowledge at the beginning of class. For example, students might be given the following prompt: *Based on the readings and video for today, what are the top one to three big ideas of this lesson?* or *What is one specific question you have about today's lesson?* Instructors then collect the responses as *entrance tickets* to register student attendance at class. Their counterparts, *exit tickets*, accomplish the same purpose but take place at the end of class and can contain appropriate prompts such the following: *What was the least clear idea from today's class?* (The previous prompt specifically is sometimes called a *muddiest point question.*)

- *What it's for.* Entrance and exit tickets provide benefits across all course design paradigms, instructional methods, and levels of technology. In a flipped learning environment specifically, entrance tickets can provide a way for students to bring focus to their understanding of the learning activities done during Guided Practice and can provide a layer of accountability for students to complete those assignments. Using technology such as Google Forms (discussed later) or classroom response systems that allow text input, entrance tickets can even be assigned to be completed prior to class. Exit tickets can be used after group space activity to allow students the chance to sum up the day's activity and engage in metacognitive activities, such as evaluation of their work and planning and forethought for the post–group space work.
- *To learn more*: Much has been written about the implementation and benefits of entrance and exit tickets. For a starting point, try this website: www.theteachertoolkit.com/index.php/tool/entry-ticket

Gitter

- *What it is*: Gitter is a chat service sponsored by GitHub, which is a web service for hosting repositories of software and source code. Its intent is to provide software developers, who are working on software applications whose code is hosted on GitHub, with the ability to engage in discussions with each other online. Users who want to ask questions of the developers and each other can also use the service. The word *Gitter* is a portmanteau of *GitHub* and *Twitter*, which indicates the intended purpose of the service—to allow small group chats consisting of short messages about GitHub projects.
- *What it's for*: Courses that use computer code can use GitHub to store and share the code, and Gitter is a natural way to engage in out-of-class discussions on student work. But Gitter also serves as a serviceable chat platform for any class. It has a simple and intuitive interface and several features for STEM-related courses that are difficult to find in other chat services, particularly syntax-highlighted code blocks and

LaTeX mathematics typesetting. This and other chat services could be valuable in a flipped learning environment by providing students and instructors with a way to engage in discussion and question-asking during individual space activities; for online courses, it could even be useful for group space activities by using it for live chats. Accounts are free (with paid subscription options), and users can sign in either with a GitHub or a Twitter account.

- *To learn more*: Sign up at https://gitter.im

Google Forms

- *What it is*: Google Forms are online forms integrated into the Google Drive office suite. Any user with a Google account has a Google Drive account as well; many users are familiar with Google Docs, and, in the same place where Google Docs are created and stored, a Google Form can also be created and deployed. Google Forms provide a simple interface to construct interactive forms that contain a variety of question types (multiple choice, short answer, long answer, dropdown menus, etc.) with some advanced features such as data verification. There is even a robust scripting system allowing users to write extensions to their forms using a variant of the JavaScript language. Once written, a Google Form can be distributed to others just by sharing a link. When a user fills out a Google Form, the data can be placed into a Google Spreadsheet and then used in a multitude of ways. There are also simple reporting tools that allow administrators to see responses at a glance. Google recently added the ability to designate correct answers and add point values to certain kinds of questions, allowing automatic grading of Google Forms so that they could be used as quizzes.
- *What it's for*: Google Forms are flexible and have a wide range of potential uses. In particular, Google Forms could be used in many ways in a flipped learning environment. In chapter 6, we described how Google Forms are used to collect formative assessment data from students as they work through individual space activities, which can then be used to make on-the-fly improvements to group space activities. Google Forms could also be used for informal student evaluations (highlighted in chapter 8) or in-class formative assessment.
- *To learn more*: Go to Google's support page for Google Forms (https://support.google.com/docs/answer/6281888). If you have a Google account (e.g., Gmail or Google Apps through your institution) the

best way to learn is to just start making a form. Also take a look at this short tutorial from Alice Keeler: http://alicekeeler.com/2016/03/24/creating-a-google-form/

Guided Practice

- *What it is*: Guided Practice, highlighted in chapter 6, is an approach to individual space work in a flipped learning environment that provides structure to student learning experiences as students are preparing for the group space. A Guided Practice assignment consists of the following parts: (a) an overview and introduction for the lesson coming up; (b) two lists of learning objectives for the lesson, one "basic" (to be learned before group space activities) and the other "advanced" (to be learned during and after the group space activities); (c) a playlist of learning resources, pulled from a variety of media including print, online text, video, audio, games, and simulations; (d) a list of exercises for students to do that instantiate the basic learning objectives; and (e) a system of submitting responses, for example, through a Google Form, along with instructions and deadlines for doing so.
- *What it's for*: The purpose of Guided Practice is to *guide* student *practice* as they come into contact with new concepts for the first time. It is a way to provide structure so that students have a framework for making sense of concepts independently, and the structure serves as a kind of proxy for the instructor as students work in individual space.
- *To learn more*: Check back with chapter 6, where this is discussed in detail.

Hypothes.is

- *What it is*: Hypothes.is (pronounced "hypothesis") is a web service that places an annotation layer over an existing web resource to allow users to leave comments and discussion threads on anything they find on the web and make those comments and discussions visible to other Hypothes.is users. This includes web objects that do not have comment threads, such as online texts of Supreme Court decisions and scanned images—or items where existing comment threads aren't well suited for academic discussion within a private group, like YouTube videos or news items. These examples show how it's used: https://hypothes.is/examples-of-classroom-use

- *What it's for*: Hypothes.is could be used to great effect in a flipped learning environment by providing a space for students to discuss items from the learning resources playlist in a Guided Practice assignment, giving students a space both for interacting and having questions and for answering writing-oriented Guided Practice exercises. It could even be used in close reading assignments done during group space activities.
- *To learn more*: Sign up at https://hypothes.is

One-Minute Papers

- *What it is*: The one-minute paper, or just minute paper, is a variation on the idea of an exit ticket (see previous section) in which students spend one minute writing a response to one or more prompts, often at the end of a class session. The responses are collected (and possibly lightly graded) by the instructor and used to collect questions, gauge understanding, and make plans for the next class.
- *What it's for*: In a flipped learning environment, where group space is used on higher-order learning tasks, students need a means of focusing and summarizing their work from the group space, as well as a way of asking questions and expressing points on which they are not clear. One-minute papers fill that need in a simple way. In a flipped learning environment, too, it is especially important to give students tasks that involve metacognition, such as evaluation of their group work and planning and forethought for how they will spend their time between group space sessions; one-minute papers give a simple means of doing so. One-minute papers can be done actually on paper, or using a Google Form or a classroom response system that allows text input.
- *To learn more*: Much has been written about the implementation and benefits of entrance and exit tickets. For a starting point go to http://provost.tufts.edu/celt/files/MinutePaper.pdf

Peer Instruction

- *What it is*: Peer instruction, first described in chapter 2, is an instructional technique based on student discussions on conceptual questions that address common misconceptions about the main ideas of a subject. Peer instruction involves repeated applications of the following cycle of activity:

o Students are given a minilecture or demonstration that sets up an essential idea of a lesson.
o Following the minilecture or demonstration, students are given a question that focuses on a common misconception of this essential idea, typically one that does not involve complex technical work like mathematical computation. The question is projected onto a screen or otherwise broadcast to students. Students are given a short time (usually just one minute) to think about the question and formulate their answer. Students then use a classroom response system to vote on their answer.
o After voting, the instructor looks at the response data. If there is broad agreement on the correct answer to the question (say, 80% of students have answered correctly) then the instructor stops the questioning, debriefs the class on the answer, and asks for any further comments. Then she proceeds to the next minilecture or demonstration.
o However, if there is not broad agreement on the correct answer, students are instructed to pair off with another student nearby (possibly with explicit instructions to pick a partner who answered differently). The pair is then given a short time (two to four minutes) to take turns explaining why they believed their response was the correct one, and to question each other's explanations and help each other understand misconceptions. At the end of this time, students vote individually on the same question a second time.
o After the second round of voting, the instructor again looks at the voting data. If there is broad agreement on the right answer—as there often is, after peer instruction takes place—then the right answer is debriefed and additional comments are collected. Otherwise, the instructor may proceed to a third round of voting or turn the question into an all-class discussion.

A typical peer instruction class session of 50 minutes would be focused around this cycle, applied to two to four essential ideas for the day.

- *What it's for.* As we discussed in chapter 2, peer instruction is considered one of the first implementations of a flipped learning environment, and it remains an excellent and research-tested means of using flipped learning that works especially well with large classes. (Eric Mazur, the inventor of peer instruction, developed it specifically to work with 200–300 student lecture sections in physics.) Students can be given a Guided Practice activity to give them preparation on the basic ideas of a lesson; then, during class time, basic ideas do not need as much attention but rather attention can be focused squarely on peer instruction questions on the advanced learning objectives.

- *To learn more*: The primary source for all things peer instruction—including a full account of the origins of peer instruction, the theory behind its use, and examples of questions and classroom activities—is Eric Mazur's (1997) *Peer Instruction: A User's Manual.* A popular video that encapsulates the origins and theory of peer instruction is Mazur's keynote talk "Confessions of a Converted Lecturer," which appears in several forms on the Internet. The version with the most views is the one delivered to the University of Maryland–Baltimore County (www.youtube.com/watch?v=WwslBPj8GgI). Don't skip the question-and-answer session at the end.

Peer-Led Team Learning (PLTL)

- *What it is*: PLTL is an instructional method that replaces all or part of standard lecture sessions with weekly small-group workshops that are led by other students in the class. Those student leaders are recruited by the professors of the course from among students who have done well in the course in previous semesters. Course instructors meet regularly with peer leaders to prepare them for the workshops and to help them develop their leadership and communication skills. Students working in small, peer-led workshops leverage a social context to help them learn and develop relationships with each other and with the peer leader that makes the learning environment more productive.
- *What it's for*: Most implementations of PLTL presuppose that significant work is being done outside the group space setting, such as online homework. In a flipped learning environment, the individual space can be used for this as well as for Guided Practice activities that prepare students for the workshops. The workshops constitute all or part of the group space of the course, and this can be spent on problem-solving sessions with a small number of students applying the basic concepts learned in Guided Practice. The group space could also be mixed, for example, with one large-group meeting per week

and one small-group meeting per week, to allow different kinds of higher-level cognitive activity to take place.

- *To learn more*: Visit the website of the Center for Peer-Led Team Learning at https://sites.google.com/site/quickpltl/

Perusall

- *What it is*: Like Hypothes.is, Perusall is a web service in which users engage in *social annotation*. In the case of Perusall, the instructor uploads a PDF text for annotation and assigns it to the students. The students can then ask questions, comment on each other's questions and comments, and engage in a discussion of the text in a completely online environment. Unique to Perusall is a system that automatically grades student responses on the basis of quality and timeliness, and an automatically generated "confusion report" for the instructor that gives a snapshot of the ideas from the text that generated the greatest number of questions. One of the developers of Perusall is Harvard's Eric Mazur, the inventor of *peer instruction* (see previous section and chapter 2); Perusall is the modern version of the online textbook annotation system he gave to his physics students for use in doing preclass assignments.
- *What it's for*: As with Mazur's physics classes, Perusall can be used as a way for students to complete Guided Practice assignments that are based on text readings rather than (or in addition to) video. Students can be assigned sections of the text, and to read and respond to that text in Perusall. The annotations are collected and graded by the system. Several major textbook publishers already integrate their texts with Perusall to make this easier.
- *To learn more*: Sign up for free at http://perusall.com

Plickers

- *What it is*: Plickers are a form of low-tech classroom response system that turn the idea of a clicker on its head. With a typical clicker, students are given items to which they are to respond by pressing a button on a device and voting. With a plicker, students do not need a device. Instead, they have printed sheets of paper (that can be printed off using an ordinary printer and ordinary paper) or special laminated cards (that can be purchased at the Plicker website) that contain scannable codes—for example, five pages, each having a code for one of the letters *A* through *E*. Students are presented with the item to which they are to respond and then they hold up the page with their response. The instructor uses an app that turns his or her smartphone or tablet camera into a scanner; the instructor simply pans the camera across the classroom and the app reads the codes that are on the pages and tallies the voting results. In this way, rather than students using a device to enter a vote, there is only one electronic device needed, namely, the instructor's phone or tablet.

- *What it's for*: Like classroom response systems, plickers can be used for classroom voting, which can then be used to motivate group discussion on advanced concepts. This would be an appropriate activity for a flipped learning environment where students have done preliminary readings or viewing of basic concepts, either at the beginning of a class as an entrance quiz or during class for discussions. Plickers might be especially attractive to schools in which student access to technology is an issue.
- *To learn more*: The associated app for iOS and Android is free and available on the App Store and Google Play, respectively. Go to https://plickers.com

Process-Oriented Guided Inquiry Learning (POGIL)

- *What it is*: POGIL is an instructional method that engages students in *guided inquiry* activities that stress learning both processes and content simultaneously through structured activities done in structured, self-managed small groups. POGIL courses focus not only on content objectives but also on *process skills* such as teamwork, oral and written communication, management, critical thinking, and assessment. In a POGIL class session, students work in small teams—often teams of four, with specific roles such as manager, recorder, spokesperson, and strategy analyst—on activities that lead students through the inquiry process on a concept. Both the structure of the activities (starting from basic information tasks through advanced critical thinking questions) and the structure of the groups (with each member sticking to his or her specifically assigned role) play a part in the instruction process, with the instructor serving as a guide and coach.

- *What it's for:* Since POGIL is predicated on having students work in groups on guided inquiry tasks that range from simple to advanced, having sufficient time to complete the tasks is essential and often problematic. In a flipped learning environment, students can learn the basic ideas and perhaps even complete part of the inquiry activity prior to the group space meeting, freeing up substantial time for the remainder of the activity.
- *To learn more:* Visit the POGIL website at https://pogil.org

Slack

- *What it is:* Slack is a software tool for team collaboration developed by software developers as part of a video game development project. The developers wanted to use IRC for discussion and collaboration among its team members, but the lack of a graphical interface led them to develop something related but more user-friendly. In Slack, users can interact through a chat interface on *channels* devoted to specific topics or through direct messages among small groups of users. Slack integrates with many existing web services such as Google Documents and GitHub (mentioned previously) to create an app-rich messaging environment that avoids text messaging and e-mail. It is still primarily used by software companies but is finding its way into other use cases, particularly education.
- *What it's for:* Slack can be used in education as an alternative to chat services like Gitter or traditional discussion boards. The chat-like interface of Slack tends to be more conversational than a traditional discussion board and promotes a freer sense of interaction among users. In a flipped learning environment, Slack could be used during students' individual space sessions (e.g., while working on Guided Practice) as a means of asking questions and engaging in discussion of preclass learning activities. The many third-party integrations available for Slack also make it a useful way to share documents, calendar events, even animated GIF images.
- *To learn more:* Sign up for an account (http://slack.com), and look for a Slack team to join at www.slacklist.info or create your own. In particular, a Slack team specifically for educators can be found at http://slackedu.slack.com

SurveyMonkey

- *What it is*: SurveyMonkey is an online survey creation and management service. Users can create surveys and questionnaires with different types of questions, transmit them to respondents, and collect the data for later use.
- *What it's for*: In a flipped learning environment, SurveyMonkey could be used in place of Google Forms for collecting formative assessment data on student work in their individual space sessions and Guided Practice work. It could also be used for entrance and exit tickets and for conducting informal course evaluations as discussed in chapter 8.
- *To learn more*: Sign up for an account at www.surveymonkey.com

Think-Pair-Share/Think-Pair-Share-Square

- *What it is*: *Think-pair-share* refers to a learning exercise in which students are given a question or some other item to think about. Then they are asked to think about it for a certain (short) period of time. Next, students form *pairs* and then *share* with each other what they were thinking in a small-group discussion. In the variation *think-pair-share-square*, there is an additional phase in which pairs pair up to form four-person groups (i.e., squares) and the pairs take turns sharing their ideas with the other pair.
- *What it's for*: Think-pair-share(-square) is a technique to spark effective small-group discussion in a group space situation. It could be used at the beginning of group space in a flipped learning environment, for instance, to help students solidify and express what they learned during the individual space or preclass work, ask questions of each other, and provide help to each other.
- *To learn more*: Think-pair-share is a teaching technique that has been around for many years and used by a vast number of teachers. For starters, read here: www.readwritethink.org/professional-development/strategy-guides/using-think-pair-share-30626.html

VoiceThread

- *What it is*: VoiceThread is a web service that allows users to share slide shows that involve documents, images, and multimedia, with its key feature being that others can leave spoken-word comments on the items that are posted.

- *What it's for*: In a flipped learning environment, VoiceThread could be used as a platform for a Guided Practice assignment (or as one or more of the learning activities in such an assignment), and students can participate in the assignment by leaving voice comments. Those comments can be the main source of assessment of the individual space activity, or they can be available merely as a means of asking questions much like Hypothes.is or Perusall is used with text items and chat services are used for interaction and questioning.
- *To learn more*: Sign up for an account (https://voicethread.com), or read this web page on using VoiceThread in education: https://goo .gl/fN9Pzn

WebEx

- *What it is*: WebEx is a platform for online group meetings that combines documents, text chat, and audio/video chat. It is often used in businesses to conduct meetings with geographically dispersed teams, or to conduct online seminars. It is quite feature-rich, including the ability to collaborate using an interactive whiteboard and to have "breakout sessions" with small subgroups meeting in online rooms while the main meeting continues.
- *What it's for*: While the primary audience of WebEx is the business community, the features of WebEx lend themselves well to online and hybrid courses and to flipped learning environments. For example, during individual space time (in between classes) office hours or small-group working sessions could be conducted using WebEx.
- *To learn more*: Go to www.webex.com (note that this is not a free service)

REFERENCES

Abeysekera, Lakmal, and Phillip Dawson. 2015. "Motivation and Cognitive Load in the Flipped Classroom: Definition, Rationale and a Call for Research." *Higher Education Research and Development 34*(1): 1–14. doi:10.1080/07294360.2014 .934336.

Allen, I. Elaine., and Jeff Seaman. 2010. *Learning on Demand: Online Education in the United States, 2009.* Newburyport, MA: Sloan Consortium.

Anderson, Lorin W., and David R. Krathwohl. 2001. "A Taxonomy for Learning, Teaching, and Assessing: A Revision of Bloom's Taxonomy of Educational Objectives." *Theory Into Practice 41*(4): 212–218. doi:10.1207/s15430421tip4104_2.

Anderson, Lorin W., David R. Krathwohl, and Benjamin Samuel Bloom. 2001. *A Taxonomy for Learning, Teaching, and Assessing: A Revision of Bloom's Taxonomy of Educational Objectives.* New York: Allyn & Bacon.

Bain, Ken. 2011. *What the Best College Teachers Do.* Cambridge, MA: Harvard University Press.

Baker, J. Wesley. 2000. "The 'Classroom Flip': Using Web Course Management Tools to Become the Guide by the Side." In *Selected Papers from the 11th International Conference on College Teaching and Learning,* edited by J. A. Chambers, 9–17. Jacksonville, FL: Florida Community College at Jacksonville.

Baker, J. Wesley. 2015. "The Origins of 'the Classroom Flip.'" Unpublished manuscript.

Baranes, Ruth, Michelle Perry, and James W. Stigler. 1989. "Activation of Real-World Knowledge in the Solution of Word Problems." *Cognition and Instruction 6*(4): 287–318.

Barba, Lorena. n.d. "Practical Numerical Methods With Python." http://openedx .seas.gwu.edu/courses/GW/MAE6286/2014_fall/about.

Barba, Lorena. 2015. "Why My MOOC Is Not Built on Video." https://www.class-central.com/report/why-my-mooc-is-not-built-on-video/

Bass, Randy. 1999. "The Scholarship of Teaching: What's the Problem." *Inventio: Creative Thinking About Learning and Teaching 1*(1): 1–10.

Baumert, Jürgen, Mareike Kunter, Werner Blum, Martin Brunner, Thamar Voss, Alexander Jordan, Uta Klusmann, Stefan Krauss, Michael Neubrand, and Yi-Miau Tsai. 2010. "Teachers' Mathematical Knowledge, Cognitive Activation in the Classroom, and Student Progress." *American Educational Research Journal 47*(1): 133–180.

Bergmann, Jonathan. 2011a. "The Flipped Classroom Is Born." https://youtu.be/v-y9vR7YTak

Bergmann, Jonathan. 2011b. "The History of the Flipped Class." http://jonbergmann
.com/the-history-of-the-flipped-class/

Bergmann, Jonathan, and Aaron Sams. 2012. *Flip Your Classroom: Reach Every Student in Every Class Every Day*. Eugene, OR: International Society for Technology in Education.

Bjork, Robert A. 1975. "Retrieval as a Memory Modifier: An Interpretation of Negative Recency and Related Phenomena." In *Information Processing and Cognition: The Loyola Symposium*, edited by Robert L. Solso, 123–144. New York: Lawrence Erlbaum. doi:10.1086/147648.

Bloom, Benjamin S., David Krathwohl, and Bertram Masia. 1956. *Taxonomy of Educational Objectives*, vol. 1: *Cognitive Domain*. New York: McKay.

Boelkins, Matthew, David Austin, and Steven Schlicker. 2014. *Active Calculus*. http://scholarworks.gvsu.edu/books/10/

Boyer, Ernest L. 1990. *Scholarship Reconsidered: Priorities of the Professoriate*. Princeton, NJ: Carnegie Foundation for the Advancement of Teaching.

Bransford, John D., and Daniel L. Schwartz. 1999. "Rethinking Transfer: A Simple Proposal With Multiple Implications." *Review of Research in Education* 24 (1999): 61–100. http://links.jstor.org/sici?sici=0091-732X%281999%2924%3C61%3ARTASPW%3E2.0.CO%3B2-Q

Briggs, Katharine Cook, and Isabel Briggs Myers. 1977. *The Myers-Briggs Type Indicator: Form G*. Palo Alto, CA: Consulting Psychologists Press.

Bristol, Tim. 2014. "Flipping the Classroom." *Teaching and Learning in Nursing* 9(1): 43–46.

Bruff, Derek. 2009. *Teaching With Classroom Response Systems: Creating Active Learning Environments*. New York: John Wiley & Sons.

Chaiklin, Seth. 2003. "The Zone of Proximal Development in Vygotsky's Analysis of Learning and Instruction." *Vygotsky's Educational Theory in Cultural Context* 1: 39–64.

Charkins, R. J., Dennis M. O'Toole, and James N. Wetzel. 1985. "Linking Teacher and Student Learning Styles With Student Achievement and Attitudes." *The Journal of Economic Education* 16(2): 111–120.

Cheshire, Tom, and Steven Leckhart. 2012. "University Just Got Flipped: How Online Video Is Opening Up Knowledge to the World." *Wired*. http://www
.wired.co.uk/magazine/archive/2012/05/features/university-just-got-flipped

Chick, Nancy. n.d. "A Scholarly Approach to Teaching." https://my.vanderbilt.edu/
sotl/understanding-sotl/a-scholarly-approach-to-teaching/

Clark, Richard E. 1989. "When Teaching Kills Learning: Research on Mathemathantics." In *Learning and Instruction: European Research in an International Context*, edited by Erik De Corte, 1–22. London: Pergamon.

Cornell University Center for Teaching Excellence. n.d. "Online Discussions." https://www.cte.cornell.edu/teaching-ideas/teaching-with-technology/online-discussions.html

Critz, Catharine M., and Diane Knight. 2013. "Using the Flipped Classroom in Graduate Nursing Education." *Nurse Educator* 38(5): 210–213.

Crouch, Catherine H., and Eric Mazur. 2001. "Peer Instruction: Ten Years of Experience and Results." *American Journal of Physics 69*(9): 970. http://link.aip.org/link/AJPIAS/v69/i9/p970/s1&Agg=doipapers2://publication/doi/10.1119/1.1374249

Davidson, Cathy. 2013. "What Was the First MOOC?" https://www.hastac.org/blogs/cathy-davidson/2013/09/27/what-was-first-mooc

Deci, Edward, and Richard Ryan. 1985. *Intrinsic Motivation and Self-Determination in Human Behavior.* New York: Pantheon.

Eager, Eric Alan, James Peirce, and Patrick Barlow. 2014. "Math Bio or Biomath? Flipping the Mathematical Biology Classroom." *Letters in Biomathematics 1*(2): 139–155. doi:10.1080/23737867.2014.11414476.

Eberly Center for Teaching Excellence. 2003. "The Educational Value of Course-Level Learning Objectives/Outcomes." https://www.cmu.edu/teaching/resources/Teaching/CourseDesign/Objectives/CourseLearningObjectivesValue.pdf

Engelmann, Siegfried. 1980. *Direct Instruction* (Volume 22 of Instructional Design Library). Englewood Cliffs, NJ: Educational Technology.

Ernst, Dana. 2015. "Setting the Stage." http://danaernst.com/setting-the-stage/

Fernandez, Vicenc, Pep Simo, and Jose M. Sallan. 2009. "Podcasting: A New Technological Tool to Facilitate Good Practice in Higher Education." *Computers and Education 53*(2): 385–392. doi:10.1016/j.compedu.2009.02.014.

Fink, L. Dee. 2003. "A Self-Directed Guide to Designing Courses for Significant Learning." https://www.deefinkandassociates.com/GuidetoCourseDesignAug05.pdf

Fink, L. Dee. 2013. *Creating Significant Learning Experiences: An Integrated Approach to Designing College Courses.* New York: John Wiley & Sons.

Fisher, Douglas, and Nancy Frey. 2013. *Better Learning Through Structured Teaching: A Framework for the Gradual Release of Responsibility.* Alexandria, VA: ASCD.

Flipped Learning Network. 2014. "Definition of Flipped Learning." http://flippedlearning.org/definition-of-flipped-learning/

Freeman, Scott, Sarah L. Eddy, Miles McDonough, Michelle K. Smith, Nnadozie Okoroafor, Hannah Jordt, and Mary Pat Wenderoth. 2014. "Active Learning Increases Student Performance in Science, Engineering, and Mathematics." *Proceedings of the National Academy of Sciences 111*(23): 8410–8415. doi:10.1073/pnas.1319030111.

Gannod, G. C., Burge, J. E., & Helmick, M. T. (2008). Using the inverted classroom to teach software engineering. *Proceedings of the 13th International Conference on Software Engineering ICSE 08*, 777–786. http://doi.org/10.1145/1368088.1368198

Ganter, S., and W. Barker, eds. 2004. *The Curriculum Foundation Project, Voices of the Partner Disciplines: A Collection of MAA Committee Reports.* Washington DC: Mathematical Association of America. http://www.maa.org/cupm/crafty/cf_project.html

Ginder, Scott, and Christina Stearns. 2012. "Enrollment in Distance Education Courses, by State: Fall 2012." National Center for Education Statistics. http://nces.ed.gov/pubs2014/2014023.pdf

Greimel-Fuhrmann, Bettina, and Alois Geyer. 2003. "Students' Evaluation of Teachers and Instructional Quality—Analysis of Relevant Factors Based on Empirical Evaluation Research." *Assessment & Evaluation in Higher Education 28*(3): 229–238.

Groot, Adriaan de. 1965. "Perception and Memory Versus Thought: Some Old Ideas and Recent Findings." In *Problem Solving: Research, Method and Theory*, edited by B. Kleinmutz, 19–51. New York: John Wiley & Sons.

Hake, Richard R. 1998. "Interactive-Engagement Versus Traditional Methods: A Six-Thousand-Student Survey of Mechanics Test Data for Introductory Physics Courses." *American Journal of Physics 66*: 64–74. http://pdfserv.aip.org/AJPIAS/vol_66/iss_1/64_1.pdfpapers2://publication/uuid/50021915-8036-40CD-A7A3-70987C4A117B

Halloun, Ibrahim Abou, and David Hestenes. 1985. "The Initial Knowledge State of College Physics Students." *American Journal of Physics 53*(11): 1043–1048. doi:10.1119/1.14030.

Halloun, Ibrahim Abou, and David Hestenes. 1987. "Modeling Instruction in Mechanics." *American Journal of Physics 55*(5): 455–462.

Henderson, Charles, and Melissa H. Dancy. 2007. "Barriers to the Use of Research-Based Instructional Strategies: The Influence of Both Individual and Situational Characteristics." *Physical Review Special Topics—Physics Education Research 3*(2): 020102. http://journals.aps.org/prper/pdf/10.1103/PhysRevSTPER.3.020102.

Herreid, Clyde Freeman, and Nancy A. Schiller. 2013. "Case Studies and the Flipped Classroom." *Journal of College Science Teaching 42*(5): 62–66.

Hestenes, David, Malcolm Wells, and Gregg Swackhamer. 1992. "Force Concept Inventory." *The Physics Teacher 30*(3): 141. doi:10.1119/1.2343497.

Huntley, Belinda, Johann Engelbrecht, and Ansie Harding. 2011. "Can Multiple Choice Questions Be Successfully Used as an Assessment Format in Undergraduate Mathematics?" *Pythagoras*, No. 69: 3–16. doi:10.4102/pythagoras.v0i69.41.

Hutchings, Pat, ed. 2000. *Opening Lines: Approaches to the Scholarship of Teaching and Learning*. Menlo Park, CA: Carnegie Publications.

Kalyuga, Slava, Paul Ayres, Paul Chandler, and John Sweller. 2003. "The Expertise Reversal Effect." *Educational Psychologist 38*(1): 23–31. doi:10.1207/S15326985EP3801_4.

Karpicke, Jeffrey, and Janell Blunt. 2011. "Retrieval Practice Produces More Learning Than Elaborative Studying With Concept Mapping." *Science* 331 (February): 772–775. doi:10.1126/science.1199327.

Kay, Robin H. 2012. "Exploring the Use of Video Podcasts in Education: A Comprehensive Review of the Literature." *Computers in Human Behavior 28*(3): 820–831. doi:10.1016/j.chb.2012.01.011.

Kogan, Marina, and Sandra L. Laursen. 2014. "Assessing Long-Term Effects of Inquiry-Based Learning: A Case Study From College Mathematics." *Innovative Higher Education 39*(3): 183–199. doi:10.1007/s10755-013-9269-9.

Kolb, David A. 1981. "Learning Styles and Disciplinary Differences." *The Modern American College* 1: 232–255.

Koller, Daphne. n.d. "Probabilistic Graphical Models." https://www.coursera.org/course/pgm

Kothiyal, Aditi, Rwitajit Majumdar, Sahana Murthy, and Sridhar Iyer. 2013. "Effect of Think-Pair-Share in a Large CS1 Class: 83% Sustained Engagement." In *Proceedings of the Ninth Annual International ACM Conference on International Computing Education Research*, 137–144. New York: ACM Digital Library.

Lage, Maureen J., Glenn J. Platt, and Michael Treglia. 2000. "Inverting the Classroom: A Gateway to Creating an Inclusive Learning Environment." *The Journal of Economic Education 31*(1): 30–43. http://heldref-publications.metapress.com/index/qu74468776t81511.pdf papers2://publication/uuid/4B0A9049-7F09-469D-ACCA-248153C24079

Lang, James. n.d. "Small Changes in Teaching: The First 5 Minutes of Class." https://chroniclevitae.com/news/1264-small-changes-in-teaching-the-first-5-minutes-of-class

Lasater, Kathie. 2007. "Clinical Judgment Development: Using Simulation to Create an Assessment Rubric." *Journal of Nursing Education 46*(11): 496-503.

Laursen, Sandra L., Marja-Liisa Hassi, Marina Kogan, and Timothy J. Weston. 2014. "Benefits for Women and Men of Inquiry-Based Learning in College Mathematics: A Multi-Institution Study." *Journal for Research in Mathematics Education 45*(4): 406–418. doi:10.5951/jresematheduc.45.4.0406.

Lokken, Fred, L. Womer, and C. Mullins. 2012. "Distance Education Survey Results." *Tracking the Impact of E-Learning at Community Colleges.* Washington, DC: Instructional Technology Council.

Lorenzo, Mercedes, Catherine H. Crouch, and Eric Mazur. 2006. "Reducing the Gender Gap in the Physics Classroom." *American Journal of Physics 74*(2): 118. doi:10.1119/1.2162549.

Lowell Bishop, Jacob, and Matthew Verleger. 2013. "The Flipped Classroom: A Survey of the Research." In *Proceedings of the Annual Conference of the American Society for Engineering Education*, 161–163. doi:10.1109/FIE.2013.6684807.

MathWorks. 2016. "MATLAB Tutorials." http://www.mathworks.com/academia/student_center/tutorials/mltutorial_launchpad.html?s_tid=ac_ml_tut_til

Mazur, Eric. 1997. *Peer Instruction: A User's Manual.* Upper Saddle River, NJ: Prentice Hall.

Miller, George. 1956. "The Magical Number Seven, Plus or Minus Two: Some Limits on Our Capacity for Processing Information." *Psychological Review 101*(2): 343–352. doi:10.1037/h0043158.

Miller, Michelle D. 2014. *Minds Online: Teaching Effectively With Technology.* Cambridge, MA: Harvard University Press.

National Center for Education Statistics. n.d. "Number of Educational Institutions, by Level and Control of Institution: Selected Years, 1980–81 Through 2007–08." http://nces.ed.gov/programs/digest/d09/tables/dt09_005.asp

Ng, Andrew, and Jennifer Widom. 2014. "Origins of the Modern MOOC (XMOOC)." In *MOOCs: Expectations and Reality*, edited by Fiona M. Hollands and Devayani Tirthali, 34–47. New York: Teachers College, Columbia University.

Nilson, Linda B. 2013. *Creating Self-Regulated Learners: Strategies to Strengthen Students' Self-Awareness and Learning Skills.* Sterling, VA: Stylus.

Nwosisi, Christopher, Alexa Ferreira, Warren Rosenberg, and Kelly Walsh. 2016. "A Study of the Flipped Classroom and Its Effectiveness in Flipping Thirty Percent of the Course Content." *International Journal of Information and Educational Technology 6*(5): 348–351.

Onwuegbuzie, A. J., A. E. Witcher, K. M. T. Collins, J. D. Filer, C. D. Wiedmaier, and C. W. Moore. 2007. "Students' Perceptions of Characteristics of Effective College Teachers: A Validity Study of a Teaching Evaluation Form Using a Mixed-Methods Analysis." *American Educational Research Journal 44*(1): 113–160. doi:10.3102/0002831206298169.

Ouimet, J., and R. Smallwood. 2005. "CLASSE—The Class-Level Survey of Student Engagement." *Assessment Update 17*(6): 13–15.

Owston, Ron, Denys Lupshenyuk, and Herb Wideman. 2011. "Lecture Capture in Large Undergraduate Classes: Student Perceptions and Academic Performance." *The Internet and Higher Education 14*(4): 262–268. doi:10.1016/j.iheduc.2011.05.006.

Palfreyman, David. 2008. *The Oxford Tutorial: Thanks, You Taught Me How to Think* (2nd ed.). Oxford, England: The Oxford Centre for Higher Education Policy Studies (OXCHEPS).

Pearson, P. David, and Margaret C. Gallagher. 1983. "The Instruction of Reading Comprehension." *Contemporary Educational Psychology 8*(3): 317–344.

Pierre, Kathy. 2014. "How Much Do You Study? Apparently 17 Hours a Week Is the Norm." http://college.usatoday.com/2014/08/18/how-much-do-you-study-apparently-17-hours-a-week-is-the-norm/

Pink, Daniel. 2010. "Flip-Thinking—The New Buzz Word Sweeping the US." *The Telegraph.* http://www.telegraph.co.uk/finance/businessclub/7996379/Daniel-Pinks-Think-Tank-Flip-thinking-the-new-buzz-word-sweeping-the-US.html

Pintrich, Paul R. 2004. "A Conceptual Framework for Assessing Motivation and Self-Regulated Learning in College Students." *Educational Psychology Review 16*(4): 385–407. http://www.springerlink.com/index/U0N624K3X6253519.pdf

Polya, George. 2014. *How to Solve It: A New Aspect of Mathematical Method.* Princeton, NJ: Princeton University Press.

Prince, Michael. 2004. "Does Active Learning Work? A Review of the Research." *Journal of Engineering Education* 93: 223–232. doi:10.1002/j.2168-9830.2004.tb00809.x.

Reichman, Sheryl Wetter, and Anthony F. Grasha. 1974. "A Rational Approach to Developing and Assessing the Construct Validity of a Study Learning Style Scales Investment." *Journal of Psychology 87*(2): 213–223.

Rose, Katherine Kensinger. 2009. "Student Perceptions of the Use of Instructor-Made Videos in Online and Face-to-Face Classes." *Journal of Online Learning and Teaching 5*(3): 487.

Rothkopf, Ernst Z., and M. J. Billington. 1979. "Goal-Guided Learning From Text: Inferring a Descriptive Processing Model From Inspection Times and Eye Movements." *Journal of Educational Psychology 71*(3): 310.

Rovai, Alfred P. 2007. "Facilitating Online Discussions Effectively." *The Internet and Higher Education 10*(1): 77–88.

Ryan, R., and E. Deci. 2000. "Self-Determination Theory and the Facilitation of Intrinsic Motivation, Social Development, and Well-Being." *The American Psychologist 55*(1): 68–78. doi:10.1037/0003-066X.55.1.68.

Sabourin, Katie. 2014. "How Much Is Too Much? Avoiding the Course and Half Syndrome." http://fisherpub.sjfc.edu/cgi/viewcontent.cgi?article=1000&context =edtech_pub

Schneider, Bertrand, Engin Bumbacher, and Paulo Blikstein. 2015. "Discovery Versus Direct Instruction: Learning Outcomes of Two Pedagogical Models Using Tangible Interfaces." In *Exploring the Material Conditions of Learning: Proceedings of the Computer Supported Collaborative Learning (CSCL) Conference*, edited by O. Lindwall, P. Häkkinen, T. Koschman, P. Tchounikine, and S. Ludvigsen, 1: 364–371. Gothenburg, Sweden: The International Society of the Learning Sciences.

Scriven, Michael S. 1967. *The Methodology of Evaluation* (Perspectives of Curriculum Evaluation and AERA Monograph Series on Curriculum Evaluation No. 1). Chicago: Rand McNally.

Sener, John. 2015. "Updated E-Learning Definitions." http://onlinelearningconsortium .org/updated-e-learning-definitions-2/

Sheridan Center for Teaching and Learning. n.d. "Entrance & Exit Tickets." https:// www.brown.edu/about/administration/sheridan-center/teaching-learning/ effective-classroom-practices/entrance-exit-tickets

Shin, Haerin. 2015. "Flipping the Flipped Classroom: The Beauty of Spontaneous and Instantaneous Close Reading." *The National Teaching & Learning Forum*, 24: 1–4.

Spencer, Karin J., and Liora Pedhazur Schmelkin. 2002. "Student Perspectives on Teaching and Its Evaluation." *Assessment & Evaluation in Higher Education 27*(5): 397–409.

Strayer, Jeremy. 2007. "The Effects of the Classroom Flip on the Learning Environment: A Comparison of Learning Activity in a Traditional Classroom and a Flip Classroom That Used an Intelligent Tutoring System." PhD thesis, Ohio State University, Columbus. https://etd.ohiolink.edu/rws_etd/document/get/ osu1189523914/inline

Strayer, Jeremy. 2012. "How Learning in an Inverted Classroom Influences Cooperation, Innovation and Task Orientation." *Learning Environments Research 14*(2): 171–193. http://www.springerlink.com/index/v56x344763202r17.pdf

Sundstrom, Ted. 2013. *Mathematical Reasoning: Writing and Proof* (Open Education Materials). Allendale, MI: Grand Valley State University. http://scholarworks .gvsu.edu/books/7/

Svensson, Lennart, and Tom Adawi. 2015. "Designing and Evaluating a Flipped Signals and Systems Course." In *Proceedings of the 14th European Conference on E-Learning—ECEL*, edited by Amanda Jefferies and Marija Cubric, 584–591. Sonning Common, UK: Academic Conferences and Publishing International Limited. http://publications.lib.chalmers.se/publication/227895

Svensson, Lennart, and Lars Hammarstrand. 2015. "Flipping a PhD Course Using Movies From a MOOC." Paper presented at the Fifth Development Conference for Swedish Engineering Courses, Uppsala University, Uppsala, Sweden, November 18–19. http://publications.lib.chalmers.se/publication/227895

Sweller, J., J. J. G. van Merrienboer, and F. G. W. C. Paas. 1998. "Cognitive Architecture and Instructional Design." *Educational Psychology Review 10*(3), 252–253. doi.org/10.1023/A:1022193728205.

Torrance, Harry. 2007. "Assessment as Learning? How the Use of Explicit Learning Objectives, Assessment Criteria and Feedback in Post-Secondary Education and Training Can Come to Dominate Learning." *Assessment in Education* 14(3): 281–294.

Vygotsky, Lev Semenovich. 1998. *The Collected Works of L. S. Vygotsky*, Vol. 5, edited by R. W. Rieber and J. Wollock. New York: Plenum Press.

Vygotsky, Lev Semenovich, René van der Veer, and Jaan Valsiner. 1994. *The Vygotsky Reader*. Oxford: Blackwell.

Walsh, Kelly. 2012. "Is Reverse Instruction Education Technology's Perfect Storm?" http://www.emergingedtech.com/2012/04/is-reverse-instruction-education-technologys-perfect-storm/

Walvoord, Barbara E. Fassler, and Virginia Johnson Anderson. 1998. *Effective Grading: A Tool for Learning and Assessment*. San Francisco: Jossey-Bass.

Wan, Tony. 2015. "No Slacking Off! How Savvy Teachers Are Turning to Trello and Slack." https://www.edsurge.com/news/2015-07-28-no-slacking-off-how-savvy-teachers-are-turning-to-trello-and-slack

Wiggins, Grant P., and Jay McTighe. 2005. *Understanding by Design*. Alexandria, VA: ASCD.

Willingham, Daniel T. 2009. *Why Don't Students Like School? A Cognitive Scientist Answers Questions About How the Mind Works and What It Means for the Classroom*. New York: John Wiley & Sons.

Witcher, Ann, and Anthony J. Onwuegbuzie. 1999. "Characteristics of Effective Teachers: Perceptions of Preservice Teachers." ERIC No. ED438246.

Yackel, Erna, and Paul Cobb. 1996. "Sociomathematical Norms, Argumentation, and Autonomy in Mathematics." *Journal for Research in Mathematics Education* 27(4): 458–477. doi:10.2307/749877.

Zimmerman, Barry. 2002. "Becoming a Self-Regulated Learner: An Overview." *Theory Into Practice 41*(2): 64–70. doi:10.1207/s15430421tip4102_2.

INDEX

research, and emerging practices in active learning classrooms. The authors' extensive knowledge and lived experience as teachers, faculty developers, and educational researchers is palpable on every page. Collectively they cover all the bases, identifying key teaching challenges in the active learning classroom and generating evidence-based suggestions and solutions. Every teacher, scholar, and administrator who seeks to understand the transformations in learning environments that are reshaping how teachers teach and students learn will find this volume a must-read and an indispensable companion."—*Mary Deane Sorcinelli*, *Distinguished Scholar in Residence, Mount Holyoke College; and Founding Director, Center for Teaching & Faculty Development, University of Massachusetts Amherst.*

"*A Guide to Teaching in the Active Learning Classroom* should be read by every faculty member or college administrator concerned with student learning."—*Ernest Pascarella*, *Mary Louise Petersen Professor of Higher Education, The University of Iowa*

Sty/us

22883 Quicksilver Drive
Sterling, VA 20166-2102

Subscribe to our e-mail alerts: www.Styluspub.com

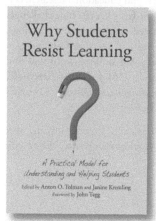

Why Students Resist Learning
A Practical Model for Understanding and Helping Students
Edited by Anton O. Tolman and Janine Kremling
Foreword by John Tagg

"This book takes the challenge head on. It directly addresses the great and central problem: student resistance to active learning. And it addresses that problem in the right way, [which] is to recognize that student resistance is a systemic problem: students do what they do for . . . reasons [that] are many and varied. But student resistance is not magic. If we can understand the reasons for their behavior, we can change it. That is the central project of this book: to understand why and how students resist taking a deep approach to learning, so that we can take a deeper approach to designing a curriculum and a pedagogy that can help them to grow rather than let them shrink into their protective cocoon of resistance."—*John Tagg, Associate Professor of English, Palomar College, and coauthor with Robert B. Barr of the seminal article "From Teaching to Learning"*

The purpose of this book is to help faculty develop a coherent and integrated understanding of the various causes of student resistance to learning, providing them with a rationale for responding constructively, and enabling them to create conditions conducive to implementing effective learning strategies.

In this book readers will discover an innovative integrated model that accounts for student behaviors and creates a foundation for intentional and informed discussion, evaluation, and development of effective counter strategies. The model takes into account institutional context; environmental forces; and students' prior negative classroom experiences, cognitive development, readiness to change, and metacognition. The various chapters take the reader through the model's elements, exploring their practical implications for teaching, whether relating to course design, assessments, assignments, or interactions with students.

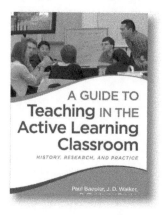

A Guide to Teaching in the Active Learning Classroom
History, Research, and Practice
Paul Baepler, J. D. Walker, D. Christopher Brooks, Kem Saichaie, and Christina I. Petersen
Foreword by Bradley A. Cohen

Active learning classrooms, or ALCs, offer rich new environments for learning and present many new challenges to faculty unfamiliar with these spaces.

"This perfectly timed book provides a much-needed and extremely useful road map of the history, innovative

(Continues on previous page)